MY STORY OF ST DUNSTAN'S

Lord Fraser of Lonsdale
Photo Fayer

My Story
of St Dunstan's

BY

LORD FRASER OF LONSDALE

With eleven plates in half-tone

GEORGE G. HARRAP & CO. LTD
LONDON TORONTO WELLINGTON SYDNEY

First published in Great Britain 1961
by GEORGE G. HARRAP & CO. LTD
182 High Holborn, London, W.C.1

Composed in Bell type and printed by Tonbridge Printers Ltd,
Peach Hall Works, Tonbridge, Kent

Made in Great Britain

DEDICATION

I dedicate this book to my wife 'Chips,' born Irene Mace.

She has had more influence over the affairs of St Dunstan's than any other woman, possibly than any other individual.

Since we were married we have hardly been parted for a day. She has 'seen' for me in all matters, important and trivial, and we have lived happily ever after.

FRASER

Preface

The first history of St Dunstan's was written by the Founder, Sir Arthur Pearson, when it was four years old. Of course, he thought it would be the last. He ended his Foreword with these words:

> The fact that this account of the work of St Dunstan's is written in the past tense does not mean that at the date of publication this work was at an end. As a matter of fact it is still in full swing and will be for at least another eighteen months.

The date line was 1919.

The work is still not at an end, and not likely to be for many years. If there are no more major wars St Dunstan's will outlive its need in the twenty-first century. I hope that something of its work will live for ever.

FRASER OF LONSDALE

Acknowledgments

I should like to thank St Dunstan's and the Editor of *St Dunstan's Review* for access to files and records; Mr W. G. Askew and Mrs N. Halliday for proof-reading and suggestions.

In particular my thanks are due to Mr Patrick Pringle for his invaluable research work and for the editorial assistance he has given me.

FRASER OF LONSDALE

Contents

Illustrations

1

When It Was Dark

THE ophthalmic surgeon stood by my bedside. I felt his cool, confident hand touch my cheek lightly, and heard his familiar and reassuring voice. But there was a difference this time.

"I'm just going to put a drop of cocaine in here. You won't feel it, and it will enable me to have a good look." Major Ormond spoke casually, but I felt it was an ominous beginning.

He opened the lids of my left eye with his finger and thumb, and I waited. Then he sat down on the bed and took hold of my right hand. "I think I had better have a little talk to you about this." Here it was at last, I thought, and I braced myself. "I am afraid that eye won't be any good to you, and of course you know that the other one—or what was left of it—had to be tidied up in France."

I was not so shocked or surprised as might be supposed, because I had half expected—and certainly feared—such a statement sooner or later.

"I'll put a shell in your socket," he added. "It will make it more comfortable." Opening my eyelids again, he inserted a piece of smooth glass the size and shape of half a marble, hollowed out behind.

This was more of a shock than his words had been, for I could feel this crude glass eye, and knew it had taken the place of a real one. My last unreasoning hope, which had been clinging to life for weeks, was finally killed. I could no longer pretend to myself that the cause of my blindness might be only that my eyes were not working properly,

13

with the implication that some near-miracle of healing and surgery could yet enable me to see again. That was out now. The harsh fact was that I had no eyes.

I had not previously thought of the personal consequences of being blinded before my nineteenth birthday. If I had half expected the verdict I had avoided considering the sentence. It's for life, I thought.

It seemed to me that there was an unusual silence in the hospital ward; then it was broken by talk and laughter, and from the other end came the lilt of a revue song played on the piano—"Oho . . . oh . . . oh . . . oh . . . oh . . ., you beautiful doll!"

The ten seconds' silence had been a subconscious expression of grief on account of what the surgeon had told me, and of which they had already been aware, for everyone knows everything about his fellows in a hospital ward. Now the ward had decided—again subconsciously—to return to normal, and the man at the piano was determined to cheer me up. He was the right man for the job, for he too was totally blind.

Nearly two months had passed since July 23, 1916, the day when I had last seen the world. I had spent that morning in charge of a burial party, finding a last resting-place for some of those who would not grow old as we that were left have grown old. We had fought in the afternoon, when I was knocked out by a bullet in the head. I am not sure if I lost consciousness, but I remember being bandaged up. I know I walked to the field-dressing station, and talked to my company commander on my way down the line. I took it for granted that I would soon be all right. I did not draw any sinister inference from being—temporarily, as I thought —unable to see.

They took me to the casino at Le Touquet, which had been converted into a hospital, and cabled my parents in South Africa to tell them that I was dangerously ill. The Red Cross brought my cousin, Lilia Howard, across from

St Dunstan's Lodge, Regent's Park

*The Clock set up at the Lodge
in Regent's Park*

*It is now back at the Church
of St Dunstan in the West*

Lord Fraser on horseback in South Africa

Lord and Lady Fraser

England, and she sat by my bedside and read to me for hours. The danger was infection with the germs of meningitis or septicæmia. Once it was clear that I was not going to fall to either of these diseases my recovery was not in doubt. Medically I was a simple, straightforward case. I was not the subject of prolonged consultations and treatment, because there was nothing to consult about, nothing much to treat. The bullet had caused no serious harm to anything except my sight, and it had damaged that beyond repair. I was completely blind, but otherwise sound.

Rightly, I think, they did not tell me this, but at first actually encouraged me to hope that I would see again. They only told me I had lost my right eye, where the bullet had gone in. Of course, I knew that my left eye had also been damaged, but I still hoped I would be able to see out of it again.

While they were careful not to destroy this hope, they did not tell me deliberate lies to keep it alive. There was no need for any, and there almost never is. So they simply evaded the question, leaving me to come to terms with reality in my own time and by myself. The only barrier between me and the truth was my natural reluctance to see it, and it was better if I overcame this gradually, and without too much outside help. The most important thing was that I should first learn that one could be blind and still lead a useful and happy life.

At first I had no idea of this, and in my more realistic moments I felt worried and depressed. Supposing I was blind, I thought, what would I do? I called to mind a sermon preached in Marlborough College Chapel two or three years before, supporting a nation-wide appeal made by someone whose name I could not remember who had himself gone blind in the middle of an active business life. There was no comfort here, for all I could remember was that the preacher had said that to be blind was one of the worst of human afflictions, and that was why we must subscribe as much as possible of our meagre schoolboy pocket-money. Then I remembered a friend with whom I used to go camping when we were in our early teens, and whose father, an old sea-captain, was blind. We boys had treated him with a certain kind of awe—whether on account of his blindness or his age I was not sure. But there was no comfort here either, for I remembered how dependent upon his wife and son the old blind sailor had seemed to be. I also remembered seeing blind men sitting or standing on the pavement selling their pitiful stock of bootlaces or matches, or blatantly begging with a child or a dog as guide or companion. There was no comfort here.

So I took refuge in the hope that I would not be completely blind after all, and as this hope dwindled I clung to it more fiercely, because at that time it was the only sort of hope I had. It kept me going for about three weeks. Then I was brought back to England and transferred to the Officers' Ward of the 2nd London General Hospital, a converted college in Chelsea, and there a new and practical message of hope was brought to me before the old, doomed, impossible hope was finally put to death.

Although it was a general hospital, the whole block was devoted to eye cases. This concentration not only made the services of specialist surgeons and sisters more readily available to those that needed them; it also engendered a fellow-feeling among the patients, who understood one another's problems—and, most important of all, it enabled St Dunstan's to get at us right from the start. It was, in fact, at Sir Arthur Pearson's request that this concentration had been arranged.

Pearson was continually in and out of the hospital, and usually he himself was the first to visit a new arrival. But I had come in August, when St Dunstan's was closed for the annual holiday and Pearson was away in Harrogate. So he wrote me a letter, and sent it with his personal assistant and guide, a V.A.D. named Irene Mace. She also brought me a braille watch.

It was an ordinary watch without a glass, and with little raised dots round the outside edge. There was a dot against each numeral, with double dots at the quarters. The hands were slightly raised, and a little flatter and stronger than ordinary watch-hands. A hunter lid shut down and protected the face.

I held the watch in my hand and felt the face with my thumb. For the first time since I was wounded I was able to tell the time.

The value of the watch to me far exceeded its usefulness. That in itself was considerable, for you tend to want to know the time often when you are in permanent darkness, and have no means of distinguishing even night from day. Of course, in hospital one could always ask. But that was the whole point. With this watch I did not have to ask anyone. I would never have to ask again. I was able to do it myself—do something that had before always been a visual act. It was an extraordinary pleasure to find that it was just as easy to do with the hands as with the eyes. Perhaps there were other things. . . .

Pearson's letter assured me there were. It was, of course, his routine letter for such occasions, and later I heard him dictating it for other new boys in almost identical words. Miss Irene Mace also had read it before. But as she read it then, as I heard Pearson's message of encouragement and cheer—man to man, blind to blind—I was astonished that someone who had never met me could know so exactly how I felt. The letter caught my mood, and I felt a great surge of new life.

Pearson was not entirely responsible for that. Three things began my recovery. The first was the watch he had sent, and the second was his message; and every newly blinded soldier received these. The third factor was personal, but so important that I cannot imagine how all the others recovered without it.

I fell in love with Irene Mace.

* * *

B

Visitors from St Dunstan's came to the ward every day, and as soon as we were well enough we had a lesson or two in braille. I was not there long enough to learn much then, but it gave me another foretaste of the ways in which a blind man could 'see' with his hands. It reminded me that I was by no means the unluckiest in the ward. Some, it is true, had lost the sight of only one eye, but there were others who were not only completely blind but had grave additional wounds. Learning that a soldier in another ward had lost not only his sight but also both his hands was a salutary cure for self-pity.

Other discoveries helped to make life more pleasant. One was that I could enjoy smoking. I had not smoked much until I was posted to France, and that was only a few weeks before I was wounded. I had smoked a lot in the trenches, and especially when burying the dead. In hospital I began smoking again as soon as I was allowed to, and found it a great comfort—especially when I had learnt to light a cigarette myself.

I was soon shaving myself, too, and this was not as difficult as it may seem. I had not had to begin shaving until I went to Sandhurst, and in France most of my shaving had been done in the trenches, often without a mirror. So I had some experience in doing it by feel when I told the hospital orderly to hand me the razor—an ordinary cut-throat—and let me do it myself. He stayed with me, doubtless watching with painful curiosity and waiting for me to slice an ear off. When he saw I could manage he left me to it, and I have shaved myself ever since. I have tried various kinds of razor, including safety and electric, but I still use a cut-throat to-day.

Learning to walk was more difficult but much more important. Not being able to move about on your own is one of the most galling of the first consequences of blindness, and I hated having to accept help every time I wanted to go to the lavatory. There was always a friendly nurse or orderly to guide me, and I had to make quite an effort to try the journey without a helping hand. Then I had to learn how to do it.

If you have ever tried to find your way about in pitch-darkness you have probably shuffled along with very short steps and outstretched hands. That is also the natural reaction of the newly blinded. If you have a stick, as we all had, you will probably wave it about in front of you in an unprofitable, ridiculous, and possibly dangerous way. That was what I did, until I realized it was not helping me along, made me look foolish, and might smash a flower-vase or lay someone out. Then I pointed the stick down towards the floor and used it to probe a little ahead while I felt my way from one obstacle to the next. This method was slow but reasonably safe, and it got me there under my own steam.

After about two weeks in the 2nd London they sent me out for convalescence. I went to Wootton Fitzpaine, in Dorset, the home of my cousin, Douglas Pass. They still did not tell me at the hospital that I had lost my left eye. There was a sort of unspoken agreement between them and me under which we talked about everything else. But I was more used to the idea that I might never see again, and much less doleful about my future now that I had heard the message of St Dunstan's.

I suppose we are all more or less schizophrenic, and youth is naturally rebellious; and there were times when I was still in violent revolt. Most came at night, when I could not sleep. Insomnia is a common complaint among the blind—partly because they do not usually take much exercise, and also, I think, because they cannot draw a sudden curtain over the waking world by switching off the light. Similarly, the condition is not so easy to put right. If I had ever suffered from insomnia when I could see I had doubtless turned on the light and read myself to sleep. Now I just had to lie there, for I did not know nearly enough braille to read a book. In the hospital I had been able to ring for the night sister, who would bring me a cup of tea and sit and chat. There was no nursing staff at Wootton, so I had to lie there until my watch told me it was day again.

On one such night I tried to see. I got out of bed and fumbled my way to the electric-light switch, and then groped for the lamp above the dressing-table, pulled it down, and pressed it where my left eye had been. The bulb felt encouragingly warm, and I strained my nerves to try to see a glimmer of light. There was none, of course. And it was sheer childishness to press the bulb against the socket of my other eye, which I knew had been destroyed when I was hit. Yet I had to do it, I had to try. The obsession had been growing for some time, becoming more insistent—and I had to do it at night, when everyone was asleep and I was not likely to be surprised in the act. Always in the early days there was this fear of looking a fool.

With it was the other fear of being the object of pity and emotional sympathy. Luckily, I was in no danger of this at Wootton Fitzpaine. And although I was fond of my parents, when I look back I think it was probably a good thing for me that they were far away in South Africa. A newly blinded person's nearest and dearest often delay rather than assist his recovery. They are so good at making everything easy for him that he has little chance of discovering what he can do for himself. In time their love may even sap his desire to be self-reliant. In fact, my mother came to see me before Christmas, and I am sure her visit did me a lot of good. But I was already at St Dunstan's then, and on the way to learning to stand on my own feet. During my convalescence I think I was better off in the care of Olive Pass.

Douglas Pass, her husband, and my cousin, was a prisoner of war in Turkey, and the news of him was sparse, unreliable, and often frightening. So she had her own emotional worries, and her sympathy for me took a healthily practical form. She talked to me, read to me, and walked with me. She also let me walk round on my own.

Wootton was a good place for me to practise walking about, for since I had come to England in 1907, at the age of ten, it had virtually been my home. Douglas and Olive Pass were like an older brother and sister to me, and I had spent nearly all my school holidays with them.

So I was extremely familiar with both the house and the grounds, and I made good progress in getting about. I was delighted to discover that going up and down a staircase presented no difficulty once the beginning of it had been found. A banister follows the stairs so faithfully that it could have been specially designed for the blind. Meanwhile I was acquiring the habit of using my other senses to help me keep my bearings.

It is sometimes said that when one sense is lost Nature compensates by sharpening the others; in particular, that a blind person's hearing becomes more acute. This is true in a sense, but not the physical sense in which it is usually meant. A blind man's ears do not become sharper—there is no increase in the acuity of his reception of sound-waves. But if the sense of hearing is considered also to include the interpretation of sounds, it is certainly improved by the loss of sight. That is because it needs to be. A businessman dictating letters does not have to hear the sound of his secretary's pencil on the paper, because he can see whether she is keeping up with him. I cannot see, so I must use my sense of hearing instead, just as for other things I have to exploit my equally normal sense of touch.

In my first efforts at walking about I learnt to make use of all sorts of sounds that I had not bothered to hear before. The difference in echo when going from a room into a corridor, or into another room; the ticking of a clock (usually indicating the mantelpiece); the crackling of a fire in winter, or the sounds of birds through an open window in summer—these are some of the sounds that only a blind man needs to hear to form a picture of his surroundings. I began to train myself to hear and interpret these and many other sounds. I also learnt the advantage of having two ears, one on each side of the head. When I dropped something like a collar-stud I could often put my hand on it at once, thanks to a purely automatic piece of range- and direction-finding by these two listening stations.

I learnt to use my other senses in the same way. I became mentally more sensitive to a change of temperature —I was quick to feel the warmth of a fire or a draught from an open window, to smell cooking and other odours that I had never consciously noticed before. And then I developed a 'sense of obstacle,' which is not a sixth sense but a combination of the other senses that somehow warns the blind man when a solid object is approached.

Thin objects are harder to detect than thick, and I have never yet met a blind man who could discern the edge of an open door. This is the nastiest of all indoor obstacles. At least, it teaches you not to wave your arms about in front of you, for it quickly comes between them, and is then ready to meet your face. I found the best protection against it was to walk with one arm just in front of the body, the forearm parallel with the ground, rather like a boxer's guard against a body blow. When I walked upright this arm protected the whole of my body and face from sharp door-edges, corners, and other such projections. Walking like this, I found I was better off without my stick indoors, although I still needed it outside.

I learnt to hold a cigarette alongside the match when striking it, so that at the moment of ignition the flame was in the right place. All blind smokers learn this trick, and that is why they are good at lighting their cigarettes in a wind. If you are sighted and have difficulty in this you might try it too. The end of the cigarette should come just below the head of the match.

I learnt to pour out a drink. If you watch a blind man pour out his own beer you will see that the first finger of the hand holding the glass is crooked just over the edge. That is so that the tip of his finger will warn him before he over-pours, or if the froth rises too quickly. But usually this precaution will prove unnecessary, because he can judge when he has poured enough partly by the sound, partly by the relative weights of bottle and glass. You could do the same if you had to, but so long as you can see there is no need.

I put braille labels on my gramophone records. I tapped a typewriter for the first time. Olive Pass, her mother-in-law, and my younger sister Betty, who was at Wootton for her school holidays, all did everything they could. It could not have been very pleasant for them. I was still resentful and sorry for myself, and not easy to help. But if I clung to the past I also looked forward to the future. I got them to read Pearson's letter to me again, and took heart from his account of what was being done at St Dunstan's. I had already accepted his invitation to go there when the doctors discharged me. I was looking forward especially to renewing my acquaintance with Irene Mace. . . .

My convalescence lasted only a few weeks. At the end of it I went back to hospital for a check-up, and it was then that Major Ormond told me that I was permanently blind. My weakened link with the past snapped, but not before I was securely bound to the future. Fearfully and reluctantly at first, then more firmly, and finally with resolution, I crossed the bridge between the old world and the new. Pearson was waiting at the other end, his hand stretched out to help me down.

2

The Pearson Story

"APPALLING as the deprivation of sight may be, it is not without some remarkable compensations."

Those words were written by a lad of twenty-four who did not know what it meant to be blind. They were the first sentence of an article called "Curiosities of Blindness" that appeared in the first number of *Pearson's Weekly*. What makes the sentence almost eerily curious now is that it was written by the proprietor and editor in his maiden publication; and he was writing much the same when he was twice as old and totally blind.

Sir Arthur Pearson—he was created a baronet in 1916— was a self-made man. That is not to say that he began life like the newspaper proprietor of legend, a ragged urchin selling papers on a street corner. Far from it. He followed his father to Winchester and received a classical education; which, incidentally, he always considered a waste of time and money. That was a pity, for his father had little money to waste.

Although extremely short-sighted even as a boy, young Pearson was good at games, especially cricket. He might have followed further in his father's footsteps and played for his school at Lord's, if his father had not taken Holy Orders. The Rev. Cyril Pearson was a country parson, and when Arthur was sixteen the struggle to pay his school fees proved too much. He had to leave Winchester, and was promised a job as a clerk in a City bank.

The prospect appalled him, but he was still at home, waiting for the vacancy, two years later, when a competition in *Tit-Bits* caught his eye. *Tit-Bits* was a new weekly magazine founded by Sir George Newnes, and it was famous for its bright ideas. This competition was in general knowledge, and it was a forerunner of the modern radio and television quiz; only the questions were harder and the prize was more original. In every issue for thirteen weeks readers were asked ten questions on subjects ranging from the payment of archbishops to the Seven Wonders of Korea. The first prize was a job on the staff of *Tit-Bits* with a commencing salary of £100 a year.

For thirteen weeks Arthur Pearson cycled three times a week to the nearest reference library, which was thirty miles away: a total of 2340 miles on one of the old high bicycles with solid tyres. For this alone he deserved to win. He won easily, and that was the end of the threatened clerkship in the City bank.

Pearson was eighteen and a half when he joined *Tit-Bits*. At nineteen he was manager of the paper with his own private secretary, the proprietor's right-hand man. He did free-lance journalism in his spare time. Unwilling to waste a minute, he worked on the train to and from the office, and because his eyes troubled him he travelled with a home-made lighting unit with a bulb fixed in his coat buttonhole. Before he was twenty-four he had a wife and two daughters and was earning over £500 a year. Of this his salary from Newnes was £350, which was pretty good for a youngster in 1890. But *Tit-Bits* was making large profits, and he thought it ought to be bigger, and asked for more. Newnes refused, so Pearson left and set up in business on his own. He had no capital, but a man he had played tennis with invested £3000, and three weeks after he left Newnes the first number of *Pearson's Weekly* was on sale. It consisted partly of old articles that he had written and failed to sell. The public bought a quarter of a million copies of the new weekly, and the publishing house of Pearson's was born.

His ideas were even brighter than those in *Tit-Bits*. One of the early competitions in *Pearson's Weekly* offered women readers a prize of £100 a year for life and a good husband, with the cost of the trousseau, wedding, and honeymoon thrown in. Then there was the eucalyptus issue. During an influenza epidemic Pearson was told by a doctor on the train that the best preventive was some stuff made from the eucalyptus tree. As soon as he reached his office Pearson bought all the eucalyptus oil he could lay his hands on, and fifty commissionaires were put to work squirting it through scent sprays on each copy of the paper as it came off the machine.

Pearson followed up his *Weekly* with other periodicals, and in 1900 he founded the *Daily Express*. He bought the *Evening Standard* four years later, and he wanted to buy *The Times*. Before he was forty he was rich, famous, and powerful. It was a traditional newspaper proprietor's success-story. But there was something else besides.

It began in 1891, the second year of *Pearson's Weekly*, when it was still largely touch and go. He collected money from his readers to provide a Christmas dinner for hundreds of children in the East End of London. His readers gave generously, and there was so much to eat that some of it went to waste. Pearson decided this was not the most practical form of philanthropy, and the next year he began the Fresh Air Fund, which gave East End children a day's outing in Epping Forest. This was one of his happiest ideas, and twenty thousand children had a picnic the first year. The next year the figure was doubled.

Pearson gave generously himself, and always bore the whole of the running costs of the fund. He also showed a distinct flair for persuading others to give.

At forty he was on top of the world, but already the darkness was beginning to fall. Two years later he was operated on for glaucoma. The operation was technically successful, but he was never again able to see well enough to read or write. His sight became steadily worse, until in 1913 he was told that before long he would be totally blind.

"I shall soon be blind," he said to his wife, "but I will never be *a* blind man. I am going to be *the* blind man."

It was hardly modest, but characteristic of the man. He never pretended to be self-effacing; there would have been no St Dunstan's if he had been.

In October 1913 he joined the Council of what is now the Royal National Institute for the Blind. It was happily timed, for the Institute was in danger of financial collapse. Three months later they made him Treasurer, and magically it became solvent.

It had been founded in 1868 as the British and Foreign Society for Improving the Embossed Literature for the Blind. The leading light among the founders was a young doctor, Thomas Armitage, who had served as a surgeon in the Crimean War. His medical career was cut short by failing sight. When he was forced to retire he decided to spend the rest of his life bettering the conditions of others who were blind. He associated himself with a charitable organization founded thirty years earlier called the Indigent Blind Visiting Society, and spent two years visiting poor blind people in their homes. He found that most were living in squalor, and maintained themselves by begging because they had no other means.

Obviously, they needed relief, but only employment could give them back their self-respect. Armitage found that most of them were untrained and uneducated, and he decided that the first step was to supply them with books that they could learn to read with their fingertips. Braille was eventually chosen as the most suitable form of embossed type, and books and writing apparatus were produced by Armitage and his fellow-workers. Although they did not confine themselves entirely to this very important but limited aspect of blind welfare, it was their main work; and even when Pearson joined the Council, in 1913, the National Institute was still chiefly a publishing house for braille.

It was at that time in great financial difficulties because

new premises had been built, and the available funds fell
far short of the cost. Pearson set himself the task of raising
£30,000. He persuaded the Lord Mayor to open a
Mansion House Fund, and gave £1000 of his own. Lord
Northcliffe and Lord Rothermere each gave the same.
Thanks largely to a great deal of free publicity in the Press,
the money rolled in.

King George V opened the Institute's new building in
Great Portland Street, and immediately afterwards Pearson
had one of his typical bright ideas. He arranged with the
Marconi Company to send out the first wireless appeal on
record to every ship at sea that could be reached by radio
from the Marconi station in Cornwall. The message included a quotation from the speech made by the King in
opening the building, and the novel appeal itself won more
free publicity in the news columns of the papers.

Pearson was the first man to organize appeals on a really
large scale, and there is no doubt about the effectiveness of
his ingenious methods. At the same time, the wording of
his appeals was always matter-of-fact and down-to-earth.
He relied on hard facts rather than sentiment. In a typical
piece in *Pearson's Weekly* at this time he made the simple
point that braille books were "so bulky and so costly to
produce that a copy of *Ivanhoe* which you can buy for sixpence in one little volume occupies in braille six volumes,
as large as a sheet of foolscap paper and nearly three inches
thick, and costs to make nineteen shillings and sixpence."
Donations were needed to make the books cheaper. "In
fact," he said, "I really want them to be so cheap that they
can almost, if not quite, be given away."

In little more than a year nearly £60,000 was raised—
compared with £8000 the year before. Pearson was made
the first President of the National Institute, and he set to
work to widen the field of its activities, to make it much
more than a publishing house for braille literature. Then
the First World War broke out, and the Prince of Wales
asked him to work for the National Relief Fund.

Few people knew what to expect of the War, but however it was fought one thing was clear from the start: some of the fighting men would lose their sight. Pearson was already thinking of the first of these while they could still see. At the first wartime meeting of the Council of the National Institute, held only six weeks after the outbreak, it was resolved that "steps should be taken to make it known that the Institute would, so far as practicable, help such men as lose their sight while in service in the war."

So far as practicable. No one knew what was practicable then, or even when the first blinded soldiers appeared.

Probably the first man blinded in the War was a Belgian soldier whose eyes were pierced by a rifle bullet on the first day of the siege of Liège. Like nearly all wounded Belgians in the early days, he was brought to an English hospital. Pearson went to see him, and chatted as only another blind man could. A little later he heard that two British soldiers had been blinded and were in the 2nd London General Hospital. He went to see them, too. And he came away wondering what could be done for them when medical science had done its best and they were ready for discharge.

He was not worried that they would starve, or have to beg, or be unwanted and unloved. Most wounded soldiers had homes to go back to, and wives or mothers to look after them. All would have pensions to save them from actual want, and for most there would be charity and compassion besides. That was the danger. Pearson wrote: "I pictured these men after their discharge returning to their own homes, where, for all the love that might surround them, they would probably slip into hopeless and useless lives. And the idea developed itself of a Hostel where they could 'learn to be blind.' "

Unless you understand what that phrase means you can never understand St Dunstan's.

It was to be a hostel, not an institution. It would put them up for a while, but not house them for life. It would provide training, but not employment. It was not to be a refuge or shelter from the world, as all the existing institutions for the blind were at that time. The aim was to enable each man to return to a normal life in a community as nearly possible like the one in which he had dwelt before he was wounded, and to make his way in the world like anyone else—to earn his own living, to create his own home, to marry and have children and, as far as possible, support his family by the products of his own work. This was Pearson's vision, the brilliant vision of a man who had lost his physical sight.

On the face of it, St Dunstan's was a paradox. Left alone, most blinded men would not have joined a community of other blinded men, but would have gone back to their former environment of their own accord. If that was Pearson's aim why did he want to winkle each of them out and put them together, creating a new community of the blind?

The answer, of course, lay in that key-phrase of his. They might make their own way back to a normal environment, but they could not recover a normal place in it until they learnt to be blind.

At that time the blind were considered what might now be called second-class citizens. They were the objects of pity, compassion, and charity. They were regarded as the unlucky victims of a terrible affliction that condemned them to a sort of passive half-life, from which the only escape was death. When Henry Fawcett, the first blind M.P., was proposed for membership of the Reform Club the committee hesitated to accept him until Thackeray, in an eloquent speech, promised that Fawcett would soon make them forget he was blind. Fawcett was exceptional not only for his personal achievement but for the fact that he did not take his blindness lying down, for the general opinion of the sighted members of society was largely shared by the blind themselves. Most of them accepted their inferiority, matched pity with self-pity, and were resigned to their fate.

That all this seems so remote from us now, even that it needs to be said at all, is some measure of the speed and completeness of the change. If St Dunstan's contributed to this change—and I think it is a reasonable boast—it is only fair to our forbears to mention that there had never been so many newly blinded persons of our age and sort before.

Most people had gone blind through disease, either when they were old and enfeebled or in infancy. Medical science has greatly reduced the incidence of blindness in both categories, but at that time most of the blind were either in poor physical shape or had never seen the world after the first few days of their lives. Only in their blindness had the men who poured into St Dunstan's anything in common with these.

With some cruel exceptions, we were not only fit but at the height of our physical powers. We were young and keen, lively and vigorous, ambitious, adaptable, and eager to get on. We not only knew what the world was like but had been on the point of conquering it. Once we got over our bad period—and we all had to go through this—we were wonderfully suitable, physically and mentally, to respond to Pearson's ideas.

The chief of these was that blindness was not a soul-destroying affliction; or, at least, that there was no need for it to be. It could and should be no more than a handicap; not a calamity, and by no means unique.

Recently the Principal of Queen Elizabeth's Training College for the Disabled, at Leatherhead, estimated that as many as two million people in this country are physically handicapped in one way or another. Less than 5 per cent. of these are totally blind. Of course, this figure includes minor as well as major disabilities, and it would be foolish to deny that blindness is a very great handicap. It is still no reason for hopelessness or helplessness. The lives of men like Fawcett and Sir John Fielding, the famous Bow Street police-magistrate—blinded at nineteen through an accident "which everyone but myself deemed a misfortune"

—prove that. It is true that these were exceptional men, but also they had had exceptional opportunities compared with the majority of the blind. Given the chance there was no reason why that majority should not lead useful and happy lives.

St Dunstan's was founded to give them that chance. They would not have got it in their homes, no matter how much understanding and sympathy they might have received. Nor was this only because they might have been smothered with love. The newly blinded person has to learn the most elementary things all over again, and in his first efforts at things like walking and eating, for example, he is as clumsy as a child. He needs help—expert help.

There is no great art in helping the blind in the ordinary things of life. It does not require long study or even much intelligence. It is merely a matter of some simple knowledge and a bit of practice. Anyone can learn in a very short time. But the knowledge has to be acquired, because the average person trying to help the blind, if left to himself, instinctively does the wrong things.

Suppose you want to help a blind companion on to a train or bus. The chances are that you will try to put him on first. You will probably grasp his arm and try to lift him up or push him on. This is exactly what he does not want. The proper thing is for you to board the vehicle first. Tell him what you are doing, and especially warn him about the steps, and stay near enough for him to use you as a guide.

Now suppose you are indoors and he wants to sit down. Again probably you will lead him to the front of the chair, and perhaps try to push him into it. That also is wrong. The proper thing is to guide his hand to the back of the chair and leave the rest to him. In lots of other ways you will, if not instructed, try to do the right thing and guess wrong. In the critical early days especially, the newly blinded needs the help of people who do not have to guess.

He also needs to be in a place where he can move about

Sir Arthur Pearson, Bt, G.B.E.
The Founder of St Dunstan's

32

St Dunstan's, Ovingdean, Sussex

Learning the Geography of St Dunstan's by studying a Model of the Building

33

The Induction of a Priest by his Bishop

with confidence—a place designed or adapted for the blind, with guide-rails and ropes, bumpers over sharp edges and corners, and no chairs left lying about for him to trip over. He needs the company of other blind men—not for an exchange of condolences but to draw encouragement from those who have been learning longer and gone farther, but were blinded recently enough for him to infer that he will soon be as capable as they are. Finally, he needs to learn to read and write, to play and to work.

Before St Dunstan's began Pearson called together a score of men and women with specialist knowledge to discuss the best trades for blinded soldiers to be taught. The traditional crafts of basketry and mat-making were obvious choices, but Pearson wanted others as well. He had some quite revolutionary ideas of his own, and the conference went on a long time before the final list was made.

The Blinded Soldiers' and Sailors' Hostel, it was called at first. Founded with the help of the British Red Cross Society, with a grant from the National Relief Fund that Pearson had helped to raise, it was originally an offshoot of the National Institute for the Blind. Its first home was in Bayswater Road, in a house lent by Mrs Lewis Hall, a continuous benefactor to the blind. Its staff consisted mainly of V.A.D.'s.

It was opened early in February 1915, with only two blinded soldiers. When it was visited by Sidney Dark, Pearson's biographer, there were four. In recalling the visit Dark told of an incident that showed Pearson in quite a typical light. He had a chat with the Matron, who told him that one of the four was rather despondent.

"Despondent?" repeated Pearson. "What on earth has he got to be despondent about?" But he sent for the man, and talked to him in what Dark called a splendid brotherly manner. Pearson was able to cheer others up because he was essentially such a cheerful person himself.

There were sixteen men in the hostel on March 26,

C

when a move was made to a much larger house—a country house in the middle of London, within a couple of miles of Piccadilly Circus and yet standing in fifteen acres of ground. It was built during the Regency, and it was in Regent's Park. It belonged to a New York banker named Otto Kahn. He placed it at Pearson's disposal absolutely free of charge. In doing so he unwittingly gave St Dunstan's its name.

St Dunstan was not the patron saint of the blind. He was appointed Archbishop of Canterbury in 961 after having once been accused of practising the black arts because of his love of books and of song and his mechanical skill. There is a legend that when he was tempted by the Devil he seized a pair of red-hot pincers and tweaked the tempter's nose. He comes into our story only because a church named after him was built in the City of London, and adorned with a famous and remarkable clock.

The Church of St Dunstan in the West stood in Fleet Street, and the projecting clock was one of the sights of London. People used to gather in the street below to watch the life-sized figures carved in wood strike the quarter-hours with their clubs.

A small boy watched these giants and longed to possess them himself. This boy became the third Marquess of Hertford, and in 1830 his dream came true. The old church was pulled down, and the clock put up for sale. The Marquess bought it, and had it set up at a house he had just had built in Regent's Park. The house came to be called St Dunstan's Villa, and later St Dunstan's Lodge, and this was the house placed at Pearson's disposal by Otto Kahn.

The house was pulled down some years ago, and our organization has long since moved out of Regent's Park. The clock is back on the rebuilt Church of St Dunstan in the West, in Fleet Street, and again draws knots of sightseers for the striking of the quarter-hours. Most of them will have heard of St Dunstan's, too. I wonder how many know the curious way in which this clock supplied us with our name.

It seemed a huge place for the first sixteen men, but all too quickly it became too small. By the end of the first year several temporary buildings, for use as classrooms and workshops, had been put up in the grounds. More paid orderlies and trained nurses had been engaged, although the staff still consisted mainly of V.A.D.'s. There were nearly a hundred and fifty St Dunstaners, and at least another fifty in hospital who would shortly join them. But fifty had already passed out, able to read and write and earn their living. They had learnt to work and to play and to enjoy life again. They were by no means the first blinded persons to do this, but never before had so many learnt so quickly.

"A little world very much in touch with the big world around it," Pearson called the hostel, and there was nothing remotely conventual about it. The men were encouraged to invite their friends and relations, for the whole aim of St Dunstan's would have been defeated if they had begun to think of themselves as a class apart. There was a welcome for all visitors who could help. It was a voluntary organization, and Pearson was always a practical visionary. Although, on his own admission, he shared the popular view that the War would soon be over, he realized at the start that St Dunstan's would need generous financial support. And the man to whom blind beggars were anathema was still the boldest and most successful blind beggar of all. Nobody could beat him at getting hard-headed businessmen to dive for their cheque-books, or cynical editors and journalists to gobble up blatant puffs and plugs.

A visit by Lord Kitchener was not only good for the men's morale, because of his prestige at that time; being chatted to by Horatio Bottomley was not only pleasant, and he extremely charming—such names in the Visitors'

Book meant more Press publicity, and that meant more money.

Yet even Kitchener and Bottomley, big names as they were then, came some way down the distinguished visitors' list. From the very beginning St Dunstan's enjoyed the support of the highest in the land. In the first year it had the privilege of being visited by Their Majesties King George V and Queen Mary, Queen Alexandra, the Prince of Wales, Princess Victoria, and other members of the Royal Family. Queen Alexandra paid several visits, and before the year was out she had become Patroness. During the next forty-five years the office of Patron was held successively by King Edward VIII, King George VI, and Queen Elizabeth II.

By the end of this first year St Dunstan's had already spread beyond Regent's Park. An annexe had been opened at Brighton, in a house in Queen's Road lent by the National Institute for the Blind. This was a convalescent home for men just discharged from hospital, and for others who needed a change or a rest. For those in need of longer convalescence—for those who had lost limbs as well as sight, for the shell-shocked and paralysed, the more sorely hurt in body and mind—an annexe was opened at Torquay, with local financial support. Sir John and Lady Stirling-Maxwell had lent their house at 21 Portland Place, for the accommodation of blinded officers. Pearson lived there with them himself. In September 1916 I went there too.

3

Learning to be Blind

I HAD stayed in Portland Place once before, so I knew
what it looked like. I think it was in the hot, dry summer
of 1911 that my mother came to England for a visit, and
I stayed with her at the old Langham Hotel.

Five years later I had only a vague recollection of the
appearance of the street, and now that has faded a great
deal more. But I was aware that it was straight and wide
and spacious, with severely plain but very fine houses on
each side.

No. 21 was one of these. It had room for about ten of us
besides Sir Arthur and Lady Pearson, who made us feel at
home. There we ate and slept and talked, but did not work,
for right from the start St Dunstan's was strictly in bounds
to all ranks. There was not the slightest distinction between
officers and men in the process of learning to be blind.

Walking to and from St Dunstan's Lodge every day was,
literally, one of the first steps in our education. It was also
very jolly and pleasant, for we were escorted by those
wonderfully charming and attentive V.A.D.'s. I suppose it
must have rained sometimes, and been cold and wet and
even foggy, but I do not remember that it was ever miserable. No one could have had any excuse to feel sorry for
us as we bantered our way along.

St Dunstan's Lodge was about a mile and a quarter
away. The first time I made the journey we walked quite
slowly, to give me a chance to get my bearings, so it
probably took us nearly half an hour. No. 21 was at what is
now the Broadcasting House end of Portland Place, so

37

there were several streets to cross before we reached the
Marylebone Road. That was a busy street even in those
days, but there was a policeman on point duty at the crossing, and he knew us and greeted us cheerily as he stopped
the traffic to let us cross. Inside the park we turned left, and
walked along the broad tree-bordered road to the western
side. With my stick I could feel a fence by the footpath. I
had made exactly the same walk with my mother five years
before, when she took me to the Zoo, and probably I had
some memory of smooth lawns leading down to the lake.

There was another cheerful greeting for us at the entrance
of the carriage-drive of St Dunstan's Lodge. This was
from the porter, who watched the traffic for blind men
going in and out. That meant that he could not be one of
us, although he was an old soldier. It was not till some time
later that I learnt he had only one arm.

Now we were walking over gravel. We followed the
hand-rail to the entrance to the building, and then passed
through the swing doors. I could hear that the hall inside
was large, and there seemed to be a lot of people moving
very quickly and surely about. One of the V.A.D.'s told me
that most of them were blind. With her help I took a few
tentative steps, and discovered that I was on a linoleum
path. The whole hall was carpeted, but paths of linoleum
ran through the carpets to help us to walk about. At first
it was quite bewildering. Blind men who were familiar with
the place moved with some speed and great certainty.
Some whistled or sang out to announce their approach,
others just brushed past. There were a few collisions, of
which I had my share when I gave my guide the slip and
practised moving about on my own.

We crossed the hall and went through open doors into
the garden. It was like being in the country, with no sound
of London's traffic, but only the songs of birds and the
rustle of leaves; no smell of petrol fumes, but the scent of
flowers and freshly cut grass. The principle of the guiding
pathway had been continued here, parallel wires crossing

the stone terrace. Wooden boards were let into the gravel at the top and bottom of steps and in front of walls and other obstacles, the blind man receiving a timely warning the moment he stepped on one. There were hand-rails, too, with knobs to mark turns, and all sorts of other aids to progress. They were mainly to help newcomers, and men who had been there a while did not use them much.

From the terrace we went down a sharply sloping bank to a wide lawn, and at the end of this there was another steep slope. My guide painted the picture for me as we went.

"There are new buildings on both sides—we go down here, there are eighteen steps." She took a pace in front of me, and I put my hand on her shoulder and counted the steps as we descended. "Now we're passing the classrooms, where you'll learn braille and typewriting. This is the massage department—I think there's a class going on." We put our heads in the doorway, and I heard a fragment of a lecture on anatomy. We continued our walk along the covered pathway. "Now we're coming to the workshops. Actually they're all in one big building, shaped like a capital E. Sir Arthur designed it himself."

First there were the basket-makers, and we stopped and listened to a blind instructor telling a blind pupil what to do. Then there were the mat-makers, and then I heard the Cobblers' Chorus—the whistling and singing of the cobblers accompanied by blows of their hammers on leather soles as they did their repairs. The joinery shop interested me most—I had not thought of being able to do carpentry, which appealed to me personally much more than any of the traditional handicrafts for the blind.

"Here's the poultry farm." I could hear it and smell it, and marvelled as I heard blind men being taught to distinguish different breeds of chicken by their sense of touch.

We walked to the lake, which adjoined the grounds, and I heard the splash of oars as blind men rowed. My guide told me about the last Sports Day, and of the preparations for the next concert. We went back to the house and through the lounges, and heard blind men playing cards and dominoes, and performing on the piano. I even heard some talking about what they would wear at the next dance, which was to be a Fancy Dress Ball. I heard shouts and laughter, humour and good fellowship. I also heard an occasional argument not always good-natured—for blindness is not a cure for bad tempers, and St Dunstan's did not undertake to turn men into saints. What I did not hear, either then or later, was despondency, apathy, listlessness, or gloom. St Dunstaners had their fair share of human faults, but at least they were vividly alive.

The thing I found difficult to believe was that they were all as blind as I was myself.

I was meant to find that difficulty. All newcomers were —it was part of the treatment. It stopped me from saying or even thinking it was too difficult when I began learning myself.

My lessons began the next day. Pearson believed in making an early start. On the other hand, he did not believe in working long hours. He broke completely with traditional time-tables in schools for the blind, and drew up a schedule allowing two and a half hours of instruction in the morning and two hours in the afternoon, with the option of an extra hour.

Only about half of this time was for vocational training. The other half was for learning to read and write in the language of the blind. So you spent either the morning in the classroom and the afternoon in one of the workshops or the other way about.

Work started at half-past nine, and I began with braille. The teaching was organized by Miss E. W. Austin, head of the National Library for the Blind. Each pupil had his own individual teacher, and at that time over a hundred of them came to St Dunstan's every day. Later this number was greatly increased. Only a few were blind themselves, but most had experience of making books for the National Library by hand. They were all women, and nearly all unpaid volunteers. They came in all weathers, and despite every difficulty. They would not like me to talk of our debt to them, for they did not lend but gave; in their own language, repaid. They and other V.A.D.'s were the salt of our earth.

It was only a classroom in the sense that we all happened to be learning the same subject. There were no desks, but separate tables, each with two chairs. Instruction was entirely individual and independent. There was no segregation of officers and other ranks. Each of us, in his own time, struggled to master the six-dot permutation of Louis Braille's ingenious but intricate system of reading by fingertips. After about half an hour of this most of us felt the beginning of a mental fatigue. That was the time to take a break in the netting room, which for this reason adjoined the classroom where braille was taught.

Netting was not considered a trade. It was a pleasant hobby that could be profitable in the pocket-money sense. It was the easiest of all handicrafts, and St Dunstan's workers went regularly to No. 2 General Hospital to start men on it while they were still in bed. At St Dunstan's they found they could, and did, sell their string-bags to the public; but only because they had been made by the blind— perhaps only because they were made by blinded soldiers, while there was still a war on. The same thing, made by a machine, was just as good and much cheaper, and there was no future for the blind in competing with machines. It would be like the blind man on the street-corner selling boot-laces, appealing to charity as an alternative to offering value for money; and one day the War would end, and loss of memory begin. So netting had its limitations, but it was still a wonderful antidote to braille.

The other classroom that everyone with hands used was for learning to typewrite, which was as easy as braille was hard. This also was not regarded as a trade, except for those who learned shorthand too. It was more important than that.

It is impossible to over-state the importance of the type-writer to the newly blinded man. When he writes his first letter home with his own hands he passes the second of the two main milestones on his way back into the world. The first is telling the time with a braille watch. The effects of these two things are symbolical as well as practical, for they mark two distinct stages in the man's recovery. With the watch and the typewriter the world is never so dark again. And happily both are within easy reach of all who have hands to use them.

Neither is specially designed for the blind. The watch has an ordinary movement, and is only adapted. The type-writer does not need to be changed at all, for the ordinary machine does everything a blind man could ask. The carriage moves the paper along automatically so that each letter falls into its right place. A bell rings just before the end of the line is reached, and a touch of a lever moves the paper up exactly the required amount. Every letter is formed perfectly, and the result is easier to read than a sighted person's longhand. It is, indeed, so suitable that it could have been invented for the blind.

As a matter of fact, it was. And not only to enable the blind to write legibly, but to produce something that they could read themselves. The first typewriter was invented to print embossed or raised letters that could be read by touch. Many more machines of the same kind had been designed and used before a typewriter was evolved that printed ordinary letters. Only then—about 1855—did busi-nessmen realize the machine's possibilities.

The subsequent evolution of the typewriter is also of interest to the blind. The first machines had only one piece of type on each key, and wrote only capital letters. The problem of designing a typewriter that would print both capital and small letters could be solved in two ways, and both were tried. Some machines were made with twice the number of keys, others with no more keys, but two pieces of metal on each, and a cylinder-shifting mechanism. For many years the competing kinds of machine ran neck and neck in popular favour, and it was not till the end of the century that the compact keyboard of the shift-key mechanism won the day. The reason was the discovery and development of the technique of touch-typing; which is, of course, another name for typing blind.

For the last sixty years all typewriters have been designed for the touch-typist, who has been taught to type without looking at the keys, so that her eyes are free to stay on her shorthand notebook or whatever else she is typing from. So no special technique is needed to teach the blind. The only difference is that the pupil has to learn the sequence of letters by heart, and the shape and the parts of the machine by touch; after that the tuition is normal.

I had already begun to learn to typewrite at Wootton Fitzpaine, on Olive Pass's ordinary machine. I found no special difficulty, although I was aware of a slight inconvenience in never being able to look at the keyboard to see where my fingers were. Even a touch-typist takes a quick glance to check her bearings: I had to stop and find them out by feel. It was a small point, but at St Dunstan's I found that even this little irritation had been removed. On each typewriter a small piece of very fine sandpaper had been stuck on each of the middle keys—Y, H, and N—so that the typist could at any time find the middle line with just a slight touch of the forefinger of either hand. Apart from the fact that the scale was embossed instead of engraved— so that the typist could tell the position of the carriage by touch—this was the only modification that had been made to an ordinary standard machine. It is still made to-day, although personally I prefer to put little blocks on the keys at either end of the row—the back-space and the fractions, and other signs that I use—and leave all the inside letters smooth. For blocks I find there is nothing better than those rubber caps that some typists fix over their typewriter keys, I believe to protect their over-long finger-nails.

There were two other classrooms, but these were for teaching trades. The first was for those who wanted to learn braille shorthand. This is quite unrelated to any of the ordinary systems of shorthand used by the sighted, and is a specially devised form of braille. It is not taken down by pencil, but on a machine.

Ordinary braille is difficult enough, and previously very few people had succeeded in becoming competent in the shorthand form. It was generally agreed in the blind world that only those who had been blind from infancy, and brought up to read braille as others were to read ordinary print, were likely to learn it. Pearson was told that to try to teach newly blinded men, many of them not highly educated, was bound to fail.

He still thought it was worth trying, especially for men who had been doing secretarial work before the War; and it succeeded well enough for many of these to go back to their former work.

The last of the classrooms was for training telephone operators; not, of course, for the light-flashing system used even then by the Post Office, but for the drop-shutter switchboard used by most big business firms. At first the blind operator would hear that a shutter or doll's eye had dropped and discover which one it was by touch; before long, however, he would be able to tell that as well merely by sound, although in theory all the shutters or doll's eyes were identical. As Sherlock Holmes pointed out, no two things are exactly alike, whether they are rifle-bullets, cigarette-ends, or finger-prints; and the observation of minute differences is the basis of scientific detection. In the same way the blind man makes uses of differences in sound that other people never hear.

The morning session finished at twelve, and then the main hall became like a railway station at holiday time.

Visitors were warned to keep off the linoleum paths—in their own interests as well as ours. The midday meal was served at one o'clock. We returned to our own mess in Portland Place, and no doubt the walk did us good. We were back at St Dunstan's at half-past two, or earlier if there was a midday concert or lecture that we wanted to hear. Then the afternoon session began.

The workshops, and indeed most other activities, were under the control of Charles Rose, a voluntary worker with unlimited energy. I had already decided that I wanted to learn carpentry, and I began it straight away.

Unlike basketry and mat-making, carpentry or joinery was not a traditional blind man's trade. It started at St Dunstan's in a typical St Dunstan's way. That is to say that it was not the result of any great deliberation or discussion, but simply happened because someone did it and was good at it, and others followed suit.

In this case the man was not a St Dunstaner at all. E. Hope Atkinson had lost his sight in Sheffield about the turn of the century. Already a skilled carpenter, he made up his mind to continue his old trade. Pearson heard about him, and had him along to do some carpentry at St Dunstan's Lodge. He was so impressed by the man's skill that he decided to add joinery to the list of teachable trades. Hope Atkinson was taken on as chief instructor, on the principle that the most suitable leaders of the blind are the blind.

For a qualified man to resume his old trade was one thing, but for novices to learn when blind quite another; but in the event it did not prove as difficult as it might seem. Mostly we used the normal carpenter's tools. Of course, some were specially adapted: our rules were marked by notches, for example, and we used laths to guide our sawing. With these quite simple aids we could do a variety of useful and satisfying work. You do not need to see what you are doing to take pride in craftsmanship when you can feel your creations with your fingers as they grow and develop.

Of course, no attempt was made to teach a man to be a complete all-round joiner. The aim was to train him to make a number of readily saleable articles, like photo-frames, tea-trays, corner-cupboards, and occasional tables. Picture-frames were made in a variety of styles to fit photographs of all sizes, and the instruction included the cutting of the glass, so that the blind joiner could make the whole article without assistance. Trays were made in oak, with brass handles and fancy moulding, and St Dunstan's became quite famous for them.

Few people downed tools in the carpentry shop when the whistle blew at half-past four, and often we worked on until quite late. Evening visitors were sometimes startled to hear the sounds of hammering and sawing executed with confidence coming from a completely dark workshop.

I often stayed late. Another keen carpenter was Captain William Appleby, who has shown as well as anyone what a full and useful life a blind man can lead. Early in 1917 he was going round the principal towns of Warwickshire, giving lectures about St Dunstan's illustrated with moving pictures. He had never been on a platform before, but was so successful that he later entered public life. He took a very active part in running the Economic League, and he was virtually one of the founders of the British Legion. After the War he helped Earl Haig to bring the various ex-Service organizations into one, and travelled round the world with him, helping to found the Canadian Legion and similar bodies in the other Dominions. He joined St Dunstan's Executive Council in 1929 as representative of the British Legion.

If you did not work late in the workshops you probably went walking, rowing, or swimming. In the summer especially these were our most popular outdoor diversions, both in the afternoon and before breakfast.

Rowing and sculling are obviously ideal exercises for the blind, and it was a piece of extraordinarily good luck that we had a lake right on our doorstep. All a man needed was a cox, and there was never any difficulty about that. Friendly V.A.D.'s came from all over London, and especially from Bedford College, and there were often fifty boats on the lake by half-past six.

One of the pleasures of rowing was that it reversed the usual order of things—we were actually taking somebody about, instead of being taken. Perhaps that is why there was no great enthusiasm for male coxes, in spite of their expert knowledge and advice on such technicalities as feathering. Most men preferred a girl in the boat, and were content with a windmill stroke, or sometimes no stroke at all. With a co-operative cox it was quite easy to bring the boat to a stop under some leafy boughs.

Riding tandem bicycles was another popular exercise. At first there were only two or three, so they were greatly in demand. Miss Irene Mace and I made do with two ordinary bicycles, which we rode from Portland Place to the lake for early-morning rowing. It was easy enough once I got the hang of it, holding her arm with one hand and my own handlebars with the other.

There are various surprises in learning to be blind, some agreeable and others irksome. It takes much less time than you would expect to learn to typewrite a letter faster than a sighted person could write in longhand, and to do apparently difficult things like distinguishing breeds of chickens and making furniture. Swimming and rowing were no problems at all. All the more frustrating, therefore, was the persistence of the problem of making our way about on foot. Bear in mind that most of us were fit and young, and that we had not only the impatience but the sensitiveness of youth, and you may perhaps imagine how we felt about having to cling on to someone else, usually a girl, when we went out into the street.

I soon learnt that it is better to hold the guide's arm than to be held. This puts the guide a few inches in front, so that you always get a warning before any change of level or course. If your guide takes your arm you are in front, and you cannot anticipate steps up or down or other hazards. The safest plan of all is for you to take your guide's arm and for him or her to tell you when you come to a step or have to change your direction. This was what we did with the V.A.D.'s, who knew how to help us best with the least possible fuss. It was still irritating to have to be helped, and in those young days I suffered from the fear that people were looking at me, probably in a pitying way. I made up my mind to get out on my own as soon as I could.

This was not easy, because first I had to give the V.A.D.'s the slip. They had a wonderful knack of spotting anyone who tried to sneak out for a solo walk—and the happiest possible way of stopping him. "Oh, hullo—which way are you going? . . . That's lucky, so am I. You can take me if you like." When this happened to me I accepted defeat, and usually took the charmer to the Langham Hotel for a drink. Very nice too, but I still had not walked outside on my own.

I had two or three defeats of this sort before I finally got away. I had found out, by asking, how the streets ran in that part, and had planned my route in advance. Turn left in Portland Place, walk about fifty yards, then turn left into New Cavendish Street; another two or three hundred yards along, then left again into Mansfield Street; left again into Duchess Street, which would then lead me back into Portland Place, left again, completing the square, and home. It might not be so easy to find No. 21, but I could deal with that point when I came to it. As a last resort I could always ask.

I turned left when I came out of the house, and set off with great confidence. This was the start of the way to St Dunstan's, which I now knew pretty well. It was so familiar that I thought I could judge when I reached New Cavendish Street almost to the step. Still, I was not taking any chances, so I felt the railing on the left with my stick as I walked. The railing stopped sooner than I had expected,

In the Carpentry Shops at Ovingdean

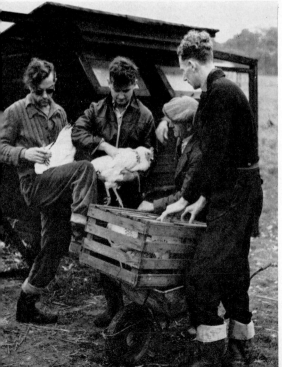

Poultry Farmers in the Making

Practising reading Braille

A First-War Instructor giving a Braille-writing Lesson to a Second-War Man

but I turned left—and fell up two or three steps leading to the front door of a house.

As I rubbed my shins I reflected how lucky I was to blunder into steps that went up and not down. I might just as easily have stepped off from the top and plunged head-long down into an area, and perhaps broken my neck; although probably not that, for I had already learnt how much safer it was to walk upright, with the shoulders well back, than leaning forward. Still, the V.A.D.'s had proved their point—or rather I had proved it for them. On the other hand, I still had to learn to walk alone, and the only way to do it was to go on trying.

In the end the V.A.D.'s must have decided either that I was safe enough or that I was beyond saving—anyway, they let me go out alone. I thought this was quite a victory, and before long I really was quite safe. Another milestone was reached and passed the first time I made my way alone to St Dunstan's, even crossing the Marylebone Road without help. The walk took me forty minutes, but later I got it down to thirty.

I still carried a stick—not a heavy one such as blind beggars used to thump on the pavement, drawing attention to themselves, but quite a light one which I used really as a sort of extension of my arm. I learnt to navigate lamp-posts and pillar-boxes, to cross roads without tripping over kerbs. I made use of the sounds of traffic and footsteps on different surfaces, and quite slight echoes that a person with sight would never need to hear. I also used my nose, and for the first time I realized that nearly every kind of shop has its own distinctive smell.

I had always been keen on outdoor exercise, and it meant a lot to me to be able to go sculling and swimming again. But my favourite outdoor sport was riding. I had been on and off horses ever since I could remember. As a child in South Africa I had ridden a pony to school, and when I came to England I had learnt properly on an old hunter

D

mare with Douglas Pass in his Dorset home. I had won my
spurs at Sandhurst, although I was an infantry cadet. I had
ridden with the Cattistock Hunt and the Cotley Harriers.
Riding was both natural in my family and a personal
delight. Could I go on riding now that I was blind? Would
I enjoy it if I did?

Henry Fawcett had ridden blind, and he seemed to have
been happy doing it. I resolved to try. I had my opportunity
that first winter at St Dunstan's during week-ends when
I was staying in Brighton. None of the others had tried
it yet, and I had to face some opposition. Finally I overcame this, and was allowed out on the Downs. At first it
was conditional on my using a leading rein, but I was able
to prove I was better off without this.

That winter I went several times to the theatre—almost
always free of charge, for St Dunstan's used to get shoals
of tickets with the compliments of the management. The
great show then was *The Bing Boys*, and I expect we were
taken there because it seemed the right sort of thing to
cheer us up. Also, perhaps, it was assumed that as we were
blind we needed something that would not put too much
strain on our intelligence; for there is an unfortunate
popular fallacy that when you lose sight you lose half your
wits as well. In point of fact a revue was the least suitable
sort of entertainment there was—except the cinema, of
course, which was silent then. The music might be jolly,
but we missed the dancing, the costumes and the spectacle
were wasted, and we had no idea what the slapstick
comedians were doing to make the rest of the audience
drown their jokes with laughter.

A straight play was different, and I was delighted to find
that I could thoroughly enjoy it. There might be one or
two things that needed explaining—if there was a man
hiding from the other characters but deliberately visible to
the audience, for example—but I rarely needed more than
an odd sentence of explanation from my companion to be
able to follow the play.

We had our own entertainments at St Dunstan's, too, of course. There were regular lunch-time concerts, and every Thursday up-patients in the 2nd General came over to share the fun and have a foretaste of St Dunstan's. Then we put on our own Christmas concert, with a programme mostly of songs and recitations. We had several pianists of varying ability, and a Belgian played some cornet solos. Later the Matron started a string band, and then a brass band. We had two dances a week—one an instruction night for beginners, the other our regular ball. This was another form of exercise that came quite easily—again, thanks largely to the V.A.D.'s.

It was the V.A.D.'s, too, who read aloud to us, and kept us in touch with what was happening in the world. Every morning after breakfast we heard the main news in the paper. Most of it was from the Western Front, where we had been so recently ourselves, and it rarely made pleasant hearing. A report of a large battle meant more men for St Dunstan's, whichever way the fighting went. It meant that more men who could see were suddenly going to lose their sight. Our hearts went out to them, with the sympathy of men who have recovered from a serious illness towards those for whom the worst is still to come. That we could feel this already, young as we were and still learning to be blind, gives an idea of how far our own spiritual recovery had progressed.

But I wondered what I was going to do about a career.

One of the books Olive Pass had read to me at Wootton was Leslie Stephen's *Life of Henry Fawcett*. I have no idea whether anyone recommended this to her, or whether she thought of it herself; but it was a happy choice, this biography of a blind man who not only overcame all difficulties and succeeded in public life but was extremely cheerful.

Fawcett was accidentally blinded in his twenty-fifth year by a stray shot from his father's gun. His first words were, "This shall make no difference," and it didn't. A few years later he was elected to the Chair of Political Economy at

Cambridge, and at thirty-two he entered Parliament. Later he became Postmaster-General in Gladstone's second Government. It is an encouraging story for anyone who loses his sight. Yet there did not seem to be anything in it for me personally at that time.

Fawcett had already finished his studies and was a Fellow of Trinity Hall before he was blinded. I had left school at seventeen, and my academic education had finished then; I had gone to Sandhurst on the outbreak of war, and the study of academic subjects was suspended for the duration. I underwent an intensive war course for six months, became an Under Officer, and was kept there to train others for six months more. None of this was of any help to me now. Nor did my own inclination fit into the picture very well. It had been my intention to return to South Africa to my father's and my uncle's business, but this seemed hardly practicable now.

I was a technically minded youngster, and I might have gone to Cambridge and read engineering or science. I should have liked this, but where would it lead? None of the men who had conquered blindness seemed to have done anything remotely scientific. There had been Fawcett and Sir John Fielding in public life. Milton had written some of his greatest poems after he went blind. Of several musicians, Dr Alfred Hollins, blind from infancy, was still vigorously alive.

Most of the others seemed to have done something for the blind themselves. Braille and Moon had invented systems of writing. Dr Armitage and Sir Francis Campbell had worked for the blind at first independently, and then had joined forces to found the Royal Normal College and Academy of Music for the Blind. There were more stirring examples alive and close at hand. Dr (later Sir) Washington Ranger, a well-known solicitor, was chairman of the National Institute for the Blind and a member of the original St Dunstan's committee. One of his most vigorous colleagues was Captain (later Sir) Beachcroft Towse, the blinded V.C. of the South African War. Finally Pearson himself. . . .

Not that I even dreamed that I might join such distinguished company as this. These were all men of exceptional talent, and I knew I was not brilliant. But with sight I might have been a reasonably useful technician, and without sight or training that seemed hardly plausible. Yet one of these ideas was buzzing in my mind.

During my convalescence I had met Sir Frank Fletcher, the great headmaster. He had left Marlborough just before I went there, so I missed him. There was still a slight bond, and we talked about teachers, and I asked him if he thought a blind man could become head of a school for the blind. I was thinking more of the organization of the teaching than of the instruction itself. He could not have known anything about the subject, but he was a good enough psychologist to encourage me to think further on these lines. My thoughts were still nebulous when I saw the job Pearson was doing in organizing a tremendous enterprise like St Dunstan's. I still did not think of any personal implications until Pearson raised the matter with me. How it developed after that I cannot remember, but I have a letter that Pearson wrote to my mother, dated February 15, 1917, which says:

"I have had long talks with Ian lately, and have decided to train him up to assist me in working for the benefit of the blind."

4

Care and After-Care

TO a blind man any new acquaintance is much more than a mere voice. When I meet someone for the first time I get an immediate impression of his height and build by his handshake, and by the height from which his voice comes. His handshake also tells me something about his character, and I learn more from the way he talks and what he says.

Pearson at first struck me as an old man; which was natural enough, for he was fifty and I was still in my teens. As I got to know him I realized that in fact he was young for his age. He was exceptionally active and vigorous. He was also extremely generous and warm-hearted—and warm-tempered, too, if you were slow on the uptake. He was quick-tempered as well as quick-witted, and if you did not think as fast as he did, or failed to see his point as quickly as he thought you should, he was liable to flare up and blow you out of the room. But the mood quickly passed, and he was never too big to apologize. He was much too kind a man to be a ruthless tycoon.

He was a good bluffer. One man went to him, having been through the workshops, and said he did not think he could do any of the trades taught. Pearson asked him what he had done before he went into the Army. The man said he had been a butcher.

"Then," said Pearson, "you have a ready-made job. You are accustomed to handling tools, to using saws and knives; carpentering is the very thing for you."

As Pearson said when he told the story, butchering and

carpentry have nothing in common, but the man fell for it, and became a first-class joiner.

Pearson believed that we should not only be as self-reliant as possible but that we should be seen to be self-reliant, and he himself would never seek help if he could avoid it. His attitude to eating was typical.

The easiest way for a blind person to eat is to have his food served in a bowl all mixed up like a dog's dinner, and eat it with a spoon. This is neither agreeable nor necessary. My own method is to find out if there is a bone, and if so to have that removed and the meat cut into a few reasonable portions, and then to eat the meal in the normal way with either a spoon and fork or a knife and fork. Pearson went further than that. He refused all help, and claimed he could deal with anything that was put on his plate, from a lamb chop to a chicken wing. This was another piece of Pearson bluff, and he only got away with it because jolly good care was taken to see that no bone was ever put on his plate. In fairness I must say that this was not done with his connivance—everyone was much too respectful to tell him.

Pearson's method certainly would not have done for taking a girl out to dinner. This was quite a ticklish affair at first, until you realized that it was up to you to put her at ease, not the other way about. This is obvious once you think about it. Most sighted people are not used to meeting blind persons, but blind people are mixing with the sighted every day. They want to help us, but usually do not know how to do it. They are scared of not doing enough, and especially of trying to do too much, and are clumsy and embarrassed. Telling them you do not need any help at all is one way, but not the best if it is followed by your chicken-bone skidding on to their lap; or, perhaps even worse, if they are on tenterhooks all the time you are eating in case it happens. One man I knew, possibly over-inspired by Pearson's example, insisted on doing everything himself, until he got into an awful mess trying to cut up his tie. Personally I have always been more practical than heroic.

Yet it was to our advantage that Pearson could bluff. His jaunty self-confidence was not only infectious among us but a good antidote to public pity and misunderstanding. When your hostess with the teapot asks your companion, "Does he take sugar?" as if you were deaf or witless as well as blind you will probably just laugh, and a good thing too; but it is important for the blind that they should not be thought more handicapped than they are. Pearson was seen more than any of us, and it was to our benefit that he cut such a good figure.

Besides his other fine qualities, Pearson was not lacking in gratitude. He appreciated the help that others gave, and he told me more than once that since he went blind his greatest debt was to the girl who was his nurse, reader, and guide, Irene Mace. She was his eyes at St Dunstan's from the start, and she became a Commandant of the V.A.D. She was appointed a member of the Committee of St Dunstan's in September 1916.

In February 1917 St Dunstan's was two years old. In this time 228 men had come and gone, trained in one or more of the eight trades; 354 were under training. We had grown and were still expanding.

The large building nearest to St Dunstan's, called Regent's Park College, had been offered and accepted rent-free. Pearson had taken another house for single officers, opposite our own, in Portland Place. Married officers were put up in flats and apartments near at hand. A house in Sussex Place had been taken for those under training as masseurs. A new convalescent home had been opened at Blackheath, and another, called West House, at Brighton. On April 6 the United States entered the War, which was no longer expected to be short.

I had passed my tests in typing, and in reading and writing braille. I was a reasonably efficient carpenter, and

I knew how to make string-bags. Now I went through the other workshops, one after another, spending about a month in each. If I was to be of any help to Pearson I needed to know at first hand what the trades were like to learn.

All the workshops were under the control of the Superintendent, Charles Rose. He had a sighted foreman in each, but the instructors were mostly pupil-teachers. They had not quite finished their own training, but were paid salaries for passing on what they had learnt. Only the brightest were chosen for this work, which had much psychological value. A beginner who might be feeling disheartened by his difficulties took fresh heart when he learnt that his expert instructor had been blinded on the battlefield only a few months before.

Basketry is the oldest of the trades for the blind, and it survived the other peasant crafts because it did not have to face any challenge by machines. We had both kinds of material, cane and willow, and I found that both stuck into my face when I tried to shape them into baskets. Then I went on to mat-making, the second oldest trade, and was initiated into the art of warping, thrumbing, and shooting the weft. I found bending over a mat-frame a bit back-aching, and after a time monotonous, but it was one of the easiest crafts to pick up.

More popular was boot-repairing, almost a new trade for the blind, but already the most largely followed in the workshops. Some men had the advantage of having done amateur cobbling at home before they were blinded, for snobbing, as we called it, was a more widely practised do-it-yourself craft then than it is now. Those of us who had not done any had to start from scratch, and learn with our hands how boots and shoes were made. We cut the leather by touch, and used most of the ordinary cobbler's tools. We had, however, ingenious little punchers for making holes for the rivets the right distance apart. With these we marked out the soles and heels, and then found the holes with our fingers and hammered the rivets in. Sometimes we hammered our fingers by mistake, but that misfortune is not exclusive to the blind.

I did not try to learn the profession of physiotherapy—massage, as we called it then—the full course for which then took a year to eighteen months, compared with the present course of three years. Only the primary instruction in anatomy and physiology was given at St Dunstan's. The bones of the body were learnt by touch. A story was current of a visitor who looked through the window into the massage classroom without knowing what it was while the bones were being passed round and the men turned them over in their hands. Instinctively they held the bones close to their faces. "Are they having their dinner?" the visitor whispered to her guide. It was the sort of story that appealed to us.

Finally there was the poultry farm, under Captain Webber, and this was another new occupation for the blind. Webber had lost his sight some years before the War, and he took up poultry-farming as a hobby. Practice made him an expert, and at Pearson's request he came to St Dunstan's and started a poultry class. He had sighted instructors to help him. Pupils also learnt rough carpentry, so that they could make things like hen-coops, sitting-boxes, and gates. I found this part of it more up my street than distinguishing breeds of poultry by feeling the birds' combs, wattles, weight, and plumage. I could have been, although I wasn't, the officer who gave the King a good laugh.

His Majesty was paying an informal visit to St Dunstan's. He said he wanted to see us going about our everyday work, without any spit-and-polish for his benefit. His wishes were respected, and at the far end of the poultry farm he surprised this officer, an absolute beginner, and not the brightest in the class. He was handling a bird with more tenacity than dexterity, and, understandably enough, the King asked him what he was trying to do.

"I am finding out the breed of this hen, sir," replied the officer, with all the misplaced confidence of a beginner.

He went through the drill while the King waited and his instructor breathed menacingly.

"Have you found out?" the King asked, when the officer suddenly stopped feeling the bird.

"Yes, sir," he said ruefully. "It's a cock."

While I was going through the classrooms and workshops I also took part in all the sports and amusements that were going on. The chief of these was rowing, and we had contests on the lake and regattas on the Thames at Putney. Indoors we played games and had talks and debates.

Our Debating Society was lively and uninhibited. I see from the minutes that I made my maiden speech in a discussion on whether blind men should marry. I followed Captain Appleby, who put in an impassioned plea for polygamy for the blind. The main argument against the motion was that a man with one handicap should not be saddled with an even bigger one. Support for the proposal came from a speaker who thought married life could not be worse than living in lodgings, while a defeatist said that as they caught men who could see them coming we had not a cat in hell's chance of escape. Another speaker said that out of a hundred girls of his acquaintance he could not think of more than two that he would care to marry. I capped this by saying I could not think of more than one, and then declared my interest by admitting that she and I had just become engaged.

At the end of July we broke up for the annual holiday. I spent the first three weeks at Pearson's house at Bourne End. He invited my sister Betty as well. I wrote to my father: "I have been getting some riding down here and also swimming and boating, so I am very fit and am well occupied all the time. Betty can ride quite well now and has been out with me two or three times. The local riding master told us she was the best pupil he had had for a long time." I spent the rest of the holiday at Canford Cliffs, near Bournemouth, where Betty went to school. I did more riding and some sea-bathing. Then I returned to St Dunstan's—as a member of the staff.

My particular task was to start an After-care Department, which would undertake to keep in touch with all who had passed through St Dunstan's for the rest of their lives. As some St Dunstaners were even younger than I was, I would think of it as a permanent job.

There was already a Settlement Department, which was responsible for giving each man a good fresh start. Masseurs, shorthand-typists, and telephonists were helped to find suitable employment. Poultry-farmers were set up on their own. Some men who had lost a limb as well as their sight were set up in tobacconists' shops. Those in the four handicraft trades—basketry, mat-making, joinery, and boot-repairing—were supplied with a complete outfit of tools and apparatus and, if necessary, a suitable place to work. Usually this meant either fitting up a room in the man's house or, more commonly, erecting a workshop in his garden. Each man was given an initial stock of materials, advertising matter, and anything else he needed before he began work. The Workshops Department of St Dunstan's continued to supply him with raw materials, and also marketed his finished products if he did not sell them himself. Instructors from the workshops visited him from time to time to give technical help and advice.

Now, however, the time had come when the welfare of the trained men in their own homes all over the land was too big and too complex a task to be undertaken as a sideline, or offshoot of the Training Departments. What was needed was an entirely new organization to give every kind of help, economic and domestic, to the men who had left. Their housing, employment, war pension claims, and family problems must all be dealt with swiftly and efficiently. I started in a small office in Great Portland Street, but soon moved to a new block of offices in the grounds of St

Dunstan's in Regent's Park, near to the Training, Settlement, and Administrative Departments. This was very much more convenient for all concerned. There were two or three hundred men already on my books and between six and seven hundred more still in training.

Part of our work was general welfare, and my first task was to build up a panel of home visitors. For this purpose the country was divided arbitrarily into a number of districts, in each of which a voluntary social worker visited all the men in the locality about once a month. These social visitors, who were women of experience and personality, reported to us on the health, progress, and general welfare of each man, so that we quickly learned of any cases of sickness or need. The ladies were skilled in netting, and knew enough about typewriters to carry out any necessary minor repairs. The men themselves appreciated their visits, which afforded them experienced advice and help on pensions, insurance, and many other matters. Also they could hear how their old friends were getting on, and generally keep in touch.

Apart from this general welfare service, men who had been trained as masseurs, shorthand-typists, and telephonists did not usually need anything. We made ourselves responsible for assuring their continuing employment. Also we kept the men informed of any new invention or discovery in medical science or mechanics that might be of use to them in their work.

Craftsmen needed more help. They were not employees working in factories or offices, but self-employed home workers; and to such persons the actual making of the goods is the least cause for worry. They also have to buy their materials and sell their products, and many sighted workers find the burden too much. For a blind man there were many additional difficulties. Our aim was to relieve him of these as far as possible, and to try to enable him to concentrate on the actual handiwork.

First of all, we did all the buying for him. We set up a

central depot, and bought very big quantities of all the materials needed—willows and cane, wood, leather, yarn, string and twine—at the lowest prices, in the wholesale market, and passed them on at cost. Poultry-farmers, for whom this part of after-care was dealt with by a staff of poultry experts, were similarly supplied with foodstuffs.

All the materials we bought were tested and checked by experts. Similarly, the finished articles were inspected by skilled technical men. These inspectors were specially trained to watch for faults that might be repeated indefinitely if they were not spotted and pointed out. It was very important that an extremely high standard of workmanship should be kept. When a sighted person does something wrong it is put down to personal ignorance or lack of training, carelessness, or stupidity. When a blind person makes a mistake there is a tendency to conclude that it is because he is blind. When the same error is repeated over and over again there is some truth in this. So I built up a staff of inspectors for each trade—again on a district basis —and they visited the men at intervals in their workshops. There they not only pointed out errors but taught new designs, arranged for deliveries of materials, and gave technical advice and information on local trade conditions. Finally we provided the men with a guaranteed market.

At the beginning of St Dunstan's there was no difficulty in selling anything. On the contrary, quite tempting orders had to be turned down. For example, one man under training produced an attractive waste-paper basket of his own design. It happened that on the day he finished the article Princess Louise, the King's aunt, visited the workshops. The basket caught her eye, she ordered several to be made for her, and she gave the man permission to call it after her. The demand for "Princess Louise baskets" became large enough to keep him busy for months. But apart from the monotony of it, he needed to be able to make more than one article, and he turned down reproduction orders so that he could complete his training. There were many similar cases in the early days, when we had to forego sales because we were primarily not a factory but a training school.

Fortunately, the men learned their trades so quickly that the supply of goods soon became more than adequate, and we had to set about stimulating the demand. As early as March 1917 we had opened a shop in Great Portland Street, and a branch was started at Wimbledon later in the year. At the same time, men were encouraged to sell all the goods they could locally, and with help in advertising and the co-operation of retail shops in the district most of them disposed of the bulk of their products. What they could not sell we took and stored until we could dispose of it, even if this meant over-stocking in some lines. The arrangements for sending the articles to our sales depot were made by the local inspectors.

When we moved to our new offices in Regent's Park we had nearly four hundred men on our books. Well over five hundred more were under training, and there were many others still in hospital and coming in from the front, where the fighting and therefore the blinding continued.

I went to see them at 2nd General as they came in. For After-care—which would eventually become practically the whole work of St Dunstan's—was not a separate service that began only after settlement, but the last and longest phase in the continuous process of recovery. However despondent and sorry for himself a newly blinded man might feel, to me he was one who would eventually be on the books of my Department.

My visits to the hospital supplemented Pearson's, but when he was unable to go to see a new patient personally I naturally acted for him, and told the man about St Dunstan's and gave him a braille watch. I also deputized for Pearson in other ways, for St Dunstan's had grown so big now that even he needed help. Quite soon after I began work I represented him at a Dickens Fellowship function at the Guildhall, and made my first public speech since I had lost my sight. Come to think of it, it was probably the first big speech I had ever made. I was only twenty.

Then it was Christmas again, and we had our own pantomime, a very topical version of *Babes in the Wood*. St Dunstan's continued to expand as more and more casualties came in from the Western Front. More buildings were put up or taken over. Fresh annexes were opened, including one at Hastings and another—for men with double handicaps—at Ilkley, in Yorkshire. The Federation of Grocers' Associations bought, furnished, and enlarged for us the Convalescent Holiday Home, called West House, in Kemp Town, Brighton. Many years later it was renamed Pearson House, in honour of the Founder.

As fast as our accommodation was increased so it was occupied. St Dunstan's was always bursting at the seams, but somehow never burst. By the spring of 1918 the number of men in the hostel and annexes passed the six hundred mark. Over four hundred others had been trained and settled and transferred to the books of After-care. Meanwhile the Germans had begun a fresh great offensive, and the eye wards in 2nd General were full.

We broke up for our annual holiday at the end of July. I celebrated the second anniversary of my own injury by getting married to Irene Mace.

When we returned from our honeymoon I wrote a little booklet called *All about St Dunstan's*. It was intended for newly blinded men who were still in hospital, and I tried not only to cheer them up but to set them thinking about the choice of an occupation right from the start.

A month or two later the War ended, and we thanked God that the supply of recruits for St Dunstan's was at last going to end. No one could guess that the first year of peace would be our busiest since we had begun.

5

At Peace

THE bare figures tell the story. By the end of 1918 we had over 1500 names on our books. Of these over 600 had been trained, and had gone back to the world. Nearly 700 were in St Dunstan's or the annexes, still in training. Nearly 200 were still in hospital. And although the War was over, we knew there was more war-blindness to come. Already we were taking in men whose sight had been damaged in the early days of the War, who had left hospital then with an adequate amount of vision, and whose sight had since deteriorated to the point of blindness. Obviously there were going to be more of these. We had no idea then that post-War attributable blindness would eventually nearly double our numbers.

Up to the present—and the list is still not closed—we have had over 2900 men who lost their sight through service in the First World War. This is out of a total of about 3200. Most of the remainder chose to be cared for at Newington House, Edinburgh, by the Scottish National Institution for the War Blinded, which was also founded in 1915, and with which we were affiliated. Apart from them almost everyone who was eligible came to St Dunstan's. So did a few who were not eligible, although they had a job to get in. It is not easy to feign blindness.

There are degrees of blindness, and some St Dunstaners were blinder than others. The qualification for admission to St Dunstan's was inability to read or write or to do ordinary work in an ordinary way. A vague definition, admittedly, but anything short of total blindness is difficult

to define. The present official definition of a blind person—
"so blind as to be unable to perform any work for which
eyesight is essential" does not seem much more precise.

About one-third of our chaps had, like me, lost not only
their sight but also both their eyes. Another third still had
one or both eyes but were also completely blind. The
remaining third could distinguish light, and a few of them
still had some glimmerings of sight—usually enough vision
to get about unaided and to recognize large objects close at
hand, but not enough to enable them to earn their living as
sighted men. Many of those in the last category were
probably the least fortunate. Their fragmentary vision
gave them no real comfort, and made it more difficult for
them to learn to be blind.

Medically we were in the hands of two of the leading
ophthalmologists of the day. One was Major Ormond, who
remained in medical charge of all cases that went through
the 2nd London General Hospital. The other was Mr
(later Sir) Arnold Lawson, who dealt with cases that came
to St Dunstan's from any other source. This association
lasted from the foundation of St Dunstan's until May 1920,
and during that time Ormond admitted 1008 and Lawson
825.

Lawson also had to reject a total of 225 as ineligible for
one reason or another, usually because they were not blind
enough. Many of these were borderline cases who still
retained a little useful and precious sight, maintained so
precariously that, in Lawson's opinion, it would probably
have been destroyed by our normal training in handicrafts.
A person who can see cannot be taught to work without
using his eyes even if he has to strain them dangerously.
Some of these men could still earn a living doing jobs not
requiring much vision, like those of messengers or care-
takers, but for others there was no suitable work of any kind.

Lawson had some hard decisions to make when such
men begged him to let them in even at the risk of their
losing what remained of their sight.

He also had to spot malingerers and scroungers who were not blind at all. As the fame of St Dunstan's spread it was not surprising that quite a few old soldiers tried to wangle themselves twelve months' free hospitality, a disability pension, and the St Dunstan's umbrella for the rest of their lives. If they feigned complete blindness they were easy to catch out, but some were artful enough to pretend only partial blindness, and to come with a cover story of a knock on the head followed by fading sight. Many genuine cases at St Dunstan's were caused by injury to the visual cortex, and showed nothing by examination of the eyes themselves, and such stories could not be disproved clinically. So Lawson admitted the men, but gave particular directions that they should be watched. Usually the malingerer kept it up for a few days, but then became overconfident and careless, and gave himself away by some simple act.

I know personally of only one more or less successful masquerade of this kind, and that was by an officer who came in while I was away on holiday with my wife. She continued her work at St Dunstan's after our marriage, so she got to know him with the others. From the very beginning we thought he was phony and could really see a bit. He did not stay very long. A few weeks after he had left my wife was walking along Piccadilly when she heard a voice call out from the other side of that very wide street. It addressed her by name, so she stopped and looked—and there he was, waving at her. He was dressed in his officer's uniform, and he rushed across the road, skilfully avoiding the traffic, to greet her.

"How are you?" he asked warmly.

My wife said she was all right, and asked rather pointedly how he was himself. He said he was fine. Either he had decided it was all over and no longer mattered, or he had completely forgotten his part; anyway, neither of us saw him again.

Between 90 and 95 per cent. of those who passed through

St Dunstan's could—and did—earn a living, or at any rate add substantially to their pensions, after they had left. Of the others some were debarred from work because of the severity of their injuries, physical or mental. The rest were simply ineffective persons whom you will find in every community and in every class—men who had never done any work if they could avoid it before they were blinded, and who thought their blindness excused them from ever doing any again. Some of these were rich and idle, others were illiterate and poor. There were very few of them—no more than you will find in any mixed community, and I like to think we may have had less. Not even St Dunstan's could reform a hardened scrounger, but he had to be virtually incurable to make no response.

When the First World War broke out pensions for disabled soldiers were awarded by the Chelsea Commissioners. In conjunction with the Army Council, they examined in detail each application for a pension and, if satisfied that the claimant was eligible, instructed another Government Department to arrange the payment of a State grant. This system dated from 1754, and I believe it worked well when the Commissioners knew every pensioner by his surname even if they could not always remember his Christian name. In the First World War it proved hopelessly impracticable, creating suspicion among disabled soldiers and causing lengthy delay. Discontent became so noisy and widespread that in December 1916 the Ministry of Pensions was formed. For the first time a single Department awarded and issued disability pensions.

Blindness is, technically, total disablement, and in 1914 the pension for this was 2s. 6d. a day for a private soldier and slightly more, according to rank, for N.C.O.'s. This was not much even in those days of relatively cheap living, and after public agitation it was increased in 1915 to 25s. a week with an additional 2s. 6d. a week for each child under sixteen born before discharge. This was slightly increased in 1917, but the cost of living rose higher; and in 1919 the basic rate jumped to 40s. with larger children's allowances and 10s. marriage allowance. Thanks mainly to the importuning of Pearson, there was also an attendant allowance for the blind.

At the beginning of the War pensions were granted only to men who could prove that their disability was directly due to their war service. If you got a bullet through your eyes, as I did, this was easy enough. If, however, your blindness was caused by disease, as it was in the case of about 25 per cent. of all St Dunstaners, your chances were remote. You had to prove that the infection was the direct result of war service, and in practice this was hardly ever possible.

The unfairness of this should have been obvious. Quite large numbers of men who went blind in the Army had been suffering from eye disease when they joined. Many of them should have been rejected as unfit. Active-service conditions, including prolonged exposure of the eyes to the cold and wet, hastened the progress of the disease.

The recruitment of potential eye cases was excusable and indeed inevitable. The eagerness of volunteers to get into the Services made the task of the doctor hard, and there were not enough doctors who knew anything about eye disease; and when there was a shortage of manpower standards were lowered to fill the ranks. It was therefore unjust to refuse a man a pension on the grounds that the original infection was not the result of war service.

This injustice was partly remedied early in 1916, when the Government brought in the famous 'aggravation' clause. This extended pension eligibility to men discharged on account of a disease which had been aggravated by war service. The onus was still on the claimant to prove Army responsibility, not on the Army to prove its innocence. Many St Dunstaners whose previous claims had been rejected now claimed again, and some of these claims were upheld. Others were turned down again, mainly because of rather narrow interpretations of the word 'aggravation.' There was a lot of friction, so when the Ministry of Pensions was formed an Appeal Board was set up. This was not a great success, as it was composed entirely of officers of the Ministry, so an impartial Pensions Appeal Tribunal was set up as the final court.

The machinery of applying for a pension and lodging an appeal involved some form-filling, and was clearly designed on the assumption that the applicant could see. Therefore we had to set up a special Pensions Office at St Dunstan's to help the men carry out the formalities. When the Appeal Tribunal was established Pearson persuaded the Ministry to nominate St Dunstan's itself as one of the Local Committees that were set up all over the country to collect and sift the necessary evidence before it was put before the Tribunal. Our Pensions Office then began a great campaign on behalf of the men who had been turned down by the Appeal Board. Many of these were absolutely penniless, and entirely dependent on St Dunstan's for the support of themselves and their families, and this was a great burden on our finances.

Our highly skilled Pensions Officer, W. G. Askew, ensured that every case was carefully prepared, and 85 per cent. of the adverse decisions of the Appeal Board were reversed. This was due in a large measure to medical evidence and the advocacy of Ormond and Lawson, who maintained that it was for the State to disprove that blindness was caused or aggravated by war service, not for the man to prove it; and who believed, as we all did, that the State would have done better to part with the little extra money needed to give a pension to every man who had lost his sight while serving his country.

We argued every case that had to go to the Appeal Tribunal, in the knowledge that when a claim was rejected St Dunstan's usually had to give the unlucky applicant some help. Our funds were limited, and as our numbers increased so did our obligations; and, although we were still generously supported, we shared something of the obvious fate of all war-based charities in time of peace. We were still determinedly voluntary, and it was a natural paradox that we should try to prise all we could out of the State for pensions in order to avoid having to accept a State grant.

St Dunstan's could only keep its independence if it was run on business lines, and, willy-nilly, I had to become a businessman myself. By 1920 about four hundred men had been resettled as home craft workers, and were producing goods of a total retail value of about £60,000 a year. They sold the greater part of these locally, but our London sales organization still had to sell goods worth between £10,000 and £15,000 a year. So we were always looking for new markets, and we found some in quite unexpected ways. Once I spent a week-end with an uncle who kept racehorses. Going round his stables, I found that the loose-boxes were lined all round with cocoa-fibre mats. I asked about, this, and was told that these were used in all loose-boxes in which valuable horses were kept. I scented business, and took details of the special sizes and shapes of mats required. We had some specimens made, and I arranged a small exhibit at the next Horse Show. With the help of some circularizing and advertising we sold over £700 worth of these mats in four months, and one of our racehorse-owning customers was His Majesty the King.

I also had to go in for insurance. We had a special section for this in the After-care Department, which was set up because of the difficulties blind men had in insuring their lives at ordinary premium rates. Before we got to work most companies charged extra premiums for blindness. We made more favourable arrangements with the leading companies, and in doing so we ourselves became their authorized agents, and received the usual commissions. We passed these on to the men by deducting them from their premiums, with the result that they could insure themselves—and their property—at even lower rates than other people.

In 1920 I became a member of the St Dunstan's Committee. About the same time Otto Kahn informed Pearson that he wanted his old home back, after he had so generously let us use it for over five years.

Fortunately, we did not have to leave Regent's Park. We got a long lease on what had been the town house of the Marquesses of Bute, in the Inner Circle, opposite the Royal Botanical Gardens. St John's Lodge, as it was called, was a fine large mansion, and in no time at all the magnificent entrance hall was transformed into offices. The Conservatory was turned into a Poultry and Country Life Section. Workshops were put up in the grounds, equipped with all the latest in ventilation and heating. At the same time they were designed for easy conversion to stores and receiving and packing rooms when the need should arise; and we knew that would be pretty soon. For the emphasis had shifted now, and new admissions were in decline. We knew that they would not dwindle away completely, that we should continue to receive fresh cases for many years to come; but they would go on diminishing steadily, year by year.

This meant that the training departments of St Dunstan's would be reduced. They could not be abolished, for newcomers needed at least as much expert help as their earlier comrades had received. But more and more of the resources of the organization would be taken up by the After-care Department, which would go on expanding, and finally become the whole of our work.

We moved out of St Dunstan's Lodge during the Christmas holidays of 1920, taking the name with us. Otto Kahn did everything he could to make it easy for us, and with good planning and staff-work we settled down in our new home almost at once. Indeed, everything ran so smoothly that I began to think of finding some other work to do as well—something preferably not connected with the welfare of the blind.

I now had other precedents besides Fawcett and Fielding and Hollins. Surprisingly enough—considering there had never been anything like it before—St Dunstan's could already boast a number of Old Boys who gained distinction.

I have mentioned Appleby, who used to work in the carpenter's shop at the next bench to me. Another fellow-officer and friend who had done big things after leaving was Geoffrey Pemberton, who had been knocked out while commanding a tank on the Somme in 1918.

Pemberton had been a chartered accountant before the War, and he took it for granted that he could never go back to the same sort of work. He came to St Dunstan's, learnt typewriting and braille, and still wondered what he could do.

"Why don't you go back to your old job?" Pearson suggested.

Pemberton was full of doubts. Could a blind man do the work? Would his partner agree to his going back? Would their old clients still have confidence in him? Could a blind man get new clients? He would be dealing exclusively with businessmen, and there was no room for sentiment in business. Had a blind man ever practised as a chartered accountant before?

Probably not, said Pearson. All the more reason for doing it.

Pearson's optimism infected Pemberton. His partner was not only willing but enthusiastic. Still cautious, Pemberton began working only from ten till four, and with a reduced share in the partnership. Within quite a short time he was working normal office hours, and eventually he became a full partner again. His hobby was apple-growing, and he made a success of that, as he did of everything else. "The chief thing you taught me," he wrote to Pearson in 1921, "was confidence; and also to use my memory and wits. Practically all the detail work in a chartered accountants' business is done by the staff. I have all the final accounts and notes read out to me, and I memorize the essential points and figures so that I can discuss them with my clients. Some people think this is all very marvellous; if it is, it is not in any way I who am marvellous but St Dunstan's which made it possible."

Then there was R. H. Hyde-Thomson, whc had passed his examinations for the Bar before going to the front, and was now building up a practice in the Temple. "The year has passed with incredible swiftness, one day in chambers being so remarkably like another," he wrote about the same time. "In addition to my routine work I am connected with several colliery undertakings, and this necessitates a general knowledge of the underground workings, and more particularly of the development work. I find the quickest method of following this is to have plans of cardboard made on a reduced scale, with string stitchings to mark the coal faces in the different districts, also main roads—direction of faults, etc." There was Blandy, too, who had gone back to his solicitor's practice in Reading. "I found what is, I believe, common to all blinded men," he wrote, "namely, that my memory had improved enormously, and so I could carry a lot of the detail of various transactions in my head. Before the war I had done a bit of advocacy and litigation, and after a short time I decided to try my hand at it again. I was terribly nervous at first, but I found that the County Court judge and officials were most kind and forbearing, and gradually I was able to get confidence and put up a fair show."

Several company directors and other businessmen had gone back to their old work. Back in his old profession also was the Rev. Harold Gibb, who went out to France in 1914 as chaplain to a cavalry brigade. After the great retreat from Mons he became a combatant officer, continuing to hold services on Sundays. Blinded in action, he came to St Dunstan's, and often preached in our own chapel while he was going through the usual course. When he left he took a living in Warwickshire. His letters were of the sort in which Pearson took the greatest delight.

"I experienced an interesting day's sport when entertaining a small house party," he wrote once. "A gallop before breakfast, followed by a rat hunt and a kill before breaking the fast, and a badger dig from ten till six, which included the bolting of Master Brock and a splendid cross-country hunt through woodland and plough after a heavy night's downpour. For me it was a case of jacket over my head and a bull-like charge through the undergrowth, a most exciting affair. Ascension Day afforded an experience which may be reassuring to those who may feel anxious as to what may happen in the event of a toss over their horse's head. Mine took it into his head, most pardonably, on that particular day to cross his legs and pray in the middle of a very hard high road. I shot over his ears, turned a topsy-turvy and landed on my feet right about. How it was done I am still wondering, but it gives one confidence as to the possibility of it happening again if necessity arises."

Rex Furness was one of the very few civilians admitted to St Dunstan's during the First World War, although no man was more surely blinded in action than he was. His work at the time was on a new form of high explosive for munitions, and he knew it was dangerous. When the accident happened he was lucky to escape with his life. There was a terrific explosion, killing everyone else in the laboratory. Furness was badly injured, but recovered with only a stiff elbow besides his loss of sight. He was a star pupil at St Dunstan's, mastering the intricacies of braille much more quickly than anyone else, and at the same time he kept abreast of the latest scientific progress. He took his brilliant brain to the firm in Warrington where he had been employed before, and, blind as he was, they knew they were lucky to have him.

All these men—and several others—had gone back to jobs they had been doing before they lost their sight, or at least for which they had already been trained. A return of this sort was always the first possibility to be considered.

More often than not the man wanted to reject the idea as impossible, and it was surprising how many of them, after reluctantly agreeing to give it a trial, made quite a triumphant return. Of course, we had to be careful in judging what might be possible, for if we made mistakes our advice would soon fall into disrepute. In the event we had almost no failures, but the credit for this was due to the men themselves. If it was always possible it was never easy, and success could only come through a determination not to be beaten.

Resettlement was obviously more difficult for those who could not go back to their old work, or who had not been trained for a job at all. This category included myself. The only profession or trade I knew anything about was soldiering, and there is no place in the Army for the blind. Still, some of our men had already shown that more doors were open to us—or at least ajar, needing just some extra push —than was supposed.

There was the law. Captain Angus Buchanan—the only holder of the Victoria Cross blinded in the First World War—was at Oxford University before he joined up, and he went back there from St Dunstan's in 1919 and read law. He became articled to a firm of solicitors in Oxford, passed all his examinations, and went into partnership with another solicitor in Gloucestershire.

Lance-Corporal Peter Sumner had begun to train as a teacher before the War, and had been accepted for admission to St Mark's College, Chelsea, to study for the Board of Education Certificate and a London University degree in Arts. He should have entered the College in September 1914. He joined the Army instead—and on Christmas Eve, 1915, he did in fact arrive at St Mark's—by then the 2nd London General Hospital—not as a student but as a blinded soldier. This seemed a cruel irony, for he had lost all hope of resuming his career. But Pearson saw the Principal of St Mark's, and Sumner picked up the threads again. By 1921 he was a qualified teacher and a fully fledged B.A.

In the same year Andrew Nugee, who had been studying for the Civil Service before the War, was ordained a minister of the Church of England. He was successful, first as a curate and then as a parish priest. He blazed a trail for a number of other St Dunstaners of both world wars, showing that blindness is no bar to the Church so long as the man has the ability and, above all, the sense of vocation.

From a purely practical point of view there is hardly a more suitable occupation for the blind than writing fiction, and F. Le Gros Clark turned to it simply because he had lost his sight and could not think of anything else. For once Pearson was cautious in his encouragement, but after reading Clark's first efforts he advised him to carry on. Clark did, with considerable success. His first published short story was a thriller with a blinded character in it. Soon he was having his stories accepted regularly. Later, he published two novels and a series of very successful children's stories which were translated into various languages. Meanwhile he had also begun applying his talent to social subjects, notably human health and welfare. For several years he was secretary of the Children's Nutrition Council, and after the Second World War he worked for the Food and Agriculture Organization of the United Nations. A stream of expert reports, pamphlets, articles, broadcast scripts, and books flowed from his pen. Then he directed his keen brain to the industrial problems of the older man and woman, doing research and publishing reports on the subject for the Nuffield Foundation. His latest interest is in the problems connected with the employment of women.

Writing would have been an ideal occupation for me, because I wanted to do something that would not take up all my spare time. I enjoyed my work at St Dunstan's, and hoped to continue it indefinitely; but I wanted something else as well. I lacked the gift for writing, so it would have to be something else. I began to think of entering what is commonly called public life—of becoming a politician.

I suppose I still had some of the inspiration I had caught at the beginning from the *Life of Fawcett*, although the idea was not really remarkable. In many departments of life the blind man is handicapped most in the least spectacular job. Fawcett could be Postmaster-General, but he could never have done a postman's round. Sir John Fielding, the Blind Beak of Bow Street, had been virtually Chief of Police of the Metropolis for twenty-five years, but no blind man could do the job of a constable on the beat. In each case it is the man in the junior position who has to see his way about himself, while the man in the administrative or executive position has many people doing his seeing for him. He has to grasp facts, form judgments, and make decisions. Blindness is no obstacle to a job of this sort of activity.

I have mentioned Captain Appleby's public career. Another of our Old Boys who made his mark in public life was Fred Martin, a journalist on the *Morning Post*. He found no trouble in going back to his old profession, and at the same time stood for Parliament as a Liberal. He won East Aberdeenshire in 1922, and became the first blind man to enter the House of Commons since Fawcett. One of our Canadian lads, Harris Turner—also a journalist—had been elected to the Saskatchewan Provincial Parliament five years earlier. During 1921 I set my own sights on a seat on the London County Council.

In entering public life I had no illusions about my own powers of oratory. I was no spell-binder, no weaver of magic patterns with words. The best I could hope to do was to express myself briefly and clearly, and I had already had much more experience of that than most youngsters of my age. Actually I had begun delivering lectures while still in my teens. When I got my commission I was still too young to be sent to the Front, so they kept me at home as an instructor, and I spent several months lecturing and demonstrating to quite large groups of men, mostly older than myself. Then I had done a lot more public speaking at

St Dunstan's since I first deputized for Pearson at the Guildhall.

The senior member on the St Dunstan's Committee at that time was Colonel Eric Ball. He was a member of the L.C.C., and he introduced me to the leader of the Municipal Reform Party, as the Conservatives were called in local government in those days. An election was due in the spring of 1922, and we talked about the possibility of my finding a constituency. Pearson approved of my ambition, as he did of everything that invited public attention to the capabilities rather than the disabilities of the blind. I could be spared from St Dunstan's to enable me to take on the extra work.

That was the stage my thinking about my own future had reached when all the affairs of St Dunstan's were interrupted by the sudden death of its Founder.

6

In The Chair

THE day before his death he had been full of life,
fitter and much more vigorous than most other men
of fifty-five. In the evening he had taken his wife
to the theatre, to see *The Yeomen of the Guard*. Nine hours
after the curtain went down he was dead.

The manner of his death was the cruellest irony. It was
a blind man's accident, and he was the last person in the
blind world to whom it should have happened. He slipped
while stepping into his bath, struck his head on the tap,
fell forward unconscious, and drowned. Only a week earlier
he had been riding over the Downs.

One of my first tasks was to fit up a large emergency
dormitory in the grounds of St Dunstan's for those who
came back, from all over the country, to show their
devotion to this most remarkable blind leader of the blind.
Nearly twelve hundred of them made this unique pilgrim-
age. The funeral service was held at our local church, Holy
Trinity, in the Marylebone Road. The theme of all the
many tributes to him was that his work would live on. It
fell mainly to me to try to see that it did.

Pearson had been Chairman of the Committee—or
rather Committees, for St Dunstan's consisted of three
separate charities at that time. There had been no Vice-
Chairman, and there was no President or Vice-President
until after his death. Then the Committees decided to
appoint a President, and there was never any doubt about
the right person for this. Lady Pearson was elected, not
just because she was the Founder's widow but for what

she had done for St Dunstan's herself. She had taken an active share in all her husband's good works, beginning with the Fresh Air Fund. During the War she had launched and organized the Blind Musicians' Concert Party, which had toured the country raising money for the National Institute and ourselves. Pearson was proud of her, and he lived long enough to share in her honour when she was created a Dame of the British Empire for her services to St Dunstan's. Lady Pearson was to remain our President until she retired, in 1947, at the age of seventy-seven. She remained our good, kind friend until her death in 1959, and she was mourned by every St Dunstaner.

Two Vice-Presidents also were appointed after Pearson's death. One was his son, Sir Neville Pearson, who was eventually to succeed Lady Pearson as President. The other was Sir Washington Ranger, then Chairman of the National Institute for the Blind. I was chosen to succeed Pearson as Chairman of St Dunstan's.

He was not an easy man to follow. True, I had been working under him for nearly five years, and besides running After-care I had represented him at public meetings, deputized for him in dealing with Government Departments, and gradually come to be his second-in-command. But he was never one to let the reins go far from his hands, and there did not seem to be any reason why he should. If either of us had stopped to think about it we might have assumed that I would be the one to take over from him if he died—but of course we did not think of such an apparently remote contingency when he was still comparatively young, fit, and intensely interested. No one could have expected I would have to take over so soon or so suddenly. And I was only twenty-four.

But I was not alone. My wife was there to help me. So were the Treasurer, Ernest Kessell, and the Secretary, Mrs Chadwick Bates; and her eventual successor in that office, W. G. Askew, was the nearest I have known to the mythical indispensable man.

F

There is no single individual member of the staff to whom St Dunstan's owes more than Mr Askew, and that is a very big statement to make. He joined us because he was himself disabled. His handicap, which he has borne bravely throughout his life, was our good fortune; for he came when we could recruit our male staff only from those unacceptable for military service by reason of being too young, too old, or unfit. Mr Askew has had a lame leg since he was a child.

Shrewd picker of men as he was, Pearson never chose better than when he invited Mr Askew to become our Pensions Officer. Done properly, the job involved ensuring that every case was properly presented and that each claimant received his full rights; a quite considerable task, but only a part of Mr Askew's conception of his duties. There was also the political side, the conduct of our higher-pensions campaign. Eventually Mr Askew delegated the administration of our War Pensions Department to Mr L. Banks and Mr H. D. Rice, but throughout his thirty-six years' service with St Dunstan's he remained my adviser on the policy to be pursued. It usually fell to me to represent our needs in Parliament and to Ministers, but I always armed myself beforehand with Mr Askew's expert advice.

Naturally, Mr Askew's administrative skill was needed for other matters besides pensions, and he played a prominent part in all our affairs. Awarded the O.B.E. in 1936 and the C.B.E. in 1951, he enjoys the lasting affection and gratitude of St Dunstaners of two generations. He now lives in semi-retirement, which for a man of his temperament means considerable activity. He is a member of the Council of the Royal National Institute for the Blind, and still represents St Dunstan's on important committees.

A man at the head of affairs, great or small, can be lonely because there are not many people to whom he can talk with the utmost frankness; but Mr Askew was one of these, and there was no matter of policy, personnel, or attitude that I did not talk over with him, certain that my confidence would be respected and that I would get good advice. If I came to appreciate him more as the years passed, I never needed his help and counsel more than when responsibility was thrust upon me at the age of twenty-four.

Pearson had been a businessman, a big-business man with an ice-cold brain as well as a warm heart. "In days when I could see I had the direction of some big enterprises," he wrote, "but St Dunstan's became the biggest individual business that I have ever conducted." He conducted it brilliantly, and it was no fault of his that the biggest of the immediate problems that I inherited was trying to keep solvent.

Compared with most war charities, St Dunstan's was rich. We were, indeed, greatly envied by many worthy causes that had failed to get what they considered, often with justice, their fair share of public support; although it could also be said justly that much of the money that Pearson had charmed out of the public would not otherwise have been given at all. And he had to have it. For all his inspiration and ingenuity, for all the selfless work of our voluntary helpers, without extraordinary financial support St Dunstan's would have failed. Large sums of money had to be raised to carry out the novel and expensive plans for rehabilitation and training essential to its success.

In the event the appeals policy initiated by Pearson was so successful that we found ourselves with a surplus on income account, and began to build up our reserves. We decided that the right thing to do was to try and 'fund' our work by collecting enough to enable us to look after all the blinded soldiers, sailors, and airmen properly for the rest of their lives.

At the same time, we were not as rich as we looked. Certainly we had substantial assets on paper, but the figures in our balance sheets were somewhat misleading. There was, for example, the very large sum standing to the credit of the Blinded Soldiers' and Sailors' Children Fund.

This Fund had been set up to supplement the children's allowances paid by the Ministry of Pensions. At that time our men received five shillings a week for the first child, four and twopence for the second, three and fourpence for the third, and half-a-crown each for any others. This did not cost the country much, because most war pensioners were not even husbands, let alone fathers, when they were invalided out of the Service; and allowances were paid only for children who had been born or at least conceived before the father's discharge.

From the beginning St Dunstan's had encouraged its men to marry and enjoy the natural happiness of a normal family life, and our Children Fund was set up to provide practical help. The aim was that an allowance of five shillings a week should be paid for every St Dunstaner's child irrespective of whether it was conceived or born in khaki or mufti.

The Fund was an immediate success, and by the end of the War nearly two hundred children were receiving allowances from it. Many towns, business firms, and private individuals made themselves personally responsible for the allowances for particular children, while the Fund's supporters included pupils at many schools. The Fund more than kept pace with the increase in the number of children, which reached five hundred early in 1921. By then enough money had been raised to meet all existing and expected future commitments, so no more appeals or collections were made. Soon there were over two thousand children on the Fund's books, but it still had plenty in hand. This was a very fine success story, an enviable one by comparison with our general affairs. The Fund was a specific trust, and neither the capital nor the interest could be used for any other purpose than children's allowances. This was all perfectly proper, although there were times—and the period just after my succession to the Chair was the most serious of them—when we began to wish that some of its money could spill over into our general funds. In the year of

Pearson's death, when everything else was running at a loss, the assets of the Fund stood at £275,000, and there was a useful balance of income over expenditure.

Another of our assets that looked best on paper was our holding of properties, which at this time amounted to about £200,000, or 40 per cent. of the total assets standing to the credit of our general funds. Financially these properties were white elephants, for the net income from them was only about £3500. But they were not bought as investments.

The first task of our Settlement Department was to find places for our men to live. Some of them, of course, went back to their old homes of before the War. But not many. Most of them had been youngsters living with their parents then, and now were married, or wanted to marry and set up homes of their own. Others had no suitable homes to go back to; either there was no space for the additional workshop accommodation they needed, or they had to move from town to country—or country to town— in order to carry on their new job. So for most men we had to try to find new homes. The time could hardly have been worse, for the country was going through the greatest housing shortage in living memory. In most cases it was found impossible to rent suitable properties, and St Dunstan's had to choose between buying houses—at greatly inflated prices—and making the men wait.

We chose to buy. Waiting would have meant unemployment, with loss of manual skill and, even more important, of spirit and initiative. Buying meant laying out a large part of our resources, and there was never any prospect of our being able to levy economic rents. Of course, rent had to be collected, if only in fairness to those of our men who were not housed in this way; but we made a very poor thing out of being landlords. We had nearly three hundred tenants on our books when I took over, and all that capital was locked up for many years.

Our financial crisis was not due to any bad management

or lack of foresight. We had expected public support to thin out after the Armistice, for war charities are naturally among the major casualties of peace. At first the decline in our income had been about what we had anticipated. But from the beginning of 1920 it became progressively more serious, and in the year of Pearson's death our expenditure exceeded our income by quite a large amount. All charities were in the same boat. So, indeed, were all private enterprises. There was a severe national slump.

We had to use some of our capital to make up the deficiency. So did most other businesses, as they always do in a time of depression, without lasting harm, provided it does not go on too long. We ourselves expected that in time we would deliberately reduce our capital by spending it, a little each year, for the greater benefit of St Dunstaners, so that there would be no funds left after the last blinded soldier had died. We were having an actuarial calculation made of the average age to which our men could be expected to live, and we intended to adjust our financial policy accordingly. But all this was for the fairly distant future. The facts of our life in 1922 were that we were in the red and had to retrench.

The first obvious economy was to reduce the number and size of our establishments, which were now spread out over the country. We had already closed the Blackheath annexe, but besides our new headquarters we still had two houses in Cornwall Terrace and our own private hospital in Sussex Place. Our main convalescent and holiday home was still West House, in Brighton, with accommodation for sixty. The four other country annexes—St Leonard's, Cheltenham, North Berwick, and Ilkley—together had room for about a hundred and fifty.

During the War our country annexes had been used partly as convalescent depots and also as holiday centres for men under training, especially those from the Dominions and others who had no homes to go to in the intervals between our working terms. There were not nearly so many of these after the War, and the annexes were used then to provide two or three weeks' holiday for men who had left St Dunstan's and were settled in their new trades. As more of these men married the need for this holiday accommodation declined, and our axe fell, without causing any hardship, first on St Leonard's and Ilkley. For convalescent and holiday purposes we kept Brighton for men in the South and North Berwick for men in the North of England and in Scotland. The Cheltenham Annexe, which was smaller, was full all the time with men with serious additional disabilities who needed special care and attention.

We were able to make other economies in our training establishment because of the considerable falling off in new admissions. In 1920 the hundred figure was topped for the last time. Two years later the number of new cases was down to thirty-one, and that remained about our average for some time. Not all our economies were so painless, and still they were not enough. With over one-third of our assets still tied up in properties let at uneconomical rents— and with the inviolable Children Fund showing a surplus of nearly £13,000—we overspent on the general account by £46,000.

Further economies were hard to make. We closed down the annexes at Cheltenham and Berwick, transferring permanent invalids to Brighton and providing other men with a monetary grant instead of a free holiday, but still taking men in at Brighton when they could not make their own holiday arrangements. Then the national depression lifted a little, and after two bad years we at last brought income and expenditure into balance. The following year—1924— we actually achieved a surplus, but this was more than accounted for by a single legacy of £45,000, a windfall that was unlikely to recur.

Rather a lot of our income came from legacies, and in most cases the wills had been made when the appeal of St Dunstan's was strongest—that is, during the War. We devoutly hoped that there were still many more such bequests to mature, but we had to expect that legacy income would eventually decrease. In any case, it was not the sort of thing to rely on to finance an enterprise with as many various commitments as St Dunstan's.

The latest of these was the new National Insurance Scheme. This was introduced by the Widows', Orphans' and Old Age Pensions Act of 1925. There were valuable benefits for employees and their widows, but no special provision for the self-employed. They could become voluntary contributors, but only by paying the employer's share of the premium as well as the employee's. We decided to pay the employer's share for all who wanted to come in. Nearly a thousand men—about 80 per cent. of those eligible—took advantage of this.

During the depression one of the main tasks of After-care was to help men to remain fully employed. This was not only to enable them to go on earning their living, either. For the blind worker unemployment cannot be measured only in terms of poverty and normal human misery—it means a slipping back from life to half-life or less. So there had to be constant vigilance. The blind masseurs already had their own association, to which we gave an annual grant. We also set up an employment bureau for our telephonists and shorthand-typists, to make sure they were never out of a job. To keep our handicraft workers fully occupied we continued to buy from them all that they could not sell, although sometimes this meant stocking our warehouses up to the roof. Much as we prided ourselves on running After-care on business lines, we could not go all the way with the law of supply and demand. It would have cost too much human happiness to curtail production by putting the man on short time. Sales difficulties were our worry, and not to be solved by putting the brake on our craftsmen's industry.

In July 1922 we opened our own shop in Regent Street, and the Royal Family led the way in patronage. This helped us to get rid of some of our over-stocks, but still the goods came in faster than they went out. We tried to encourage the public to buy more locally, with limited success. In 1924 we had to try to sell goods worth nearly £27,000, and the next year the total value was over £35,000. From the corresponding rise in the value of raw materials supplied to the men we found that the increase was due not to any slackening of local sales but to greater individual output.

This was something we had to encourage, although it was doubly at our expense. Not only did we have to buy and store more goods than we could easily sell, but we had to bear a greater loss on the handling and transport of the raw materials, which we supplied at net cost price. The more money the craftsman made for himself, the more he cost us in this indirect subsidy.

No doubt our common dread of pity and magnanimity made those of us who ran the place incline to be hard-headed and realistic, but St Dunstan's was anything but an institution without a soul. We did not shout about our spirit of comradeship because we did not want to create blind enclaves in the sighted world, but that spirit was none the less real for that. One expression of it came in the form of reunions in different parts of the country, which were arranged and attended by those of us who were running After-care. We took a room in a convenient centre and laid on tea and entertainment for twenty or thirty old St Dunstaners from the district, together with their wives and friends. They were social occasions, but a good deal of useful shop was talked as well. I attended these reunions myself whenever possible—in the first place because I thoroughly enjoyed them, but also because they enabled me to learn what the men thought of our current practices and policies. If they were critical or discontented there was something wrong, no matter how good the record might look; for the single aim of St Dunstan's was the happiness of the men.

* * *

In 1922 we parted company with the National Institute for the Blind. It was the N.I.B., with the help of the British Red Cross Society, that had started St Dunstan's. Pearson was President of the N.I.B. then and until his death, and throughout this period St Dunstan's was an integral part of the work of the N.I.B. Our co-operation in money-raising activities was to our mutual advantage, but it also led to some confusion in the public mind about the respective functions of the two organizations. So, in the friendliest possible spirit, we agreed to part. Henceforward St Dunstan's cared for all blinded ex-Servicemen, and the N.I.B. for the much larger number of civilian blind. With a nice touch of irony the N.I.B. celebrated its divorce from the military by electing Captain (later Sir) Beachcroft Towse, V.C., to succeed the civilian Sir Washington Ranger as Chairman.

Blinded in the South African War, Towse had promptly offered his services in any capacity when war broke out again in 1914. He went to France to comfort men who had been blinded on the battlefield. Few people had the slightest idea of the great amount of good he did; not just because he could talk as one blind man to others, but because he had something to say.

On the Executive Council of the N.I.B. since 1902, Towse had supported Pearson in the foundation of St Dunstan's and could convey its message to turn despair into hope. Many future St Dunstaners were saved days, even weeks, of distress and anguish by their first brief contact with him. James Rawlinson, a Canadian, described his own feelings in a book he wrote called *Through St Dunstan's to Light*. He was at Boulogne when Captain Beachcroft Towse broke the news to him that he was blind for life.

"I gathered myself together as best I could under the circumstances," he wrote, "and said, 'That's a h—— of a thing to tell a guy!' "

Towse then asked him a string of questions.

"While the Captain was questioning me I heard a rapid, clicking sound following each of my answers. The noise fascinated me, and I made bold to ask him what it was.

" 'It's a braille machine,' he replied. 'I am taking down your answers.' " Towse then began to explain its use, and gradually it dawned on Rawlinson that you did not have to be useless just because you were blind.

Captain Sir Beachcroft Towse remained Chairman of the N.I.B. until 1944, when he became its second President. During the twenty-two years when he was Chairman of the National Institute, and I of St Dunstan's, we were personally good friends. This happy association continued when Towse was succeeded by General Lord Ismay, who remained Chairman until 1952, when he handed over to Godfrey Robinson, M.C., who was created C.B.E. in 1953.

Robinson is a St Dunstaner, and has been a personal friend ever since I visited him in hospital in 1918 and told him of what lay in store. Very badly wounded as well as blinded, he won a great victory over physical disablement and went back to his family business. He also entered public life, becoming Sheriff of Hull. A lifelong tireless worker for both the British Legion and the civilian blind, his appointment as Chairman of the N.I.B. was naturally very welcome to St Dunstan's. During the years the two bodies have naturally had their disagreements, but I think probably there has been less uncharitable bickering between us than there is between most such similar and potentially rival charities.

Meanwhile the Government had accepted a share of the responsibility for helping the blind. This had previously been left entirely to voluntary effort, although as early as 1914 the House of Commons agreed without a division that the State ought to help. A Departmental Committee reported with detailed proposals in 1917, but three years later almost nothing had been done. Public opinion was already well ahead of authority when Pearson pressed the Government, and two hundred blind men marched from

Manchester to London and held a demonstration in Trafal-
gar Square. The upshot of all this was the Blind Persons
Act of 1920. This humane piece of legislation made it
compulsory for each local authority to look after its own
blind, with the option of employing existing voluntary
agencies to do the work. The local authorities were paid
block grants by the Exchequer, and in the event they nearly
all delegated the work. This consisted mainly of education
for the young, training and employment for adults, and
social welfare for the old.

At the same time the Register of the Blind was compiled,
and the first published estimate of the number in the
United Kingdom was between 30,000 and 40,000. The
latest total is more than three times the latter figure, but
that does not mean there has been an increase. The first
register was simply incomplete. It still is, for registration
is not compulsory; but the benefits are now so great that
the number of unregistered blind must be quite small.

The work of the R.N.I.B., as it has been called since
1953, is another story. It has already been told, and told
well.[1] It is an outstanding example of the contribution a
large voluntary organization has to make in a Welfare
State. The St Dunstan's story is a variation on the same
theme.

It is sometimes argued, and argued sincerely, that all
charities ought to be abolished and their work taken over
by the State. If the cause is good, the argument runs, it is
the duty of the State to support it. This would relieve the
cause of financial uncertainty and spread the charge over
the community as a whole, so that the generous would not
have to pay twice or more to make up for failure of the
mean to give at all. It is also said sometimes that it is
humiliating for an individual to receive private charity.

The second point depends, of course, on the spirit in
which help is given. If it is in any way patronizing the

[1] *The Royal National Institute for the Blind*, by Mary G. Thomas
(R.N.I.B., 1959).

argument is valid. But I think that sort of charity is out of date. Literally millions of Servicemen in both World Wars were in no way humiliated in accepting the help of the Red Cross, the Y.M.C.A. and Y.W.C.A., the Salvation Army, and other similar voluntary organizations. They were never patronizing, and I do not think St Dunstan's ever has been either.

The answer to the first point is less obvious but, in my opinion, even more compelling. Of course, a great deal of welfare to-day must be provided by the State. Any idea of transferring a scheme like national insurance into the hands of voluntary enterprise would be putting the clock back; and that really is the key to it all. Almost every social welfare activity began as a private charity. The State only came in after the public conscience had been sufficiently aroused. The care of the blind is a typical example of this progressive evolution. Voluntary agencies had been at work for over a hundred years when at last the State came in with the Blind Persons Act of 1920. This process is likely to continue whenever a new need arises, even in the age of the Welfare State. Every social advance has been inspired by an enlightened minority, and the whole community would be the poorer if such private benevolence was snuffed out.

The blinded Servicemen of the First World War would certainly have been poorer, for no State scheme for them had been devised. There was no precedent for war blindness on such a scale. Doubtless if no voluntary action had been taken the Government would have been prodded into doing something, but only after early neglect and public agitation; and then the authorities would have had to consider the blind not as an individual problem but in the context of all the war-disabled. And I am quite sure that blinded Servicemen have received better and more generous care from St Dunstan's than they could have had from any Government. Not only has more money been spent on them than they would have been allowed by the Treasury, but they have had expert personal services that would have been outside the scope of a Government Department.

You cannot expect the State to assign public money for any purpose without deciding how it should be spent, and that is why we went to such lengths to keep St Dunstan's purely voluntary, and not ask for a grant. At the same time we got our men all we could in the way of pensions. When I followed Fred Martin into the House of Commons I often used—perhaps abused—my position to press for more.

This book is not my autobiography—I wrote that about twenty years ago[1]—and this is no place for details of my public life. All I need say is that in spite of Pearson's death, and my sudden appointment to the Chairmanship of St Dunstan's, I went ahead with my plans for the 1922 L.C.C. elections, and won a seat. Two years later I stood for Parliament and just scraped home.

I was not an independent Member, but accepted the Conservative Party Whip. I was accountable to my constituents just like any other Member, and if I took time off from their affairs, to further the interests of a particular section of the community, the local branch of the Party could very well call me to order. In the event it never did, and, far from being rebuked for taking up the cudgels for the ex-Serviceman, I was encouraged to do still more. I was happy to do it, although I got a bit fed up always being referred to as "the blind M.P."

The blind world benefits when one of its members does something like getting into Parliament, but some of the benefit is lost if his blindness is dragged in automatically whenever his Parliamentary activities are reported. I was very pleased when *The Times* newspaper decided its readers had had enough of it and just called me by my name. In practice being blind is little handicap in Parliament. I found that it does not even make it difficult to catch the Speaker's eye. Height, not sight, is what you need there and I have plenty of that.

[1] *Whereas I was Blind* (Hodder and Stoughton, 1942).

7

Lines of Communication

THE further man has progressed, the more he has
come to depend on his eyes. Our remote ancestors of
the cave and forest needed sharp ears and keen noses
in order both to eat and to avoid being eaten, and a good
sense of touch to be able to move in the dark of the night.
Nowadays we are in no great danger of being eaten, and
instead of hunting we choose our food by looking at it in
shops; and darkness can be destroyed by a flick of a switch.
Again in the Middle Ages a student learnt mainly by
listening, and the story-teller entertained the common
people. Now, it is much quicker to read lectures than to
hear them, and instruction and entertainment alike are
disseminated more and more by means of pictures and
printed words. Even wireless, one of the greatest of all
boons to the blind, has become for many people a mere
adjunct to television.

A modern psychologist has estimated that 85 per cent.
of what is learnt is acquired through the eyes, and we live
in an increasingly visual world. The eye is so much the
swiftest and most effective of the messengers of the brain
that the others are not used much so long as it can do its
job. That is why loss of sight seems at first to be so much
worse than it is. Learning to be blind is, to a great extent,
learning to use the other gateways to the mind. It is a great
comfort when you find these are much more valuable than
you expected. Only the blind can appreciate what a wonderful gift the sense of hearing is, for only the blind have to

discover how many things normally done by the eyes can be done by the ears instead.

The blind are generally good mixers because they have that incomparable social asset of being good listeners. This is not because they are any less interested in themselves than everyone else. It is just that they like to know what is going on in the world around them, and they have no other means of finding out.

They are gluttons for information about everything. They like to have books and especially newspapers read to them—and they tend to be critical of the way you read them unless you know how. When I was newly blinded and young I used to get very impatient at having to spend so long listening to a piece of information that I could have read in a quarter of the time if I had been able to see. I became positively irritated if the reader tried to brighten the piece up by punctuating it with comments.

Reading a newspaper to the blind is something of a skilled occupation, and my secretary has brought it to a fine art. Clarity is the first essential, and after that speed. The reader should not try to put too much expression into it—the listener does not want her to interpret the item or to let her personality come between him and the writer. My secretary's reading speed is between two and three hundred words a minute, and most sighted people who hear her cannot keep up. It still takes two or three times as long as it would if I could see to read myself, but it is a valuable discipline. I have to keep alert to absorb the gist at once, and this makes it easier to remember. For very many years Miss E. Westmore has done most of my reading, latterly on tape recordings which she makes each morning, covering those parts of the daily news-papers which deal with politics, ex-Service or 'blind' affairs, South Africa or my other interests—and very skilled she is at this work.

Blindness undoubtedly stimulates and trains the memory. In ancient Japan the Government exploited this fact in a unique way. Blind persons were employed as a sort of living national library or repository of archives. Each learnt the equivalent of a number of volumes, and was available for consultation on any relevant historical fact. A younger blind man served as his apprentice or assistant, and the older man passed on to him his quota of history. This employment was reserved for the blind simply because they could do it better.

Exactly when blind people first thought of reading with their finger-tips is uncertain, but it was long before braille, and even before the invention of printing. The earliest attempts were made not with raised letters but with string. First in Peru, and later—but independently—in Edinburgh, string alphabets were devised with various knots and loops. In schools for the blind in Italy and Spain letters carved in wood were used, and in France a reading system was devised with movable letters cast in type.

All these methods were slow and laborious, and no real progress towards modern touch-reading was made until one memorable day in 1786 when a pupil at a newly opened blind school in Paris happened to be handling some printed sheets that had come fresh from the press. As one sheet was passing between his hands he felt a bump in the smooth surface. He stopped and passed a finger-tip over it, and deciphered a letter of the alphabet in reverse. It had been made by the pressure of the type on the other side. He reported his discovery to the founder of the school, Valentin Haüy, who grasped its significance at once. Haüy, who was not blind, soon produced type that would emboss characters on paper clearly enough for them to be easily read with the fingers, and from this came the first books for the blind.

The next chapter in the strange story was written many years later and quite unintentionally by a French artillery officer named Charles Barbier, who invented a system of reading by touch for troops receiving messages under cover

G

of darkness. He used a phonetic alphabet, and each sound was represented by a combination of embossed dots. The Academy of Sciences suggested that Barbier should show his system to the Head of the blind school founded by Haüy. He did, and it fell into the hands of a blind teen-ager, who had entered the school as a pupil and was now an instructor, named Louis Braille.

Barbier had used up to twelve dots for each character, making it too tall to be deciphered with any ease. Braille cut it down to six. He also rejected the phonetic principle, arranged the characters in logical sequence, and finally devised a system that could be written as well as read by the blind themselves. This was braille, and it still is.

The basic cell is simply the six of dominoes, two columns of three dots. If you work it out mathematically, as Braille did, you will find there are sixty-three possible combinations of one or more dots. After assigning one combination to each of the letters of the alphabet he allotted the others to common words like *and*, *the*, and *for*, double letters like *wh* and *th*, and so on. In a sense, there-fore, you might call it a kind of literal shorthand.

It is not easy to learn. There is no great difficulty in memorizing the various signs and contractions, but the fingers have to undergo quite long and intensive training to be able to distinguish them. Of all the things I did at St Dunstan's when I was learning to be blind, I liked nothing less than this, and almost everyone who has learnt braille will say the same.

I had an excellent teacher. She was sighted, as most of the braille instructors were then; nowadays they are mostly blind, and this is better, for obvious psychological reasons. However persuasive and understanding a sighted instructor may be, the pupil is bound to feel sometimes that she cannot quite understand the difficulties of reading blind. The blind instructor has the great advantage of being able to show all the time that it really can be done.

We began learning with big dots, almost the size of

peppercorns, and by degrees got down to dots of the normal size. We differed quite considerably in the time we took to master braille, and it was not always the brightest who were the quickest to learn. Intelligence and education naturally played a part, but the most important factor was individual sense of touch.

It is sometimes thought blindness improves one's sense of touch, just as it is supposed to improve one's sense of hearing. Again, it merely makes you use it more. Your sense of touch is something you are born with, and if you have the good luck to keep the use of your eyes you will probably never know whether it is good, bad, or middling; for you will never need to know. The blind find out when they join the braille class.

A sensitive touch is not necessarily a mark of delicacy or refinement, or long, tapering fingers more sensitive than short, chubby ones. Many with a rough background displayed an exquisite sense of touch and mastered braille reading in a few weeks. Others, often much more sensitive types, had the greatest difficulty in identifying the dots.

Some men had hands roughened by manual labour, and several of these greased their fingers with "Vaseline" at night and slept with gloves on. But in any case the effect was usually temporary. Put a manual labourer in hospital for three months, and all those callouses and hard patches on his fingers will grow off, leaving them as soft as a woman's. The only men we have had whose sense of touch had been physically impaired were those who had been in Japanese P.O.W. camps in the Second World War, and whose blindness was due to beri-beri. This deficiency disease also causes some diminution of the nerves of acuity, and most of these men had to struggle very hard to master braille.

One of the first blind instructors we had at St Dunstan's used to wear thick woollen gloves in cold weather, and read braille comfortably without taking them off. But the most remarkable sense of touch I ever came across was that of a clergyman named Arthur Lloyd. He came to have dinner with us once at Portland Place in Pearson's time, and read braille at high speed through four thicknesses of a handkerchief.

My own sense of touch was about average. I passed the reading tests, and eventually was able to enjoy a book. Our source of books was the National Library for the Blind, which generously decided to lend books free—and free of postage—to blinded ex-Servicemen for the rest of their lives. Quite apart from the cost, few people have enough space for a private braille library; the Bible takes up seventy-four volumes, and *David Copperfield* twelve.

The National Library got its books from the National Institute and the Scottish Braille Press, and especially from a large number of sighted voluntary braille writers who devoted much time and skill to the transcription of individual books.

The National Institute also began to publish text-books in braille to meet the needs of St Dunstan's men who wanted to go to a university or train for one of the professions. Previously there had been almost no demand for technical books of any kind.

I did not read much braille myself. I was lucky enough always to have someone to read to me, and using my ears rather than my fingers was quicker as well as less tiring. Yet there were times when I was alone or could not sleep, and then I was immensely grateful that I could read. The ability also restored a little more of the independence that I had lost through being blinded.

Paradoxically, I never liked to be seen reading braille in a public place—I never took it in a train, for example, because I would have had the feeling that the rest of the carriage was watching me, and that would have reminded me too forcibly of my blindness. This was something I grew out of—I was more sensitive when I was young— and now I have no compunction about taking braille anywhere. I have even read it in the House of Commons—

most improperly, I am afraid, as one is not allowed to read anything there; but when an all-night sitting developed into a marathon of boredom the temptation was irresistible.

I was also easier to teach and quicker to learn than I would have been later in life. As you get older it becomes harder to learn anything, and we have found that men who go blind over forty, and still more over fifty, have much more of a struggle to master braille than do the youngsters. Some of our older men have had to give up the attempt, and have learnt Moon instead. This system, which was devised by a blind man named William Moon, is much easier to learn but much slower to read. It is a type based on the printed roman capital, and, of course, it is even more cumbersome than braille.

In the early days of braille, books were transcribed one copy at a time—indeed, one dot at a time, for it was all done with a single-pointed hand punch. One old blind man, John Ford, brailled the whole of the Bible in this way, making between twenty and twenty-one million strokes. Now there are mechanical writers with six keys, and the operator makes the whole of each character with a single stroke. Books are produced mainly by stereotyping, the characters being embossed in the first instance not on paper but on a double zinc plate, from which any number of copies can be printed.

Theoretically, an electronic brain is able to translate one set of signals into another set even though the relationship between them is quite arbitrary. It may be, therefore, that in the future the master braille copy will be written by a machine without human intervention, the original being the "Monotype" tape or even the printed copy itself.

For individual braille writing there are pocket frames, and I carry one of these as a sighted person carries a diary or note-book. I often use it to make notes when I have to give a speech. It has to be small to be portable, and I might have ten or more bits of paper in my hand, each with two or three notes on it, when I stand up to speak. In this respect, at least, I have an advantage over many sighted speakers—however else I may annoy my audience, I cannot irritate them by continually looking down at my notes.

We have a braille writing test as well as a reading test at St Dunstan's, and some men have become extraordinarily adept. Those who have set up in business of their own have found it especially useful, and many of them keep their accounts in braille. Of course, the braille writer does not replace the typewriter, and the latter only fails when the user himself needs to be able to read what he has written. It is for this reason that our typewriting instructors, unlike our braille teachers, have always been sighted.

Most men pass the St Dunstan's typewriting test after about six weeks. They are then given a typewriter to keep for the rest of their lives. Before they leave they are taught simple maintenance, including changing the ribbon and brushing the machine.

Unlike some aids for the blind, the typewriter becomes more rather than less important as the years go by. A person who has been blinded may for a while be able to continue writing by hand more or less legibly, but he is unlikely to keep this up. From the start he will probably make the letters too small and too close together, and these and other faults will become accentuated because he cannot see what he is doing wrong. Even with regular supervision and the use of one of the writing frames made for the purpose, his handwriting will almost certainly deteriorate until it is virtually illegible.

Fortunately, the typewriter can be used by nearly all the blind, including those who have had the misfortune to lose one or even both hands. In the very early days of St Dunstan's a machine was constructed for the one-armed man, with a special mechanical guide to enable him to keep the paper straight when he put it in.

Much more drastic amendments were needed to enable a man with no hands to type, but he does not need a specially constructed machine. He uses a standard portable typewriter, with a metal plate fashioned in a series of terraces, or steps, superimposed over the keyboard. Each terrace has a number of shallow gutters, or grooves, with a quarter-inch hole in the centre of each, positioned immediately over each key. A metal L-shaped striker, or "bent finger," is fitted to each of the man's artificial arms, and he types by inserting these strikers through the holes and pressing the keys beneath. The tricky part of it is finding the right hole. He has to use his artificial finger first to feel for the correct terrace, then to slide it along the gutters, counting them until he comes to the letter he wants, and finally to locate the hole.

No doubt it sounds painfully laborious, and your heart might bleed for a man with no hands if you saw him having his first typing lesson. You would feel better if you went back and watched him after a few weeks' training, and if you talked to him you would soon find he neither wanted nor needed your pity. Speed, after all, is relative, and with practice he will be able to type at a useful rate. He will feel a thrill of achievement when he types his first letter home, without anyone sitting by his side. He may also turn his newly acquired skill to profit.

Publications for the blind now include many periodicals as well as books, and rotary presses are used to print braille newspapers and magazines. These include our own monthly house magazine, the *St Dunstan's Review*, which is published simultaneously in ink-print. It was only added to the list of braille publications after the Second World War. Before then there were not enough good braille readers among us to make it worth while.

The *Review* is nearly as old as St Dunstan's. The first number was published only a few months after the move to St Dunstan's Lodge. It was light-hearted and often facetious, with articles on rowing on the lake, Visitors' Day, and the V.A.D.'s, and a poem, the inevitable parody on Kipling's *If*. I have been unable to discover who started it, but his first Editorial, dated July 1915, seems to reveal quite a lot about the spirit of St Dunstan's at the start. Here it is:

St Dunstan's as you all know is a hostel for blinded soldiers and sailors. What then could be more desirable than a magazine for their benefit which is useless to them? Nobody wants it, and so I consider it my duty to bring one out.

It is not an advertisement of cheap wit, nor is it meant to make you laugh at the expense of others. It merely chronicles a few of the actual happenings at St Dunstan's. You will, I am sure, agree with me in saying that when one sees such a large number and such a quaint assortment of people as one does here, their doings and sayings should not be allowed to sink unrecorded into utter oblivion.

It is hoped that none of our articles will be considered impertinent or personal, but everyone here is so jolly and full of fun that they cannot help being amused by all who come and go, and even those who stay.

It will probably be remarked, "Why do they not bring out their magazine in Braille, so that the officers and men can read it?" That is what we also say, and so, dear reader, if you happen to know Braille we shall be more than grateful to you if you will carry out your own suggestion.

We should also much appreciate any articles for our next issue, and we hope—there being no tax on the hope—to answer all letters and inquiries, which may be addressed to "The Editor, 12, Kensington Gate, W."

Alas for the articles! Only four were offered, two from the same man, and in the next issue, published three months later, the Editor threatened to stop publication unless there was better literary support. Presumably there was not, for he carried out his threat. St Dunstan's was without a magazine for the next six months.

Then one of our first masseurs, William Girling, revived the idea—according to his own account, just for his own amusement. He was not fit enough to take part in games, and he indulged a taste for scribbling. The first edition was modest enough, consisting of a single typewritten copy;

and I wish I knew where that is now. It was an immediate success, and a month later Girling brought out his second number, with a print of a thousand which sold out within a week. It was a nice mixture of local news and fun, beginning with two pages of "Notes by the Chief"—with the initials C.A.P. at the end of them in case anyone did not know who the Chief was. Girling promised to publish monthly, and it has come out monthly ever since. The only month it does not appear is August, when St Dunstan's shuts down for the annual holiday.

Girling passed his final examination in massage before the end of the magazine's first revival year. Soon afterwards it had a sighted Editor, the Workshop Superintendent Charles Rose. After a few months he also left, and Richard King Huskinson took charge. He was both a professional journalist—he did a weekly book review and essay for the *Tatler*—and, like Rose, a voluntary helper at St Dunstan's. He had no official rank, but we called him the Adjutant. He was a good friend to all of us, and he wrote a chapter for Pearson's book on the psychology of the blinded soldier that does not look the least bit old-fashioned to-day. I helped him with the magazine—actually, we were put down at the start as joint editors, but at first he ran it— and I took over from him in February 1918.

I kept the job for a year or two. I think now that I did it rather badly, although at the time I considered myself rather good. I was keenly interested in everything technical, and took it for granted that everyone else was too. Any new mechanical device that affected the blind was bound to get a long report under my Editorship, while blank spaces in the magazine were filled up with little items about aeroplanes or ships, engineering or electricity, that had nothing to do with us at all. Probably a great deal of this bored most readers, although they were kind enough to suffer in silence.

In my career as Editor I had a scoop—namely, Corporal Mason's account of how he was torpedoed on his way back to South Africa after his training. He was in a ship's boat for nine hours, and handled one of the heavy oars that pulled the survivors—who included his mother— to the safety of a British destroyer. His rowing in Regent's Park stood him in good stead. A typically modest hero, when he arrived back at St Dunstan's unexpectedly he only apologized for having lost his typewriter and poultry outfit.

We had gramophones at St Dunstan's from the beginning, just as we had pianos and indoor games. You had to wind the instrument up by hand and put in a new needle after each record, and the more or less musical noises emerged from an enormous horn shaped like a trumpet. The word "fidelity" did not exist in this context; if we ever compared the noises that came from one gramophone with those from another we used to say that one instrument had the better tone. Singers sounded hardly human, but it was possible sometimes to make out the words of their songs. It ought to be possible, I thought, to record human speech. Theoretically it should be possible to record whole books. . . .

I took my dream to the Columbia Graphophone Company and the Pathephone Company. Was there a means, I asked, of making the records run longer than the usual three or four minutes? We experimented together. The disk was run a little slower than the normal 78 revolutions per minute, and the threads were cut a little closer together. We succeeded in making a record that ran six minutes, then one that lasted ten minutes. All this was in 1919, long before anyone had heard of long-playing records . . . or talking books.

The reproduction was vile. Recording was done mechanically, the speaker's voice being received by a trumpet down which the sound waves travelled to a diaphragm, making it vibrate. On the diaphragm was a needle that cut the wax. You had to speak right into the trumpet to get enough force to cut the wax, and the reproduction was ruined by resonance. Yet those primitive records we made were in fact the first beginnings of talking books.

"If books could only talk!" Everyone who ever tried to learn braille must have said that at some time or other, for listening is so much easier and quicker. To pass the St Dunstan's elementary braille reading test you have to average about fifteen and a half words a minute. The advanced test works out at about twenty-six words a minute. With practice you might, in time, achieve a reading speed of as much as eighty or even a hundred. Now switch on the radio and listen to a B.B.C. News Bulletin. Time it, and you will find the reader averages about 135 words a minute. He does not gabble, but, on the contrary, keeps below the maximum comfortable speed. Push it up to a hundred and fifty, and you will not find it difficult to take in. And that is twice as fast as you are likely to read braille, if you belong to the 20 per cent. of the adult blind in the country who master it well enough to read at all.

If you have someone to read aloud to you whenever you wish you will not need Talking Books; provided, of course, that your reader is an expert. But to pay for this service will cost you quite a lot, and if your reader is voluntary you are again dependent. Remember that at the time I am speaking about there were no regular wireless broadcasts, and the blind man's world was silent as well as dark unless there was someone to talk to him. No wonder he wished that books could talk!

When we made our experiments with those early gramo-phone records the results were imperfect because the idea was before its time. That time had still not come when, a few years later, I met an inventor who had found a way to make a film talk, and was trying to persuade the big companies to try it out. They all turned him down, and both the film trade and the public were derisive about the idea of moving pictures that would talk. I wondered if we might have the talking without the pictures, and I asked the inventor to make me a piece of his film. Again, the technical problems were too great for reasonable reproduction.

Then electrical recording was introduced to the gramophone industry, and what had been a visionary ideal suddenly became a practical possibility. No longer did the speaker have to bellow down a trumpet to make a diaphragm vibrate. He spoke into a microphone, and the engineer put it on to the wax with whatever power he thought necessary. He could go further than that. He could, if he wished, cut out all the deeper chest tones, reducing the lateral vibration of the needle, and therefore the necessary width of the groove.

Electrical recording brought with it many other exciting possibilities, and I set up an experimental laboratory at St Dunstan's where we could carry out some research. By omitting the bass tones from the voice we succeeded in cutting the threads at 200 to the inch instead of the standard 100. This doubled the playing time of a record running at what was then the standard speed of 78 revolutions per minute. We set about lowering this speed, and eventually got it down to 24 r.p.m.

We ran into all sorts of technical problems. We had to find the right material for the records, and a needle that would last the unheard-of playing time of twenty-five minutes; and we had to find a means of keeping the speech clear as the needle approached the centre of the record, where it tended to become muffled. Finally we had to devise a record-player that would be cheap, simple, and suitable for operation by the blind.

The matter of cost was always a restraining factor on inventive originality, for the blind world is not big enough itself to provide a mass market for anything. Any article that has to be specially made for such a relatively small community cannot be mass-produced, and therefore will never be cheap. In devising any apparatus, therefore, the aim must be to adapt what exists rather than to invent something new. If standard equipment cannot be used as it is, any new equipment must as far as possible be made with standard components. The main reason why we concentrated on talking records rather than talking films was that equipment for playing them was already mass-produced.

St Dunstan's was not in this on its own. It was a matter that affected the whole blind world, and, indeed, affected others even more than us, for our standard of braille-reading was relatively high. So we worked in co-operation with the Technical Research Committee of the National Institute for the Blind. In 1932 this Committee tried to persuade the leading gramophone companies of the advantages of records that would play for half an hour instead of a few minutes, but the gramophone companies were unconvinced. The era of long play for the sighted had not yet dawned, so we had to go into it on our own. We shared the cost with the N.I.B., and in 1934 we produced our first talking books. With the very generous help of Lord Nuffield, we began to build up a Talking Book Library such as I had dreamed of fifteen years before. Mr L. S. Pinder, Senior Recording Engineer of the famous Decca Company, joined our staff to take charge of the project—the British Talking Book owes more to him than to any other single individual for its progress and success during the following twenty-five years. He retired in 1961, having been awarded an M.B.E. for his services.

About the same time a similar project was begun and developed in the United States by Robert B. Irwin, the blind Director of the American Foundation for the Blind. We reached similar conclusions independently, and then exchanged visits and views, and finally records.

In this country records, like braille books, can be sent by post at greatly reduced rates. The United States Post Department carries both free of charge.

Being easily breakable, talking books have to be packed in special containers, and they bulk rather large. A short novel occupies about ten double-sided records, and longer books may need fifty or more. Like braille books, this is all very cumbersome, and from the beginning we have been constantly seeking simpler and cheaper methods. I was experimenting with recordings on a moving steel wire in the early days of the Blattner-phone, and we began research with magnetic tape when it first came into use.

After the Second World War St Dunstan's set up a committee of eminent scientists to advise on sensory devices to substitute for sight, more particularly in the matter of reading and walking. This committee devised a talking-book machine that used tape instead of disks. Its unique feature was the tape cassette. Little larger than an average novel, it could contain twenty hours' recorded speech, and was extremely simple to operate.

In 1959, with the R.N.I.B., we started a pilot scheme under which one hundred experimental models of the new machine were tried out in the homes of blind persons, half St Dunstaners and half civilians. This field test proved successful, and in 1960 the change-over from disk to tape began. Naturally, this could not be done in five minutes; it is expected that it will take five years to complete. I again approached Lord Nuffield, and through The Nuffield Foundation a further gift of £100,000 fortified the finances already set aside by the R.N.I.B. and St Dunstan's to pay for the change-over. Meanwhile the two systems are run in parallel.

The Nuffield Talking Book Library for the Blind—as it is now called, in very proper recognition of its benefactor— is firmly established as one of the greatest modern boons we have. To-day it has a membership of over 6500, including 650 St Dunstaners, and a catalogue of well over seven hundred books. About seventy-five new titles are added every year, and in a sense they all come under the heading of 'Desert Island Disks.' They were originally chosen by the Sound Recording Committee, of which I was the first Chairman, and before we drew up our first list we canvassed a number of blind readers to find out what they

wanted. Their lists had too little in common to help the
selectors much, but they gave us some idea of what the
readers did not want. One of them was particularly explicit.
He ended his reply to our questions with the plea "but
no poetry, and no prose."

We were lucky in not having to worry about copyright
once the necessary safeguards for the owners had been
arranged. Authors and publishers have always been generous to us about copyright, almost without exception
allowing their property to be put into braille free of charge.
They wanted to be equally charitable over talking books,
but some caution was needed here. No one who can see
print is likely to read braille, but there was no reason why
only the blind should listen to books on records. To avoid
any danger of abuse of their generosity, safeguards are
written into permissions and a nominal fee is paid.

When we had chosen our first talking books we had the
task of finding suitable persons to do the talking. During
experiments we had done this ourselves, and undergone
the somewhat mortifying experience of hearing our voices
played back to ourselves shorn of the bass tones. However,
we had found out what seemed to us the best style of reading.

The ideal voice should be exceptionally clear, for technical reasons, not too expressive, and yet not monotonous.
As in reading aloud, the speaker should not impose his
personality between the book and the listener, nor should
he over-dramatize it. On the other hand, his voice should
not be too flat, or devoid of character portrayal.

This is a pretty tall order, and we had quite a lot of
difficulty in finding the right sort of person for the job. In
the end we discovered that professional readers were the
best, and most talking books have been made by B.B.C.
announcers. Much of the 'proof-reading' has been done by
a St Dunstan's man, who listens carefully to the recording
and types a report. There is nothing remarkable about
that, except, perhaps, the fact that he is one of the men
who is practically handless.

Two or three talking books have been made by a blind man. This is the Rev. Arthur Lloyd, the same man who astonished us at Portland Place in Pearson's time by reading braille through four thicknesses of handkerchief. He wrote to me from Wales and said he wanted to make a talking book, and he was so earnest that I agreed to try the experiment, although I felt rather sure it was not really an occupation for the blind. He made a very fine bid to prove me wrong. The only sign in his recordings that he was not reading ink-print—and you were not likely to notice it unless you were looking for it—was a slight pause every two or three hundred words that indicated he had come to the end of a page of braille and was feeling for the top line of the next page. He read two or three talking books, all extraordinarily well, but he had still not proved me wrong. Making talking books is not an occupation for the blind, because the original must be in braille, and that is a limiting factor. Saying that in no way detracts from Arthur Lloyd's remarkable feat.

Wireless, of course, had come several years before the first talking books, and it was a popular hobby at St Dunstan's before there was any B.B.C. For this I was partly responsible, as I had been a wireless fiend when I was still at school. I was about sixteen when I made my first receiver—and to build a set in those days you had to make the components first. Several schoolfriends helped me, and I remember our winding many hundreds of feet of enamel-covered wire round a cardboard tube given to us by a friendly linoleum salesman. We did the wood and metal work in the carpentry shop, and took the all-important crystal—it was probably a piece of copper pyrites—from the Chemistry Laboratory when Old Stinks's back was turned. The one thing we had to buy was an earphone—of course, we could not afford a pair. We took it in turns to listen to the news in Morse from the Eiffel Tower.

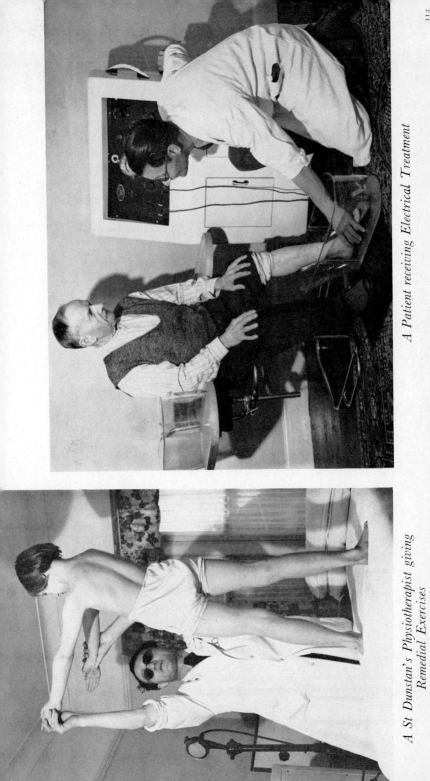

A St Dunstan's Physiotherapist giving
Remedial Exercises

A Patient receiving Electrical Treatment

A Deaf St Dunstaner's Hobby—building a Model Ship

In the Training Workshops: Men using the Capstan Lathes

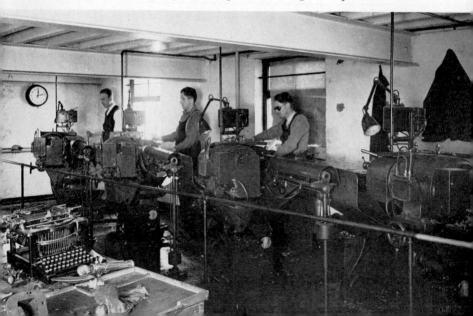

That was back in 1912 or 1913. In the Army I became a signals officer, but I never got as far as wireless. At St Dunstan's, when I found I could do carpentry, I took up my old hobby again. Others shared my interest and began to build receivers, for wireless was still a technical pastime rather than a form of entertainment. "A very large number of men are now the possessors of wireless sets of their own," ran a note in our Annual Report of 1924, "and find, we know, the most intense pleasure in the science." They were encouraged by the supply of apparatus and component parts at a good deal less than the normal cost.

By then we had gone far beyond the days of listening to dots and dashes from Paris, and were on the threshold of something tremendous. I remember the thrill—and it was a far greater thrill for us—of hearing voices from the head-phones instead of Morse. I also remember building my first transmitter, and sitting up till the early hours of the morning exchanging greetings with other enthusiasts all over the world. This was an exciting activity in which sighted and blind were on equal terms. There were several St Dunstaners among the first radio hams, as we came to be called, and I was very proud when I was elected President of the amateurs' association, the Radio Society of Great Britain.

Broadcasting was one of the subjects about which I nagged Ministers most at Question Time in the Commons, and—perhaps to shut me up—they appointed me to the Crawford Committee on Broadcasting in 1925. Our main recommendation was that the old British Broadcasting Company should be replaced by a Corporation with independent Governors, and I little thought then that one day I would be on that Board.

In 1926 I drafted and piloted a little Bill that allowed every blind person to have a wireless set without a licence. This was one of two Acts of Parliament for which I must admit responsibility, the other one being the Blind Voters Act, 1934. This second measure was so obviously necessary that it was difficult to understand why it had never been brought in before. It enabled the blind voter to have what everyone else had long since taken for granted as his proper right—secrecy of the ballot. Before this Act the blind voter's ballot paper was marked for him by the presiding officer. So he had to tell the presiding officer his voting intention—and, presumably to make quite sure that the presiding officer did not cheat, this declaration had to be made in the presence of representatives of all the candidates. Under the Blind Voters Act the number of persons he had to tell was reduced to one, and that was a relative or friend of his own choice.

To come back to wireless: thanks to the initiative of Sir Beachcroft Towse and the very willing co-operation of the B.B.C., a braille edition of the *Radio Times* was published as early as April 1927. It has come out ever since; indeed, it was the only edition when the ink-print *Radio Times* was suspended because of a printing-trade dispute.

Wireless could have been invented specially for the blind, so exactly does it fulfil our needs. The news-bulletins are a talking newspaper, stripped of inessentials and boiled down to the hardest possible facts. Talks are the equivalent of essays and magazine articles, short stories are short stories, and plays are plays. Both plays and documentary feature programmes are written and produced specially to exploit the audience's ear far more than is necessary when they are using their eyes as well, and this puts us on terms of complete equality with the sighted. Broadcasting came not only as a wonderful new source of entertainment and instruction, but it helped us to remain informed members of contemporary society.

As wireless meant so much to us, it was clearly necessary that every blind person ought to have the opportunity to listen to it regularly, just as every sighted person has, through free libraries and reading rooms, the chance to read books and newspapers. Right from the start, therefore, we decided that every St Dunstaner should be provided

with a receiver if he did not already have one. So when the
B.B.C. was born almost every St Dunstaner was equipped
with at least a crystal set and two pairs of headphones, a
total initial cost to us of nearly £4000.

Other blind persons were not so lucky, but again Sir
Beachcroft Towse took the initiative, and under his Chairmanship we set up the Wireless for the Blind Fund. St
Dunstan's joined the National Institute for the Blind in
this, and a joint broadcast appeal for the Fund was made
on Christmas Day, 1929. The speaker was Sir Winston
Churchill, and the occasion inspired one of his many happy
turns of phrase. He asked listeners to make it possible for
everyone to boast, "The blind all have wireless sets. It is
the custom of the country."

This Christmas Day broadcast appeal became an annual
event. We have indeed gone a long way towards achieving
this boast, but, of course, funds still have to be raised.
Wireless sets wear out or become obsolete, and every year
several thousands of new names are added to the registers
of the blind.

No one who is not blind would think of asking what
sight is, and yet there is more in it than using your eyes.
Sight is only partly physical. A blind man can usually
visualize—more or less clearly, according to his mood—
faces and things he can remember from the time when he
could see. He can also visualize a new scene, if someone
will take the trouble to describe it to him. Silence is not
golden to the blind, and on a walk one always likes to be
told what everything looks like and what is going on so
that he can form a picture in his mind.

Some blind persons can create more vivid images than
others, but there is one time when they can all see as well
as the sighted: when they are asleep. "Good night,"
Milton said to his daughters once, "and may it indeed be
as good to you as to me. You know, night brings back my
day; I am not blind in my dreams."

8

A Job of Work

"THERE is a fellow I met the other day," Pearson wrote in the *St Dunstan's Review*, "who, though he holds some bootlaces in his hand, is frankly nothing but a blind beggar. He is typical of many thousands throughout the country, and in my view a very serious blot upon the blind community."

Pearson blamed the country, not the beggar. If the man was capable of work he ought to have been trained and employed. If he was incapable there was an equal obligation to house and care for him. It was as easy as that.

We had some men who were too badly injured to be able to work. In a few the damage was mental, which is not surprising when you consider how near the eyes are to the brain. We had special convalescent homes for them, and they received every kind of help it was possible to give.

Happily, there were few of them. Happily, too, Pearson succeeded in inspiring almost everyone who could work with the *desire* to work.

What makes St Dunstan's unique is that nobody ever had to come, and yet almost everyone eligible came. No other organization of its kind has so nearly attained a 100 per cent. membership. And not only did they come, but they stayed until they had been trained to go out and do a job.

When St Dunstan's was two years old a deputation came from a very large, well-known institution for the blind in the North of England. "We have come all this way," said their leader, "to ask you to tell us how it is that

116

you teach men in six months as much as it takes us four years to teach them."

Pearson was never at a loss for an answer. This time he had four.

"Firstly, our pupils are exceptional among the newly blind," he said. "They are mostly young and fit, high-spirited, eager and impatient for life. Secondly, most of our instructors are exceptional in that they are blind themselves. We have developed the pupil-teacher system because a blind man can overcome his feeling of helplessness most easily when he knows that his guide and leader is in the same position as himself. Thirdly, we work much shorter hours than any institution. The men are put to play before they can feel brain-fag and mental strain. Fourthly, there is the handicap ideal."

They asked him what he meant by the handicap ideal, and he told them the story of a recent visit he had made to a school for blind children. Over two hundred of them were assembled in the hall, and they sang like angels. Then the chairman of the school, a good and benevolent man, made a little speech to "the little afflicted ones," as he called them, and introduced Pearson as one who "shared their affliction."

Pearson could hardly wait to get to his feet.

"Now, children," he said, "I am going to ask your chairman as a personal favour to me, and as a memento of my visit here to-day, to promise never to mention that beastly word 'affliction' when speaking of or to a blind person again."

The children rose and clapped and cheered, they shouted and stamped their feet. Teachers blew whistles and ran among them, calling for silence, but the uproar continued for several minutes. Meanwhile the chairman quite broke down. He had been working for blind people for thirty years, and was horrified to learn how he had been hurting their feelings. He added that he would make it his business to remove the word 'affliction' from the school vocabulary.

"Call it a handicap," suggested Pearson. "That's some-thing that can be overcome." There you have the handicap ideal, on which the whole work of St Dunstan's has always been based.

Earlier in this book I mentioned some of the individual St Dunstaners who achieved exceptional success in spite of being blind. St Dunstan's can be proud of them, and of several more like them, and they may feel grateful to St Dunstan's; and yet they were probably the least of our achievements, for most of them would have succeeded—as many other blind men have succeeded—without us. It would be wrong to judge us by the records of a few out-standing men. The proper yardstick is what St Dunstan's did for the ordinary man.

Most of the men who came to St Dunstan's were of average intelligence and education—and the general educa-tional standard in the First World War was considerably lower than it is to-day. It would have been foolish to try to train them for work beyond their capacity. So the first occupations taught at St Dunstan's included the traditional handicrafts for the blind.

The word 'traditional' needs some qualification. All traditions must begin some time, and the idea of blind persons doing any work at all is distinctly modern. The Poor Law of 1601, the first English statute in which the blind were mentioned, allocated responsibility for "setting to work the poor and the giving of relief to the lame, impotent, old, blind, and such others amongst them being poor and unable to work." The State continued to regard the blind as totally unemployable for the next two hundred years.

The history of the training and employment of the blind begins at the same place as the history of braille—the National Institution for the Young Blind in Paris, founded by Valentin Haüy in 1785. Some years earlier, when he was interested in work being done for the deaf, Haüy walked through a market and saw a group of blind men being publicly exploited and ridiculed. Their miserable plight touched his heart, and led him to open the world's first school for the blind. There he discovered that certain kinds of manual craft-work, such as basketry and mat-making, were within the capacity of the blind.

The first training establishment in Britain was founded by Edward Rushton and James Christie in 1791. It was called the Liverpool School for the Indigent Blind. Both the founders were blind themselves. Rushton was a poet and bookseller, and Christie a musician; but their pupils, like Haüy's, were taught basketry and mat-making and other crafts. During the next fifteen years four more institutions were opened in other parts of the country, all based on the Liverpool model and teaching the same trades.

These establishments were training schools, not workshops. After they had learned the crafts the pupils went back to their own homes to work—not because they were blind, but because home-working was the normal trade practice at that time. The Industrial Revolution had brought new weaving machines to Lancashire's cotton industry, but they were operated by manual power and worked in the weavers' own homes.

In the next twenty years—from 1790 to 1810—mechanical power was harnessed to the weaving machines, and the concentration of work in factories began. The blind continued working by hand in their own homes for another fifty years, during which time the factory system developed and the peasant crafts were steadily depressed. Many trained blind handicraft workers were reduced to soliciting alms because they could not earn a living by working at home.

The first workshop for the blind was founded by Elizabeth Gilbert, the blind daughter of a bishop, in 1856. It consisted of a cellar rented for eighteen pence a week, and the first workers were six blind beggars from off the streets. Other sheltered workshops were opened soon afterwards, most of them attached to training schools for the blind.

These workshops were not self-supporting, and when

the First World War began there was not nearly enough workshop accommodation for all the blind civilians. St Dunstaners could not have been placed in existing sheltered workshops even if this had been thought desirable. It was not. If it had been, additional sheltered workshops could have been built—as they were in Edinburgh and Glasgow, by the Scottish National Institution for the War Blinded. It was through deliberate policy, not force of circumstances, that men who had been trained in handicrafts at St Dunstan's went to work in their own homes.

So the wheel had turned a full circle, and we were back where we had been before Miss Gilbert rented that cellar sixty years before. There was just one difference, and it was all the difference in the world. It was, of course, After-care.

Although many attain great skill, blind craftsmen generally work more slowly than the sighted, and for shorter hours. That is one reason why sheltered workshops have to be subsidized. St Dunstaners were well above the average in skill, and did not receive any direct subsidy; but there was quite a lot of indirect help. There was the supply of raw materials at cost prices or under, and the humping and dumping of them were paid for by the department. So were carriage and overheads when the finished goods were bought by St Dunstan's. Whether they could be resold to the public then or not, the workers were paid by return of post at the highest market rate at the time. Further, each man was entitled to a fortnight's holiday a year, entirely free of expense, at one of our convalescent homes. Finally, cash grants were made in cases of sickness, accident, and business difficulties.

About 60 per cent. of the men who came in from the First World War were trained as craft-workers, and we did all we could to give each man the maximum possible earning power. There was nothing remotely arty-crafty about our attitude to handicrafts; we were quite mercenary and realistic. It was nice to hear compliments about the beauty of our men's products, but the clink of money was what we wanted to hear. So basket-makers and mat-makers were encouraged, like carpenters, to specialize in making one or two types of article for which there was a definite demand, and by repetition to achieve a speed and accuracy that would not have been possible with a more varied range. We kept the popularity of different kinds of baskets and mats constantly under review, and carried out what would now be called market research. We found that the demand for various articles varied from one district to another. So, as each man entered the basket-making or mat-making workshop, we asked him where he intended to settle down, made local inquiries to discover the types of article most in demand in that part of the country, and instructed him accordingly.

We did the same with netting. Although we encouraged the men to regard it as a paying hobby rather than a full-time occupation, we did our best to make it as profitable as possible, and we found there were better things to make than string bags. We published the results of our researches in the *St Dunstan's Review*, which became a trade paper as well as a social magazine. For example:

We have recently been inquiring into the matter of machine-made nets, with the object of avoiding competition. . . .

Fine mesh netting under $1\frac{1}{2}$ in., such as is used for boundary and other garden purposes, can be made in very large sections on machines, so that there would be only a low profit for hand-made nets of the same description.

Tennis nets in their entirety can be machine-made at too cheap a price for us to make them in large quantities. But apart from the above kinds of netting, there is a clear field for hammocks and every kind of netting done on a larger mesh than the $1\frac{1}{2}$ in.

Heavy farm-nets, swings, and all other fancy articles must be hand-made, and we can therefore be sure of a permanently good sale price. Our latest enterprise is the manufacture of rick nets. . . .

Later the Netting Department was extended to include rug-making, and cable and turkey wool rugs of the most intricate designs were produced. Again, rug-making was not an ideal full-time job from a financial point of view, but, like netting, it was useful for severely disabled men who were not up to the heavier crafts. Our rugs sold well until housewives began making rugs themselves.

Boot-repairing remained the most popular occupation, and the main economic problem here was the fact that, like all services, the work was liable to be irregular. Our answer was to train the cobbler in another trade, such as mat-making, so that he could do this when there were no boots to be repaired. This meant, of course, that he had to spend longer under training, and a high standard of workmanship was particularly important for a cobbler because he was on his own and our central depot did not see his finished work.

Poultry-farmers also were encouraged to learn another trade, as they were usually kept busy for only part of the day. Many of them took up basketry or mat-making. As they also learnt rough carpentry, so that they could run up chicken-houses and other such equipment, they were in a fair way to being jacks-of-all-trades.

Altogether nearly two hundred of our men from the First World War, including quite a high proportion of officers, were trained in poultry-farming. The number was a bit too high. The results ranged from brilliant success to complete failure.

No one failed because the work was too difficult, for in fact it is admirably suited to the blind. So long as you have at least one hand—and I remember a one-armed man of ours managed very well with three fingers and a stump—you can do nearly all the jobs required on a poultry farm. You do not need eyes to recognize the different breeds of fowl, or to collect and grade eggs. Nor is sight necessary for the correct mixing of poultry feed and mash, provided you use all the other four senses. With the help of a few simple but ingenious devices specially designed for him, the blind poultry-farmer could do almost every job himself —mating and breeding, managing incubators and foster-mothers, trussing and preparing for the table. He needed a little help in the actual care of the incubator, and usually his wife or some other member of the family read the temperature of the thermometer and trimmed the lamp. For the sake of a demonstration it could have been arranged for him to dispense with even that amount of help, but practically it would have not been worth the cost.

The main reason why there are not more blind poultry-farmers is the outlay. For the civilian blind without private means or financial help this is not a plausible occupation. Land must be leased, and the initial cost of stock, houses, and appliances is high. Then the return is slow. The new poultry-farmer cannot expect to make any money at all the first year, and the second year his profit will be quite small. So he needs some capital behind him, and in this the St Dunstan's man had a great advantage.

It did not take long to train a blind poultry-farmer. Our Country Life Section, initiated by Captain Webber and sighted assistants, gave instruction in two courses, each of six weeks. There were examinations, oral and practical, at the end of each course. The training was very thorough, and included subjects like the prevention and cure of poultry diseases. The men were also taught about ducks and turkeys, and even rabbit-breeding; and there was some simple market gardening, mostly growing vegetables and foods for the birds. The last month of the training was done on a real poultry-farm, first at Dollis Hill, Finchley, and then at King's Langley, in Hertfordshire, where we set up a farm of our own. Each man could bring his wife or other relatives who were going to help him, so that they could learn their part of the work under sighted supervision.

Unless a man had somewhere to go back to, our Settlement Department searched for a suitable place for his farm.

The man went to inspect it, and if he thought it would suit him the site was leased. We put up the chicken-houses, wire nettings, runs, incubators, and all the rest, but the man took over the farm before the fowls arrived. These were reared on our own farm, and one of our sighted experts was with the new poultry-farmer when he received them. Then he was left to carry on. He was visited regularly by one of our staff or expert visitors, and After-care supplied him with foodstuffs at cost price.

The way poultry-farms developed varied tremendously. For some men it was never much more than a backyard holding, which provided eggs for the household, and perhaps for sale to passing motorists. Others, more ambitious, developed quite large farms and eventually employed labour to do the physical work while they concentrated on the business side. Some of these men are still running their farms to-day, and are regarded with great respect by their sighted competitors.

Others gave up poultry-farming soon after they began. They were only a few, happily, and as they either had another trade or could come back to St Dunstan's to learn one, no harm was done. But you might say a little of our precious money had been misspent, a minor mistake had been made. The reason was that we had not been careful enough in selecting the men.

It was not for lack of trying but simply through ignorance. We thought that if a man was physically and mentally fit, keen on the job, recommended by the teaching staff and successful in his examinations, he had everything needed for success. The missing factor was love of the land, which does not necessarily follow enthusiasm, and which is not always shared by husband and wife. We should have settled each poultry farmer temporarily, for a period of a year. Only after living in the country through the worst as well as the best season could he and his wife know if they wanted to live there for good.

From 1925 our poultry-farmers were stimulated by com-

petitive Egg-laying Tests under the National Poultry
Council Scheme, and even those of us who did not know a
Rhode Island Red from a White Leghorn read the published
results regularly to see how our old friends were getting
on. Perhaps because there are no ex-St Dunstaners, because
one never becomes an Old Boy of our club, our comradeship is uniquely enduring.

Besides poultry some of our farming members kept
various animals and other birds. Pigs and rabbits were
popular. So was dog-breeding, for different purposes. A few
men kept goats, making their own goat-feeding nets. F. Tait,
of Bolton, bred canaries that won many prizes. Others bred
squabs, or young pigeons. Yet others bred racing pigeons.

Jerry Jerome, an Australian who settled near Christ-
church, was the first to take up bee-keeping, and this was
another typical piece of St Dunstan's empiricism. He was
poultry-farming, and decided to add to his income by
gardening as well. His ex-V.A.D. wife was enthusiastic,
and they did not let lack of knowledge stand in their way.
Then they discovered they had chosen the wrong spot to
live. It was in the middle of a heather moor—and heather,
they found, was not only very beautiful but also very
selfish, and reluctant to let anything else grow with it or
after it. So they had to choose between spending a fortune
on lime and fertilizers, moving somewhere else, or giving
up gardening. This would have spelt failure but for a piece
of inspired observation by Jerome. He noticed that from
July to September the heather buzzed with bees. The stuff
apparently contained an inexhaustible supply of nectar, and
Jerome decided to treat it as a friend instead of an enemy.
He stopped trying to burn it out, and bought a hive of bees.

He told himself he should have done this in the first
place, for while he was ignorant of gardening he had
experience with bees. His father had kept several hives in
Australia, and made him his unwilling assistant. In spite
of his lack of interest as a boy Jerome could not help
learning a lot about the management of an apiary, and

when he read modern text-books on the subject in Christ-church he found nothing had changed very much. So he got off to a good start, and after three years he reported that his original hive had multiplied itself by twenty-two. "With luck I hope to double this number again this year," he said. "I do all the manipulating of the bees myself, and never wear gloves—but my wife has to tell me how the bees are looking, if the queen is laying or not, how much brood there is, which frames contain brood and which honey, etc.—but I can tell if the hive is strong, also if they have much honey by the weight of the frames in my hands; and by putting my ear to the hives I can tell if all is well with them by the noise they are making. The contented humming roar of a healthy happy hive is unmistakable to those who know them. I can also tell if they are preparing to swarm by listening in the same way to catch the quaint little piping note of the young princesses in their cells; they pipe incessantly for a day or two before they emerge from the queen cells, and the old queen swarms."

Most poultry-farmers did some market gardening, and many others gardened either as a paying hobby or just for fun. The Guild of Blind Gardeners was started in 1920, and at its first exhibitions most of the prizes were won by St Dunstaners. Probably over half of all our men have done gardening in some form or other.

About a hundred and thirty First World War men, including several officers, qualified as physiotherapists—or masseurs, as they called themselves in those days. Most of them had good physical qualifications for the work. They were fit and strong, and in learning to be blind they had learnt to develop their sense of touch. The physiotherapist needs both muscular strength and delicacy of touch. Deep massage is laborious and quickly exhausting; a fine sense of touch and resistance is needed, because too much pres-sure will hurt the patient and may even cause damage, while too little will be ineffective.

Massage was by no means a new occupation for the blind. In Asia especially it has been practised by them since quite ancient times. It is on record that in Japan for many centuries it was virtually a closed shop for the blind. In this country there were no certified blind masseurs or masseuses until right at the end of the nineteenth century, and organized training began only in 1900, with the foundation of the London Institute of Massage by the Blind. The moving spirit was Dr Fletcher Little, a West End physician and Medical Officer of Health for Harrow. After eight years it changed its name to the National Institute. It then had twenty-one blind men and thirty-six blind women on its register of graduates. Fletcher Little died in 1914, and in February 1915 his school became a branch of the N.I.B., and was given accommodation and up-to-date equipment at the new buildings in Great Portland Street.

Henceforth blind students took the same examinations as the sighted. These were set by what is now the Chartered Society of Physiotherapy. At the examinations held in 1916 every blind student was successful, and out of nearly two hundred candidates, mostly sighted, a blind man actually came top. This was Percy Way, one of Fletcher Little's pupils and, among many other things, a Fellow of the Royal College of Organists. He became Principal of the N.I.B. Massage School, and held that position for thirty-two years. Every St Dunstaner who was trained in this profession was in his debt.

Another man to whom the students owed much was Dr Lloyd Johnstone, the librarian. He had lost his sight while in medical practice, and, like several other doctors who became blind, learnt massage. He was another of Fletcher Little's pupils. Other students, lacking his knowledge of the structure and working of the human body, needed textbooks in braille, and he built up a fine library for them.

But the students needed to see the various parts of the body, at least in their minds' eyes. They could learn something from braille diagrams, but these alone were not quite adequate. Happily, there were two other things to help them, and these were the proudest possessions of the Massage School.

They were kept side by side in a tall, narrow cupboard, which any over-curious sighted person could open at his peril. One was a skeleton, one of the finest specimens imaginable, six feet in height and perfect in every detail. The joints were arranged so that the lecturer could demonstrate every form of dislocation as well as all the ordinary movements.

Next to the skeleton stood the anatomical figure, specially designed for the instruction of the blind. The muscles and superficial structures had been cut away on the left side to show the deep-lying arteries, veins, and nerves, and the student could trace the exact course of these with his finger, from start to finish. On the right side the muscles and structures had been left in place, and could be examined manually in their correct positions. The head of the figure could be taken to pieces, and all the various passages in the throat and nose examined in the same way. All the internal organs could be taken out, their relative positions to one another studied, and their details noted. Some of these opened and showed the internal structure of the organ.

Again we saw the value of the principle of the blind leading the blind. Percy Way both inspired confidence and automatically understood all the special problems of the blind masseur. He taught with the easy, relaxed manner of the self-assured blind. "Do you see ?" he would ask. "When the bicep muscle is contracted the radial and ulnar bones are raised. Now put your fingers there." He guided the pupil's hands on to the anatomical figure. "That's the bicep muscle—do you see it now ?"

"Yes, I see." Only the sighted find our use of the verb 'see' strange. It is natural for us to use it not only in the sense of understanding but also when we talk of meeting

Running his own Tobacconist's and Sweet Shop

A Cheerful and Efficient Switchboard Operator

Lord Fraser with Members of the St Dunstan's Band

Some Braille Playing Cards

people, and newly blinded men are discouraged from making self-conscious efforts to avoid it.

During the War and for about five years after it our men filled all the vacancies at the Massage School. "The course of training may be regarded by many as somewhat lengthy," Percy Way wrote in an article in the *Review*, "lasting as it does from nine months to a year or even longer if ill-health prevents regularity of attendance; but massage is not a simple subject to master, and a shorter period would be quite inadequate." Now the course is three years, so by present-day standards the training then must have been sketchy.

Training on patients was done at the Middlesex and Hampstead Hospitals. After passing their examinations our men usually worked first in military hospitals and convalescent depots, and they proved some of our best ambassadors.

"Your blind masseur has been with us now two months, and of the staff of twenty-three he is the best. I should like you to send me three more as soon as you can let me have them." That came from the commanding officer of a hospital in the North early in 1917. About the same time the principal of the massage department of the largest Command depot in the country wrote: "Of my staff of thirty-two masseurs your four blind boys are incomparably the best, and we want four more."

Our prize letter came from Sir Robert Jones, the father of orthopædic surgery in Britain:

"The work which your blind masseurs do is very exceptional in quality. They are in every sense of the term a great success. I find them all intelligent and possessed of a wonderful gift of touch together with keen enthusiasm for their work. Apart from their qualities as masseurs I think they have an extraordinarily good psychological effect upon their patients. I consider institutions which secure the services of these men trained at St Dunstan's very fortunate."

I

Sixty of our men were earning good salaries as masseurs before the end of the War, and this number was eventually more than doubled. In 1918, on the initiative of Pearson, the Association of Certificated Blind Masseurs was formed, to protect the interests of all qualified blind masseurs and masseuses. In no occupation have St Dunstan's men been more successful than physiotherapy.

I started working for St Dunstan's about the time when the first masseurs were trained, and one of my first jobs was to get them started. I soon realized a potential limitation to their work in the development of electrotherapy, or medical electricity. I was told that was beyond the power of the blind.

"Why can't they do it?" I asked.

"Because they can't read the milliammeter."

I saw the point. A milliammeter is an instrument that records the amount of electricity passing through it, which in this case was the amount passing through the patient. Clearly an electrotherapist could not work without access to this knowledge, and on the face of it this ruled out the blind. Their exclusion would not have mattered greatly at the time, but I thought electrotherapy might develop further, and it seemed important for the blind to keep abreast as far as possible.

I took the problem to my workshop. The ordinary milliammeter had a dial like that of a watch, but it was not so easy to take a reading by feeling the delicate needle as it was to tell the time by feeling a watch's hands.

I had to devise some method by which the blind masseur could feel this highly sensitive needle without damaging or shifting it. Eventually I made a clamping device that did the trick. It only remained to convince doctors that the work could be done safely by blind masseurs, and to get public bodies to recognize the fact.

This was not so easy, and at first it looked impossible. The doctors still said it would be dangerous for the blind to do this work—that they could not see their patients' reactions, and so on. The masseurs' organization, partly out of prejudice and partly out of deference to the doctors' views, refused to examine our men or to give them a certificate for medical electricity. Then Dr Murray Levick took a hand.

In exploring circles he was better known as Surgeon-Commander Levick, for he had been with Scott to the Antarctic—not only as surgeon but also as electromagnetic expert. He was one of the first doctors to take up medical electricity. We explained our problem to him, and he said he would back his own judgment whatever anyone else said. We suggested that he should set an examination and award a certificate to any St Dunstaner who passed, and he did. A number of our early masseurs worked on this certificate, in defiance of the other doctors and the whole of the massage profession. In the end they recognized us, and allowed us to enter their examinations and obtain their certificates. Thanks to Dr Murray Levick, the battle was won, and electrotherapy was added to physiotherapy as an occupation for the blind. My little device, since improved, is still in regular use to-day.

After the War some of our physiotherapists took jobs in civilian hospitals which gave them the advantage of regular hours and a fixed salary. Others—the majority—preferred to chance their arms in private practice. Where necessary we found them a suitable house and provided them with equipment, had it regularly inspected and maintained in good order, and gave them professional advice and introductions to doctors. Some built up most successful practices, and were earning four-figure incomes before the Second War.

A few went into osteopathy, and also did extremely well. Toft and Lowry were outstanding.

Captain Gerald Lowry, the first officer blinded in the 1914-18 War, became a member of the Order of St John of Jerusalem in 1931. Edmund Toft was a private in the Royal Sussex Regiment. He built up an excellent practice in the West End of London, first as a masseur and then as an osteopath. He was a great team man, and when the Second World War broke out he immediately asked me if I wanted his help. I could not resist the offer, although I knew it would mean considerable financial sacrifice. So he came back to St Dunstan's to start instruction in physiotherapy for a new generation of war-blinded. He stayed with us until his death in 1941, at the early age of forty-six.

Then there were the office jobs.

We all learnt typewriting, like braille, for our own benefit, but by itself it could not be a means of earning a living. A blind man could not be a copy typist, and in those days few offices had recording machines. The St Dunstaner who wanted to go back to secretarial work had to learn braille shorthand.

This is taken down on a small portable machine which is fed with a thin paper tape. The machine was invented at the beginning of the century by a remarkable man, Henry Stainsby, who also devised the ordinary braille writer. He invented both machines while he was General Superintendent of the Birmingham Institution for the Blind, and he pioneered the employment of blind women as shorthand typists over fifty years ago. He was Secretary-General of the National Institute for the Blind from 1908 till his death in 1925, and a member of the founding Committee of St Dunstan's.

The Stainsby braille shorthand machine can be operated quietly at high speed, and the men who learnt to use it had to go through a test of dictation at 100 words a minute before they were passed out. We could fairly claim that our men were able to take down shorthand as fast as a sighted secretary, and to type as quickly; but they were bound to lose some time in the actual process of transcription, because they had to read back and type alternately, phrase by phrase, instead of simultaneously. The loss of time through this is much less than you might think. From the point of view of employment, however, the blind shorthand-typist can be at a disadvantage through not being able to do copy typing or filing and other clerical work.

The blind telephonist has no such handicap. On the contrary, he can compete with the sighted operator on equal terms. He keeps a braille directory of the numbers he has to call, and because he is blind he can usually carry an exceptionally large number of the commonest numbers in his head. Actually there is a trick of remembering four-figure numbers that the sighted can also use. Just think of them the way the French do, in pairs—thirty-six twenty-five is easier to remember than three six two five. The blind telephonist learns braille shorthand, so that he can take down messages at dictation speed; and many employers prefer the neatly typed verbatim messages they get from a blind operator to the hastily scribbled abbreviated (and sometimes garbled) messages that are the best sighted telephonists can manage. The comparison is not quite fair, because the average sighted operator is not professionally trained, and seldom stays long on the job. The blind telephonist—and this is the thing that makes many employers prefer him—goes through a stiff course, and regards the job as a career. He tries to be not only efficient but pleasant and tactful, because he is taught that he is in the front rank of the public relations department of his firm.

The first man we trained as a telephone operator was a very young "Old Contemptible," Dick Spry, who had joined the Coldstream Guards in 1907 at the age of sixteen. He was severely wounded in 1915, and only a marvellous operation by Ormond saved his life. After training as a telephonist he began work, appropriately enough, as assistant on our own busy exchange. Almost at once our regular man, who was sighted, fell sick, and the St Dunstaner had to take charge. It was very important that Spry should succeed, and we were all delighted when he showed he was

on top of the job. Later he worked as telephone operator
for the Gas Light and Coke Company in Kensington, where
he stayed for nearly five years. They were sorry when he
left, and we all mourned a fine man when he died of his old
wounds soon after. He was only thirty-one.

Over a hundred of our men from the 1914–18 War were
trained and placed in this occupation. Most of them stayed
with a single firm for years, often with increased responsibilities, and some were still in the same job when the
Second World War began. None of them lost his job
through inefficiency. During the depression some were
displaced through their firms closing down, but we never
had much difficulty in finding them vacancies.

Shell–Mex have probably employed more St Dunstan's
telephonists than any other firm, and eventually there were
enough for the Company to give them an annual party.
When some of their big exchanges went over to the
flashing-light system we asked if this would make any of
our men redundant. "We shall always have work for St
Dunstaners, and we're not letting any go without a
struggle," we were told; and so it has turned out.

The first man we had at Shell–Mex, Jack Lynch, stayed
for thirty-one years before ill-health forced him to leave.
He retired with a B.E.M. So did Patrick Garrity, who
operated at headquarters of the British Legion. If you rang
them up any time between 1919 and 1947 he probably
answered your call, for he was there all that time.

Sidney Dyer, who joined the Municipal Mutual Insurance
Company in 1920, did not stay quite so long, but that was
no fault of his. He lived and worked in London all through
the Blitz. In October 1940 the firm was evacuated to the
West Country, and Dyer went with his job. He and his
wife were living in a boarding-house when he completed
his twenty-first year of service with the firm. Then a bomb
hit the house and killed them both. It was one of the most
vicious twists of war. Dyer's son Dennis served in the
Royal Navy. When the war was over he came to see me

and said that, having no living relatives in Britain, he wished to emigrate. I got him a humble job with a firm of which I was a Director in Durban. He is still there and is now Marketing Manager.

Shopkeeping was not on the original list of jobs for St Dunstan's boys, but it soon edged its way into our scheme of things. First of all there were the men who had been shop-assistants, and wanted to use their experience to open shops of their own; or their wives had worked in shops, and the two thought they could manage together. If we shared their optimism they were given the chance. Some made mistakes, but none ever let us down.

Then there were the men with multiple injuries, who were physically incapable of any of the other occupations. Usually they had lost one or both arms, or perhaps legs, and were much more severely handicapped than the rest of us. About a hundred of our men from the First World War lost a limb. Given a competent wife or other sighted assistant, a shop was often the right solution for them, and jolly good shopkeepers they were. Once on board ship I put my fingers into an electric fan that was revolving quickly, and my right hand was tied up for a few days and I was told to make do with the left. Simple things like shaving and dressing took twice as long, and I had a glimpse of the meaning of a double handicap—and of how brilliantly it is often overcome.

The easiest kind of shop for a blind person to run is a tobacconist's. It may also be a sweet-shop, and the shop-keeper may stock periodicals and do a newspaper round. The fact that he is a disabled ex-Serviceman will not make up for inefficiency or failing to give the customers what they want. When Bill Shakspeare of Sheldon, near Birmingham, was asked for a recipe for success for blind shopkeepers he said at once: "The right stuff, the right place, the right time, and the right price." He knew what he was talking about, for he was very successful himself.

He learnt mat-making at St Dunstan's, but soon opened a paper shop and built up a good business. Eventually he had two shops, and was President of the South Birmingham Branch of the Retail Newsagents' Association. In his spare time he worked vigorously for St Dunstan's and the British Legion, and for his services received the M.B.E.

Bill Shakspeare's shops owed nothing to his mat-making, nor did we think of linking shopkeeping with handicrafts until some of the men showed us the possibilities.

This was one of those curious twists in our story that caught everyone by surprise. Some go-ahead handicraft-worker—perhaps a boot-repairer or basket-maker or carpenter—went further than most in building up a circle of local customers, and had the idea of selling them other goods besides those he made himself. If he was a boot-repairer he might sell sundries like boot-polish, laces, and all the other footwear accessories known in the trade as grindery; a carpenter could sell photo-frames and artists' materials; a basket-maker might sell various fancy goods; and so on. In other words, he could run a small shop.

Exactly when and where it first happened no one seems to know. The idea seems so obvious when you look back that I expect it occurred to a number of men independently about the same time. At any rate, we took the hint quickly enough, and helped these pioneers to stock their shops. It proved good business for us as well as them. They found they could make more money out of shopkeeping than their handicraft, and so cost us less in indirect subsidies. Nor did it stop there. After the man and his wife had been running the shop for a while they found they could expand their business, and took on staff; and in this way some of our home-workers rose by their own efforts to become successful businessmen.

F. G. Braithwaite of Guildford was an outstanding example.

"You will see by my bill-head," he wrote in 1921, "that I have gone a step further than boot-repairing. I have quite

recently started in the wholesale trade. I don't think this
will be too big an undertaking, for there must be no limits
to my business. I now rank amongst the three largest boot-
repairers in this town; also you will see above that I am
allowed to use the King's Seal, for I employ all disabled
men."

Three years later he was still on the King's Roll of
Honour with a staff of eight, including a traveller. He
became a prominent freemason, and did a great deal of
voluntary work for ex-Servicemen.

Once we had seen the success of transitions of this kind
we modified our training. Those men who seemed competent to keep shops were instructed in this as well as their
craft, which was then only a hobby and a demonstration.
This development was, I think, typical of a voluntary
enterprise like ours. A State-run show would probably not
have reacted so promptly when the need for a change of
plan first appeared.

Team-spirit has nothing to do with dull conformity, and
St Dunstan's has always taken a pride in its odd men out. I
forget what Bombardier Pink was trained for, but it could
not have been in delivering coal in the winter and taking
people for outings in the summer. That was what he did,
using the same transport for both services. He did very
well, and was always making beastly puns about being in
the pink, and he bred chinchilla rabbits as a side-line.

Another unusual success story was that of Private L.
Jackson of the 11th Cheshires, who went back to his home
in Rock Ferry. He had been a hairdresser before the War.
At St Dunstan's he learnt basket-making, and he had hardly
opened his own little workshop when an order for fifty
baskets came in. So did his old customers—demanding a
haircut or a shave.

Jackson struggled for a while with centre cane and willow,
and then, rather diffidently, got out his scissors, clippers,
and razor again. His old customers egged him on. His
heart was not really in basketry, and soon he was again

giving haircuts and shaves. One thing led to another, and before long he had one of the leading hairdressing establishments, for both men and women, in the district. He employed several assistants, and spent most of his own time in supervising and running the business. Only very favoured customers had the privilege of being shaved by Mr Jackson himself.

The success of a blind shopkeeper depends quite a lot on the help he gets from his wife, and ours have been wonderfully lucky. This does not mean that the husband is just the nominal shopkeeper. On the contrary, I suspect sighted shopkeepers leave at least as much of the work to their wives, and I have never heard of any of our chaps having to close his shop because his wife was busy bringing up baby—or, for that matter, bringing baby into the world.

Handling money is not much trouble, because our currency is very suitably designed for our needs. Banknotes are of different sizes, and it does not take long to learn to tell a pound note from the smaller ten-shilling note by the feel. Coins can be identified by both size and the milled edges. Of course, there are greater difficulties for the man with no hands, but special machines have been invented to enable him to give change and identify coins.

Sometimes men with an additional handicap, such as the loss of a limb, were trained as public speakers or organizers, and were employed by St Dunstan's itself to help collect funds. I have always been a bit chary about this, and I have never appointed a man to this work unless I thought he had a genuine talent for it. It would be bad for both him and us, and indeed for the disabled generally, if he was merely put on show to attract public sympathy, and therefore charity. At the same time, if our man has such a disability I certainly would not ask him to try to hide it, and if it should move someone to double a contribution I would not send half the money back.

No one could say Sergeant Alan Nichols had his job with

Appeals because he had no hands. He was an Old Contemptible, and very proud of it, and one of only three St Dunstaners who lost both hands in the First World War. He lectured on St Dunstan's for thirty years. He was far too cheerful and humorous to attract any pity on account of his grave double handicap. Instead he aroused admiration for his very definite conquest of disability, and set a shining example for the larger number of handless St Dunstaners who were to come.

The list of occupations followed by St Dunstaners from two World Wars runs to over fifty professions and trades. It includes missionary and bookmaker, actor and paviour, newspaper proprietor and travel agent, flower-farmer and fish-trader.

A large number of these occupations have been followed by one or two individuals who were already trained and employed in them before they lost their sight. Our main task has always been to find work suitable for men who could not make use of skills already learnt.

Pearson was always looking for new jobs for the blind. "Arrangements for teaching the men to be divers have been made with two well-known firms engaged in this work," he wrote in the first Annual Report. "This is a new industry for blind people, and is likely to prove highly satisfactory."

The idea was not so far-fetched as it might seem, for most of the waters in which our divers go down are so muddy that they have to work entirely by feel. So a salvage firm in Hull agreed to engage T. P. Drummond, an Australian, who soon sent us photographs of himself in diving-dress taken while he was working on a sunken wreck.

Then he came back. It seemed that his employers had not been able to put full confidence in him, and the other divers did not let him take his proper share of the duties, so that he went down only once in a while. Naturally, he got bored by the idleness, and gave up the job. He trained and qualified as a masseur, and then returned to Australia, where he later took up casual diving again.

Drummond's diving failure reflects no discredit upon him, but illustrates the point that every specialist must also to some extent be a jack of all trades. Between the Wars, before the use of radar, approaching aircraft were apprehended by a crude listening-device with two enormous gramophone horns set apart and directed by ear to the approaching noise. When both horns were "on" the target a bearing could be taken and the aeroplane could be spotted with binoculars. The War Office consulted me as to whether blind persons, whose hearing was supposed to be abnormally acute, could do this work better than others, and a group of St Dunstaners with our sports instructor, Corporal-Major Tovell, went to camp for a test. They did very well, perhaps a little better than less concentrated persons, but not so exceptionally well as to justify their employment in war when a soldier, apart from being a specialist, has to turn his hand to any task in an emergency and look after himself into the bargain. One remembers many occasions in Britain's history when the thin red line had to be reinforced by Army cooks and bandsmen.

Some time in the 1880's Dr Thomas Armitage visited two Glasgow shipyards and found six blind men at work. They were cleaning bolts, polishing rough castings, and spinning oakum. Armitage was keenly interested by this early example of the employment of the blind in open industry.

In 1918 Dr Wheeler and his wife walked through the factory of the Crocker-Wheeler Electrical Company of New York. Mrs Wheeler stopped to watch some of the workers who were taping coils for armatures. They were wrapping tape round several strands of copper wire. It was a simple occupation, and many of the workers did not need to look at what they were doing.

"That job could be done blindfold," Mrs Wheeler said
to her husband. "Blind folk could do it." The idea flashed
in her brain. "Why don't you try them out?"

"I will," said Dr Wheeler, and he did.

His wife was right. It was a very suitable occupation for
the blind. An account of the experiment was published in an
American scientific journal. A copy reached Pearson in
London. Immediately he got in touch with an old friend,
Hugo Hirst, the Director of the General Electric Company
of London and Birmingham. Hirst knew Wheeler, and he
promptly cabled for full particulars. Wheeler replied by
taking the next boat for England.

He visited St Dunstan's the day after he landed, and
showed Pearson the nature of the work. Two days later
they went together to Hirst's office in Queen Victoria
Street for a meeting with the heads of the biggest electrical
firms in the country. Pearson demonstrated that a blind
person could do the job, and suggested that the Birmingham Royal Institution for the Blind might like to start the
occupation experimentally in their workshops. They were
near the Birmingham works of the G.E.C., which Hirst
said would supply the material and pay for the work. Dr
Wheeler promised to go and show them how to do it.

The work appealed to Pearson especially because no
raw material had to be bought and no finished goods
marketed. Yet he did not think there was anything in it for
St Dunstan's. "The industry can only be satisfactorily conducted on factory lines. It is not suitable for home work. I
think it will be made an addition to existing industries
practised in the Institutions for the Blind which are situated
in cities in which there are electrical works." The only
alternative to home industry was still the sheltered workshop.

But home industry was fast becoming an anachronism.
The cost of supplying materials and marketing the goods
had always made it uneconomic, and competition by the
machine was becoming increasingly keen. We were living

in a machine age, and mechanical mass-production was seen as a threat to the blind man's ability to gain his livelihood.

By a happy irony it also offered him a new way of earning his living. The essence of mass-production is standardization, and for the factory worker that means repetition. Costs are cut by stereotyping products and making them in long runs. This involves much work that is so unvarying and mechanical in itself that, as Mrs Wheeler shrewdly observed, it could be done blindfold. For the sighted it has been called monotonous and soul-destroying; to the blind it has opened the gates of industry.

They were not exactly flung open, however, and it was some time before we even got a foot in the door. Mass-production began in the United States, and I think it was the Ford Motor Company of America that first found room—or rather made room—for blind workers in the machine shop and on the assembly line. Shortly after the First World War, Henry Ford had a survey made of handicapped people and issued a decree on the strength of the results. "If one out of every thousand persons is deaf," he said, "then one out of every thousand Ford workers must be a deaf man. If one out of every six thousand is blind then one out of every six thousand Ford workers should be blind." Like all his orders, the rule was strictly observed. Not only that, but it was never a question of charity. Each handicapped person received full pay and was expected to give full value for his wages. If his disability prevented him from operating a machine efficiently it was up to the Company to try to adapt a machine so that he could do a good job.

The first blind persons in Europe to work alongside the sighted in open industry were the Germans; in particular, German blinded ex-Servicemen from the First World War. In their case it was a question of a desperate situation being given a desperate remedy.

Germany had no organization comparable with St Dunstan's, and most blinded ex-Servicemen were left to the care of local institutions for the civilian blind. There was very little vocational training during the War, and the only central effort of any kind was the employment of some of the men in minor operations in munition factories. By 1918 there were forty of them working at the Royal Munitions Factory at Spandau, in the examining and packing department of the cartridge section. They worked eight and a half hours a day for a maximum daily wage of five shillings. When the War ended the factory was closed down, and they were all thrown out of work.

The civilian blind were not much better off. Although many of them were trained in the traditional handicrafts, they had trouble in plying their trades, as materials for basket weaving and brush-binding were difficult to get. Against this background the State Insurance against Accidents passed a law permitting the employment of blind persons in factories. A later Act compelled large firms to employ a certain percentage of disabled ex-Servicemen. The Siemens Electrical Works in Berlin then followed the example of the Royal Munitions Factory and engaged as many as fifty men on the factory bench. At first they were given simple checking and packing work; later they operated boring machines and stamping presses.

The Siemens experiment attracted the attention of the Government, and other firms were encouraged to employ the blind in similar ways. By 1921 the German blind were reported to be employed in cigarette and chocolate factories, a gramophone factory, a worsted yarn mill, a cutlery factory, a motor works, and a factory that made alarm clocks. Wildly enthusiastic reports of these activities spread abroad, and in November 1922 my wife and I went to Germany to see for ourselves what was being done.

I was able to make a fairly complete study of the training and after-care of Germany's war-blinded men, and on materialistic grounds alone I could be extremely thankful that I was British. Pensions were much smaller than ours, and voluntary organizations had only meagre funds. Of Germany's 4000 war-blinded soldiers, about 500 had been through a training school in Berlin that taught many of the St Dunstan's subjects, but with little success. They had trained only ten masseurs, who did so badly that the subject was given up. The same happened with telephone-operating, which was used only by men who worked in the Post Office before. Their only success was in stenography, and about eighty or ninety men were employed as short-hand-typists. Poultry-farming, boot-repairing, carpentry, and shopkeeping had apparently not been tried.

Of the remaining 3500 a few had found their way into civilian blind institutions, and had learnt brush-making and basket-making. Some had stayed; others had returned home and tried to do handicrafts there, but without an after-care organization they could make little headway.

Of the men in open industry most were engaged on dull, unskilled, and monotonous work. They were employed because the State said they should be, and sighted labour was very cheap. When I talked with some of these fellows I knew there was nothing for us to learn here.

The Siemens Electrical Works was a different story, almost in a class of its own. I was greatly impressed by what I saw there—but let me quote from what I wrote at the time:

In one workshop where small metal parts are manufactured, amongst two or three hundred sighted employees are eighty blinded soldiers. They fit into the routine of this factory, each doing an automatic job with an electrically driven machine, specially adapted for his use. The machines in use are fundamentally the same for the disabled men as for fit men and women, the only differences being special devices for quickly clamping materials to be machined, and protecting devices.

The thing which strikes one about Siemens is not the skill of the blind men, which though good is not surprising, not the cleverness of the machines, but the goodwill of the firm, which has obviously set out to do the thing thoroughly and with every possible consideration for the blinded men. It is true that they were compelled to do something, but they would appear to have gone out of their way to handle the problem as much from the men's as their own point of view. Originally these men were engaged upon handwork, i.e., fitting screws into parts, assembling parts, winding coils, etc., etc., but this was so dull that men did not take to it eagerly. This has now been discontinued at Siemens, and machine work has taken its place. The Director says that the sound of quickly moving machinery, the necessity for the blind man's concentration, and the feeling that good production is being procured alongside of and under similar conditions to sighted workers has produced good moral effect and led to an increase in the men's interest and diligence.

Some are engaged on more complicated work than others; for example, a few work two slow-running drilling machines simultaneously. Perhaps this indicates that the Director will move the best men on constantly to more difficult jobs, which will add to their remuneration and interest.

Putting eighty blind men in the same workshop is not the best arrangement; they get more individual attention and make more friends among the sighted workers if they are distributed in ones and twos, and that was the policy we followed in the Second World War. But this was 1922, and there was nothing like the Siemens experiment anywhere else in the world.

A pathetic incident occurred at the end of this visit. I had entertained a German blinded soldier who had given me much information about his life, his work, his guide dog, and his war pension. Christmas was coming and I said I would like to give him a present for his family. What would he like? He said "A goose," and I gladly agreed and provided it. The goose cost some hundreds of thousands of marks and represented a month's war pension for this man and his family—a warning against runaway inflation, I thought.

When I visited Germany again in 1936 I found blind men in other open factories doing a fair variety of work

K

side by side with the sighted; and we still had nothing of
the kind. I must add quickly that in every other respect our
war-blinded were much better off, thanks to the generosity
of our supporters and the help of many industrialists. It
would be a great libel to say that British industry had let
us down. What got the German blind into the factories
was the law that compelled large employers to provide
jobs for disabled ex-Servicemen.

We had nothing like this until the Disabled Persons
Act of 1944, and even then we had to mobilize the back-
benchers and twist the Government's arm. I would be the
last to deny that it was long overdue. The British Legion
had pressed for it since 1922. I did my share of the pressing,
and of the final arm-twisting, when the Minister of Labour
wanted the matter left as a hope. Yet it is no cause for
national shame that this humane piece of legislation came
so much later here than in Germany.

The pressures were far greater there, for their war-blind
were in a desperate plight. Voluntary assistance was barely
enough to save them from poverty and degradation, let
alone help them to be happy and useful again. So the
Government had to step in, and then it only shifted the
onus to the richer companies. It did not say how the help
should be given, and the credit for the results is due to
enlightened employers.

The successful development by St Dunstan's of so many
quite different occupations saved the British war-blinded
from similar need and distress. It also made it more difficult
for our men to reach the factory bench when it became
clear that home handicrafts were losing their place as
economic jobs in the machine age. A character in one of
Somerset Maugham's plays said that no one learns from
anyone else's experience, and the half-truth is valid for
nations as well as individuals. The results of the American
and German experiments did little to undermine the common belief in this country that there were no factory jobs
suitable for the blind.

The N.I.B. challenged this quite early, and from 1927 conducted a searching investigation of a number of trade processes to find out if they came within the blind worker's capacity. The findings were largely positive, and in the nineteen-thirties further fruitful research was carried out by the Institute with the co-operation of the National Institute of Industrial Psychology. After all this no one could say there was no factory work within the scope of the blind. But that did not get them any jobs.

It could be objected, reasonably enough, that a blind worker took longer to train. All right, then, we would train him. So in 1935 St Dunstan's set up its own Machinery Department, in the workshops at Kentish Town, where we taught men to operate router and borer machines, a circular saw, and a vertical belt sander. We showed, to anyone who cared to look, that these men could operate machines in open industry side by side, and on equal terms, with sighted workers.

Employers came and looked, and we caught their interest at once. Of course, there were objections, but these were easy to answer because they were always the same. Accidents . . . surely we would admit that a blind man was more liable to accidents than the sighted when working with machinery? We would not admit it. We assured them that, if anything, it was the other way about. Elementary precautions would have to be taken at the start, but after that they could rely on the man to look after himself. Most accidents were caused through carelessness or inattention —surely we did not have to tell them that? The blind were much more safety-minded than people with eyes. Because we could not afford to take risks, being careful had become second nature to us.

How would blind men find their way about in a factory built for workers with eyes? All right once they got the hang of the place, we said. No, they would not need an escort every time they wanted to go to the lavatory. They did not need any concessions or special privileges.

The Trade Unions, like the employers, were friendly and willing to help; but they had another nagging fear. Might not the blind become a source of cheap labour? We could assure them that they would not, that the sighted had nothing to fear from their competition, that they would be on equal terms.

Then we came to the heart of the matter, and there was nothing we could say to this. There were no unfilled jobs. There was widespread unemployment. Whenever a vacancy occurred a queue was formed. To employ a blind man meant refusing a sighted man a job. It was too long after the War for any idea of employment-preference for those who had made great physical sacrifices.

We had reached a brick wall. In an age in which pacifism was fashionable, and full employment unheard of, the future looked bleak. We needed a labour-shortage and an acceptance of the special claims to consideration of disabled ex-Servicemen, and we were not likely to get either without another war. But that was all too near.

9

Fun and Games

"WHAT is this life," asked the poet W. H. Davies, "if, full of care, we have no time to stand and stare?" Such inactivity is less attractive to the blind, for they can only stand. If they are young and vigorous they will not yet have acquired a taste for the pleasures of contemplation, and if they have only recently lost their sight it is not the best medicine for them. They need a full life in the most literal sense of the phrase. They want to be doing something all the time.

The easiest way of solving the problem of leisure is by getting rid of it. Emulate Isaac Watts's busy bee, improve the shining hour, keep your nose to the grindstone and shoulder to the wheel, and the problem disappears. Leisure is reduced to a minimum, and you are so tired that you need all that for sleep.

The comparatively short working hours at St Dunstan's left us all with much time to fill. Happily, we also had many ways of filling it.

Some years ago St Dunstaners were invited to vote on their favourite sports and pastimes so that they could be placed in order of popularity. This is how they came out:

1. Walking	7. Swimming
2. Cards ⎫	8. Cycling
Dominoes ⎬ tie	9. Darts
Reading braille ⎭	10. Chess ⎫ tie
5. Gardening	Fishing ⎭
6. Rowing	12. Golf

149

The list is not complete. But it seems long enough to correct any lingering illusion about our not being able to enjoy ourselves like other people.

Perhaps Nature makes us like walking most because we need it. The average sighted person has quite a lot of exercise every day, merely through walking about. He takes this for granted, and it never occurs to him how dependent it is on his eyes. If he loses his sight he discovers this as soon as he is up and trying to get about, and he may start thinking gloomily that he will get soft and flabby. But pretty soon he makes another discovery that more than compensates for this. This is that he can still take part in sports.

They may not be the sports he was used to when he could see, but he is not likely to complain about that. A man who must either have a guide or else grope about to perform the simplest journeys is thrilled at the idea of any kind of sport. Few of us had any experience of rowing, but once we found it was within our capacity nothing would keep us away from the lake. Here was an activity that satisfied all our frustrated needs. It demanded physical effort, and there was exhilaration in feeling the boat glide forward, responsive to the power behind the stroke. There were the distinctive and evocative sounds—the soft splash of the oar dipping into the water, the creaking in the row-locks, the gentle flurry of feathering—and these, with the smell of the lake and the surrounding park, created a vivid mental picture of the scene.

You could idle dreamily and romantically, if you had the right cox. Or you could row quite furiously to work off all your surplus energy without having to worry about bumping into someone or something. You were no longer the victim of your blindness, you had reduced its importance, and the things you couldn't do faded before something you could do.

It has often been said that you can tell a St Dunstaner by his bearing. He does not shuffle along clumsily, or carry his head awkwardly up in the air, and he takes a great pride in looking well-groomed and smart. There is no pose in this. It is a reflection of his spirit—a spirit of sturdy self-reliance and ability to do things that was originally nourished on that lake in Regent's Park. It was not only his body that glowed when he stepped out of the boat after a hard row, and no man returned from his first row without a squarer set of his shoulders.

No wonder that rowing was so popular. Almost everyone could do it—even the one-armed could paddle canoes or row in pair-oared boats, and their triumph was even greater than ours.

Another factor came into this sport. It could be competitive.

Competition was something to fire enthusiasm, and to make you forget your own private little battle against what wasn't as good as it had been. It was something to make you look out instead of in, to make you take the conquest of blindness in your stride because you had to think about conquering someone else.

Impromptu races took place on the lake from the beginning, and the sport caught on so quickly that in the first summer of St Dunstan's a contest was held on the Thames. It was between St Dunstan's, who issued the challenge, and the Worcester College for the Blind. Worcester, who practised on the Severn, were proud of their rowing, and St Dunstan's trained hard for weeks beforehand. The forthcoming contest was talked about and aroused public interest, and of course Pearson did not miss a trick. When the day came Press reporters and photographers turned up in force, and crowds on the towpath cheered the competing crews.

St Dunstan's won, but that did not matter. It did not even matter when one of our eights rowed in Marlow Regatta and defeated two or three River Clubs. I stroked this eight, and the real joy was the rhythm of the rowing, the feeling of harmony, the team-work spirit, the bond between us that had nothing to do with the fact that none of us could see.

We liked to be treated on equal terms by sighted crews, we wanted them to try their hardest to beat us, and then it did not matter greatly who won. Of course, it was good publicity when we were victors, and I cannot blame Pearson for the number of times after his death that we told the world we had beaten the London Fire Brigade. I suppose the truth is that it was a long time before we beat another sighted crew, so whenever we published news of our activities, and there was the usual paragraph or two on rowing, this victory was reported again. Our regular readers must have thought we were beating the gallant firemen again and again. It was really very thoughtless of us to go on boasting like that.

Every year we had our own big annual regatta at Putney, and old St Dunstaners came from all over the country to take part. Sometimes we had over three hundred entries, and there had to be eliminating races in Regent's Park. Nor was the excitement limited to the contestants. Teams represented houses, and each had their loyal and noisy supporters who were there on the day to cheer their champions on.

We had races both among ourselves and against sighted teams in swimming, too. The Marylebone Baths reserved periods for us, with free admission, and large numbers of men learnt to swim for the first time. Most of us swam in the sea at Brighton as well, and we revelled in the freedom of movement you have in the water; but this is something only the blind can understand. When we walk about on land we must always be more or less on guard and take precautions against obstacles, even though habit makes these virtually automatic, so that we are no longer aware of our vigilance. We remember it quickly enough when we enter the water and suddenly find we can cast it off, and strike out boldly and vigorously without fear of hitting anything.

Usually one swims in a party, and the talking and splashing and shouting of the others enable you to keep your bearings. Sometimes I have been the only one in the water, and again I could keep my sense of direction by the noise of people on the beach and of the surf breaking on the shore.

There are plenty of useful noises and echoes in the bath, too, which the blind swimmer soon learns to interpret. Again he can have that glorious experience of striking out fearlessly in any direction, simply by going in from the middle of one end and swimming straight out. Usually he can hear other swimmers and avoid them, unless the baths are crowded; and anyway, bumping into someone is nowhere less painful than in the water. It is better not to swim side-stroke, as with one ear under water it is harder to hear. Most baths have a chute, which makes a recognizable splashing noise. It is easy to find the steps in the corner of the baths, too. There is a waste-pipe there, to take the overflow. The swimmer sends a little wave ahead of him, and when this reaches the walls it splashes back and gurgles down the waste-pipe and guides the swimmer right into the angle. This gurgle is one of those unobtrusive but distinctive sounds that help to give the blind what often seems to the sighted a quite uncanny sense of direction.

Then there is diving, with another thrill of glorious abandon which the sighted can perhaps share with us. I used to dive regularly off the springboard and the seven-foot platform, although I always took the precaution to ask if it was all clear before I plunged. Other St Dunstaners have dived from greater heights and, I am assured, much more gracefully. But I loved it, and was very sorry when I had to give it up because of inconvenience under water from the old wound in my head.

Captain Gerald Lowry was one of our finest swimmers, as he had to be to win the Bath Club's two lengths annual handicap. Another keen swimmer was A. E. Bettaney, of Stoke-on-Trent, who enjoyed the sea. On his first swim of

his summer holiday on one occasion he swam out alone
about two hundred yards. He was just turning back when he
heard a woman cry for help.

Bettaney turned and swam rapidly towards the sound.

"Help him, not me," the woman said, and that was the
first Bettaney knew that there was a man there as well. The
woman was exhausted with the effort of trying to hold her
companion up. Bettaney took over from her, and soon
discovered why. The man might be half-drowned, but he
fought and struggled like mad. Bettaney fought back, and
managed to hold the man's head above water for ten long
minutes. He tried to swim with the man, but he struggled
again, and Bettaney was becoming exhausted himself. He
was nearly at the end of his endurance when three men with
a life-saving buoy came on the scene. Bettaney was awarded
the honorary testimonial on vellum of the Royal Humane
Society for his heroism.

On July 15, 1917, almost a year after I was blinded, I
went with over two hundred others to the grounds of
Ranelagh Club for my first Annual Sports Day. This was
the culmination of regular Saturday morning sports programmes held in Regent's Park throughout the year, and I
knew the standard would be high. The spectators had not
been warned, and they reacted like victims of a confidence
trick.

One hundred yards sprint, said the programme, just like
any other programme. To the public, with its image of a
blind man shuffling and groping along, the idea of a sprint
would have been comical if it had not been pitiful.

"What a wonderful spirit these boys have got! . . .
They'll never say die, will they? . . . A blind man's sprint,
of all things! . . . I hope there won't be any accidents,
though. . . . No, dear, they won't go fast enough for that. . . .
Ah, here they come—you know, I've a feeling we're in for
a surprise. . . ."

In fact, they were in for the shock of their lives. On your

marks, get set—"It's just like the real thing," said one woman—then the gun cracked, and half a dozen men ran hell-for-leather along the track. Winner's time—10.8 seconds. A second and a half more than the world record, but for a small Sports Club it was still pretty good. The winner, who had always been a keen athlete, confessed it was better than anything he had done before he lost his sight. "It's the training that's done it," he said.

In those days we used guide-wires to enable sprinters to run in a straight line. For each runner a steel wire was stretched very tightly between posts for the whole length of the course. Five or six such wires were placed parallel with one another, and a ring was threaded on each. A tape of strong material was attached to the ring, and the runner held this tape as he ran. The ring slid along with him, and so kept him in his lane. You could say that he felt his way along, although hardly in the way—and certainly not at the speed—the good ladies watching the event had expected.

In later years we exploited the sprinter's sense of hearing instead of touch. There were no guide-lines, but the finishing tape was reinforced with a whistle or an oscillating bell.

The recorded speeds showed that our runners lost very little time through not being able to see, and it was good to hear the gasps of astonishment, still better to hear the murmurs of sympathy and compassion give way to spontaneous applause. But it is only fair to say that it was not as easy as that for any of the runners when they had their first practice sprints. However much you may trust the person who shows you the guide-line or rings the bell, running flat out when you cannot see where you are going calls for some pluck the first time.

No one knew this better than Bill Tovell, the Corporal-Major of the Royal Horse Guards who joined the staff of St Dunstan's on a temporary posting in 1917 and stayed till his death in 1937. Tovell came as a sort of P.T. instructor, without any previous experience of training the blind. You could not say he proceeded by trial and error, for he made few mistakes. He had a natural flair for the job, and he dedicated himself to it. He organized and prepared our regattas, walks, sports days, swimming contests, dances, camps, and even trips abroad. He knew all his boys, as he called them, and most of their wives and children. He was everyone's friend and adviser, always cheerful and helpful, a man who knew instinctively when to joke and tease and when to hold his tongue.

Our sports programme included every kind of novelty race, of course—wheelbarrow, egg-and-spoon, three-legged, sock, and so on—and putting the weight and throwing the cricket-ball. As some of our chaps could hurl a ball over eighty yards, they had to be shown rather carefully which way to hurl.

While we were still at St Dunstan's Lodge visitors were astonished sometimes to see a dozen or so men apparently attempting the quite hopeless task of pulling one of our fine old oak-trees up by the roots. In fact, they were just tug-of-war teams practising the scientific use of their weight. The fact that it is a team competition made the tug-of-war an ideal event for us. Some of our teams have taken part in the Royal Tournament at Olympia.

Then we had the standing long jump, climbing the rope, and tandem cycling—more, we had one monstrous bicycle for six riders that used to startle innocent pedestrians as it was propelled with much shouting and laughter round the Outer Circle of the Park.

We were allowed to hold our annual Sports Day in Regent's Park long after we had moved our training department to Brighton, and men came from all over the country. Sports Days were also held, of course, at Manchester, Birmingham, and other centres, and those who could manage it went to them all. As our average age increased the times became slower, and men who had been among our keenest sprinters were seen only in the wheelbarrow race, being trundled protestingly by over-enthusiastic wives. More and more of the running was

handed over—to the children of St Dunstaners, who made
the day for everyone. My wife and I were pleased when
our daughter Jean won the race for the under-fourteens.

For many years competitors were divided into two
categories, labelled 'T.B.' and 'S.S.' The former meant
'totally blind,' the latter either 'semi-sighted' or 'slightly
sighted'—neither of which, of course, was remotely true.
If they had had any really useful sight they would not have
been admitted to St Dunstan's. But some men, although
technically blind within the official definition, could see
enough to distinguish vague objects or shadows, and in
sports like rowing this was obviously an advantage. The
distinction was worth keeping, but the initials caused mis-
understandings through being printed on programmes at
our Sports Meetings. Some of our men were assumed to be
tuberculous, while others were presumed to have half
ordinary vision. But it was not so easy to think of a good
alternative, and for both fun and utility I offered a prize of
a guinea for the best suggestion.

The winning entry was really quite obvious—'A' and
'B' instead of 'S.S.' and 'T.B.' respectively, to be memorized
as 'A for Almost, B for Blind.' The only trouble was that
the letters meant even less to those who had not been told
what they meant, and in the Second World War we went
back to T.B. and S.S.

In the summer of 1922 someone suggested a competitive
walk from London to Brighton, on the same lines as walks
held by the big clubs. Padre Williams, our Sports Captain,
was sceptical about the probable response, but tremendous
keenness was shown. That was all very well, but the Padre
rightly decided that would-be entrants would have to pass
a stiff test before they were allowed to attempt the fifty-two
miles to Brighton. Training for this began at once, and in
October a test walk was held. It was three times round the
Outer Circle—nearly nine miles—and it had to be completed within one and three-quarter hours.

Fifteen men entered, and they all passed the test. The following month the first Brighton Walk was held.

The Surrey Walking Club put off a special walk of their own to help to organize the event, and at 5 A.M. the fifteen men—followed by a great crowd of supporters—set off from Big Ben. Each walker was accompanied by a cyclist and guide, with whom he maintained contact by a tape tied lightly to the wrist. It was a great event, without precedent in the blind world. People turned out to cheer all along the route.

Not all the men finished the course. Some had to retire through foot trouble, others because of their old wounds. One man covered forty-six miles before his weak ankle gave way. Yet eight men finished the course, and the winner, F. H. Cassidy, took only a shade over ten and three-quarter hours. My wife and I held the tape when he was cheered home by an immense crowd.

This gave St Dunstan's walking fever. The following spring the Birmingham St Dunstaners held a twenty-five-mile walk from Stratford-on-Avon; in London the famous Queen's Park Harriers competed against us over three laps of the Outer Circle. Then our walkers went to Wembley and won prizes in the British Legion Empire Sports, and we finished the year with the second Brighton Walk.

For a time the London-to-Brighton Walk was an annual event, and it was hard to give it up. It had raised morale among St Dunstaners, and it had been very good publicity. You will not find many persons capable of doing fifty-two miles on their own two feet in less than ten hours, which was what Jock Ingram did when he won the event in 1925. But it was in this fact that the weakness of the event lay. It was not a race but a test of endurance. Few were fit enough to start, and fewer to finish, and as we grew older the standard was bound to fall. In the fifth year of the race only six men qualified, and two of these had to retire.

By now shorter walks were held annually at Manchester as well as Birmingham, and we regretfully gave up the

London-to-Brighton event and organized a twenty-five-mile circular walk at Maidenhead to take its place. This was a great success, and it remained the last event of our walking season for many years. Later it was replaced by a fifteen-mile walk at Wembley, which was still more popular. But what pleased us most was the fact that several St Dunstaners had joined ordinary clubs and were competing with sighted athletes on equal terms—and winning prizes. Some of our best men have competed regularly in the annual Stock Exchange London-to-Brighton walk. Billy Miller has twice finished second, and Archie Brown, our champion walker for twenty-five years, was still putting up a great show in this event at the age of sixty. Archie Brown is now a Centurion, as also is Les Dennis. A Centurion is one who has walked a hundred miles within twenty-four hours.

We continued to hold our annual sports in Regent's Park and our regatta on the Thames and Putney until the Second World War, and for both events St Dunstaners came from all over the country. But the fun and games were not confined to the metropolis. There were similar reunions at other centres. One of the liveliest and most famous was the annual Stratford-on-Avon Camp.

It grew from the Birmingham St Dunstan's Club, which was started in 1921, and had members from all over Warwickshire and beyond. They met for socials and sports in Birmingham, and went on trips to Stratford and held regattas on the Avon. It was all good fun, but spoiled by having to break up early to catch buses; then someone had the bright idea of a week's camp.

Up went the marquees and tents. They were connected by a rope, so it was easy to move round without help. A canteen opened, a piano appeared in the mess tent; the local Boat Club provided boats, the British Legion Club threw open its doors and put on extra dances. A picnic in the Cotswolds, a trip to Worcester for a regatta there, an impromptu concert—there was all this and much more at the annual St Dunstan's Camp at Stratford-on-Avon. Appropriately, the life of the party was the successful Birmingham shopkeeper with the name of William Shakspeare.

The year after the first Camp at Stratford another was started, at Little Gaddesden, near Berkhamsted, and this also became a happy annual event. Some St Dunstaners joined forces with sighted campers, of course. One of our men, W. H. Thorpe of Canterbury, became the first blind Scoutmaster.

Ball-games are obviously unsuitable for the blind, until you take nostalgia into account. Of all games football was the one our boys knew and loved best when they could see. If they had never played the game they would probably not have been very interested—but they had enjoyed that peculiar feeling of kicking a leather sphere filled with air, and they wanted to do it again. So they did, and so they do to-day.

In its simplest and most practicable form blind man's football consists simply of shots at goal on the principle of the penalty kick. A sighted goalkeeper stands in the middle of the goal, and claps his hands to indicate his position; and, from a distance of about fifteen yards, the blind man kicks. Teams can be of any number, and the one that scores most goals wins.

It is good fun, even if a very limited interpretation of football. It has always been extremely popular at St Dunstan's. I have boasted enough about our sporting successes, so I ought to admit that when Arsenal played against us—kicking blindfolded for the first time in their lives—they won 4-0.

We also tried playing football with a bell inside, but this was not so much a game as light amusement. On the other hand, keen football fans got a very real enjoyment from going to Arsenal or Chelsea or Fulham for a League match or Cup-tie. The big clubs generously let us in free, and a sighted escort gave us a running commentary. The M.C.C.

kindly invited us to Lord's for the cricket, and the National
Sporting Club to boxing contests, and again commentaries
enabled our chaps to visualize the whole thing. The pleasure
we took in this sort of thing is probably more compre-
hensible to the sighted now than it was then, although the
next generation may find it stranger. In that brief period
in our history—less than three decades—when nearly
everyone had a wireless set and almost no one had television, literally millions of people listened to sporting
events in exactly the same way. They do not need to be
told how near you can get to the real thing if you have a
good running commentary with the roar of the crowd in the
background, punctuated by the referee's whistle, or—
perhaps the most strongly associative sound of all—the
crack of leather on willow that denotes that the ball has
been struck with the middle of the bat.

Golf for the blind may sound almost as far-fetched as
football, for the first maxim of the game is that you should
keep your eye on the ball. So you should, but there is no
reason to jump to conclusions and infer that the ball must
be seen. As a beginner you are told to keep your eye on it
because that is the easiest way to stop you from moving
your head while you are making your stroke. The blind
golfer must keep his head just as still. If he does that he
can manage without seeing the ball.

Pearson was a golfer, and after he lost his sight he used
to amuse himself driving balls off a tee. He became very
good at it. Harris Turner, of Saskatoon, became still better.
He used to explore the boundaries of the driving mat to get
his bearings, tee his ball and place the head of his club
directly behind it, and then, without moving the club,
recover his standing position and drive. If his body and
arms were in the right position he would make a good
clean shot, and he had as much right as any golfer to cuss
himself if he did not smack the ball a hundred and fifty
yards up the fairway.

L

Other blind golfers would get their caddies to tee the ball and place the head of the club in position, and indicate the line of direction. Even Turner could not manage without the help of his caddie after leaving the tee.

"How far is it to the hole?" The question puts the golfer at the caddie's mercy, and few men can judge distances with any accuracy. But at least the caddie can show him the direction of the hole, and he will reach the green in the end. Now he can pace out distance to the hole himself, and even find out where the green rises or dips. But he still needs his caddie or opponent to rattle the flag-rod against the iron lining of the hole, and he putts by ear. To be precise, by the left ear, because he still has to stand square to the ball.

Many of our Canadians besides Harris Turner have played golf, and St Dunstaners have a fine record in the Canadian and World Blind Golf Championships held at Toronto. At home, W. H. J. Oxenham, one of our osteopaths, got down to a handicap of twenty after playing for only five years—he had never held a club in his life before he lost his sight. This reached the wide-open ears of Ripley, the famous "Believe it or not" cartoonist, who invited him to the United States to play in exhibition matches with men like Walter Hagen and Gene Sarazen. To reach the largest possible radio audience Oxenham demonstrated in the evening. The course was floodlit, to give the others a fair chance, and running commentaries were broadcast of his onslaught on a hard bogey 3 hole of 225 yards. He played it twice, each time holing out in 4.

The Canadian Blind Golfers' Association was for long proud of the record score of one of its members of 105, but one of our Second-War men, Gerry Brereton, went round in 92, and then in 82. With his handicap down to 23, his professional coach gave up arguing with people when they questioned him about Brereton's scores. "Nobody believes it till they see it for themselves," he said.

Bowls is another game that many blind men enjoy,

especially if they have handled woods before. A sighted
marker stands behind the jack and gives the position of the
wood, usually by the clock method—"Three o'clock, four
feet," for example. The bowling mat is adjusted so that
the player can get his direction by running his hand along
one of the edges. The marker may talk or make some other
noise to help the player to judge line and distance. The
game was taken up with great enthusiasm in Australia,
where the Victorian Blinded Soldiers' Bowling Club has
played regularly against sighted teams.

Sport of a more vigorous kind almost thrust itself on one
of our Canadians, A. Glasspool, of Montreal. He had been
trained in boot-repairing, and each winter there was a slack
period when everyone wore rubber over-shoes as a protection against the snow. Tired of waiting for customers,
Glasspool shut up his shop and went off to the winter
sports, tobogganing and skating for the first time in his
life.

Skating was one of my own favourite pastimes, and
several of us used to go to one of the London ice-rinks. But
my favourite form of exercise was riding, though lately
fishing has taken its place.

Riding is an unexpectedly good sport for the blind. It
can be learnt and enjoyed by a blind man who has never
been on a horse before. We had several of this sort in
addition to the officers and cavalrymen with riding experience. I never heard of any of them coming to grief. Again,
if we are physically more exposed to accident, that is offset
by our mental attitude towards safety and risks. The trick
of riding blind, like doing most other things blind, is to
accept your limitations and keep within them.

So you do not go in for jumping or bronco-busting or
any stunts, but content yourself with a good ride in an open
paddock or on the downs. You choose your horse carefully,
making sure it is a decent, steady mount.

Of course, you cannot just get on a horse and ride off
alone. On the other hand, if you have ridden before you do

not need an expert companion—unless you want to ride on a leading rein. In my opinion this is not only unnecessary but, unless you are with a really good horseman, positively dangerous. It places a considerable extra burden on your companion, and as you are not free to handle your horse yourself you cannot deal with him if he is restless.

On the other hand, you need two horses that do not mind going together, so that you can keep in company without any trouble. It is better to ride on the inside of your companion, and you can stay within a reasonable distance by using your ears.

No one with eyes could imagine the number and variety of sounds a horse makes when walking along a road or cantering over a field. Hoof-beats may not be quite as loud as they are in radio plays, and over turf they may be quite inaudible; but there is also the jangle of the bit when the horse tosses his head, the creak of the saddle, the swish of the tail. There are echoes, too, which tell you how far you are from buildings on the side of a road. But the most important sound of all is your companion's voice.

He does not need to direct you all the time, although at first he will often have to tell you to move over more to the left or right. Otherwise it is enough for him to keep talking, and you will stay with him without any conscious effort.

I would not claim that I taught my sister to ride, but she was still learning when she accompanied me over the Sussex Downs during my first winter of blindness. That was forty-four years ago. My wife and I still ride sometimes, both in England and in South Africa; and the last time I was on my Basuto pony I reflected I could, if necessary, make such a journey on my own. Those ponies can always find their way home alone. Then my toe touched a rock, and I was reminded of the three things a blind man can never teach a horse. It does not realize that your leg and foot are wider than its flanks, so it can give you a nasty knock. It does not realize you are higher, and is quite capable of going under a tree-branch that will knock you off its back. Finally, it does not know its own speed or how long it takes to pull up before a ditch or hedge. Unless it is checked it will go on until it has no choice but to jump or swerve violently away. For these reasons I have not ridden alone. But Clutha Mackenzie has, in New Zealand, with a quiet horse over territory that he knew very well.

Fishing is another good sport for the blind. I say this as a beginner, for it is only recently that I have taken it up myself. Sir Beachcroft Towse was quite an expert, and Captain Angus Buchanan made a habit of catching the first salmon of the season in the river Wye. I blame myself for having missed many good years of this sport. I had some most attractive invitations, and there are two good fishing rivers in my old constituency of Lonsdale, and yet I kept putting it off. Partly this was inertia, but there was also the fear that I would do it badly and make a fool of myself. As a result I am still only a novice, but I get a great deal of pleasure from the sport—and I can more than hold my own in talking about it.

Most blind fishermen use a wet-fly, and no special apparatus is necessary. Casting is more difficult when you cannot see the line, but I think we have the advantage in hooking a fish—it is easier for us to resist the temptation to strike him. In the last few years I have enjoyed fishing of all kinds—including tunny-fishing in False Bay, off Cape Town, where I once caught three tunny in the roughest sea I have known. One of the fish was attacked by a shark while I was pulling it in. It jumped four or five feet in the air to avoid the menace, but lost its tail.

I would not have thought shooting was a likely sport for the blind, but Harris Turner, of Saskatoon, told us of a remarkable exploit by a blind friend of his named Ross while out on a shooting expedition with a sighted companion. "Ross heard a wild goose flying towards them. It was in the evening, and the other hunter could not see the goose. Ross took the gun. Unfortunately for the goose, it squeaked when it was almost directly over Ross, and he located its position exactly and brought it down."

There is an historic link between outdoor and indoor recreations at St Dunstan's. The boys wanted to show their gratitude to their lady coxswains, so they decided to give a dance in their honour. Before the invitations were sent, however, they had to find out whether they themselves were able to dance.

A dancing teacher and her assistant were roped in to help, and they came and sorted the boys out. Their first discovery was that many of them had never danced a step in their lives. Some of the old soldiers said they never would. Those who were willing to learn proved the best pupils, because they instinctively let the instructors take the lead. Some toes were trodden on, but it was soon clear that there was no reason why they should not all dance very well. It was just a matter of practice.

This created a slight problem. The obvious persons to ask to practise with were the V.A.D.'s for whom the ball was to be given. Fortunately, they did not know of the honour in store, so it seemed all right to ask them to come to the series of practice dances that the instructor said were needed to prepare for the event. Soon dancing fever gripped St Dunstan's, and even some of the old soldiers were caught taking secret lessons. Finally the ball was announced, the invitations were sent, and the great day came.

It was a tremendous success, and from then onward dancing was the most popular indoor recreation St Dunstan's had. We put on at least two dances every week, one of them mainly for beginners, even in the summer months. Competitions were included, and famous dancers came and acted as judges and presented the prizes.

Then there was music, and the moving spirit here was Lady Pearson. Intensely musical herself, she encouraged St Dunstaners to learn, to play, to perform, and incidentally to raise funds. So we had, at various times, a brass band, a

string band, a jazz band, and a full orchestra; to say
nothing of a choir. We had performers on every known
instrument, from the double bass to the penny whistle.
Between the wars the St Dunstan's Dance Band achieved a
fair measure of fame, getting good engagements, making
gramophone records, and broadcasting several times. The
Prince of Wales engaged them for a staff party at York
House, and I had the pleasure of introducing them the first
time Henry Hall put them on the air.

Dannie McLoughlin, with a lilting voice full of brogue
and blarney, sang regularly from Radio Dublin. He was a
born entertainer, and loss of sight did not prevent him
from becoming a first-class conjurer. It was a happy irony
that his fellow St Dunstaners were almost the only ones
who could not fully appreciate his sleight-of-hand. It is nice
to think of sighted people paying sincere money to see a
blind man entertain them with a purely visual performance.

There is a famous story of a blind traveller who was
embarrassed to hear his fellow-passengers discussing him
unfavourably because he had been seen marking a pack of
cards with a pin. As he does not seem to have had anyone
reading the cards to him, perhaps the passengers were
right and he was not really blind. Otherwise the story is all
right, for that is just how cards used to be adapted for the
blind.

Almost every player had his own system of braille
marking, and it seemed to me that it should not be very
difficult to devise a standard procedure. Systems in which
the cards were embossed on the back failed because the
player could not manipulate them without laying them
down. The obvious places for the markings were the top
left-hand and the bottom right-hand corners, just where the
suit and number appear, enabling the blind player to hold
his cards in the normal shape of a fan. When I was Chairman of the Inventions and Research Committee of the
N.I.B. I worked out an efficient system of marking, and

then had dies made so that a whole pack could be pressed at one time.

Here for once was a means of making special apparatus for the blind at an economical cost. This is a rarity, because the blind are relatively few in number, and mostly poor. As, moreover, the majority are old and cannot learn braille, apparatus using it almost always has to be heavily subsidized to be made generally accessible. The braille cards were a happy exception. We bought the packs wholesale and sold them retail, and the profit paid for the brailling!

Nearly everyone at St Dunstan's could use braille cards, at least for some games. Pontoon and cribbage are the easiest, because of the small number of cards to read. Those who wanted to play whist or bridge usually began with nap, because it includes all the elements of these games, but involves the use of only five cards in each hand. In all these games the normal practice was for each player to name his card as he played it. In bridge the dummy had to be called out and memorized as far as possible, but a good player would soon master this and compete with sighted players on equal terms. Naturally, all this shapes the memory, and it is not surprising to us that St Dunstaners at whist drives have often walked off with the prizes.

I had never cared for cards as a young man, and it was some time before I had a go at bridge myself. I hesitated for fear that I would make a mess of it—fumble with the cards, or forget what had been played or what was in dummy, or otherwise make a fool of myself. No doubt I did all these things at first, when I took advantage of one or two kindly people who were willing to put up with a beginner's blunders. There was no bridge group at St Dunstan's then, and it was not till 1938 that we founded our Bridge Club, of which I have long been President. My own game never rose above family bridge, but some St Dunstaners have reached match-play standard, which is far higher than that of the average sighted player. A blind player in an otherwise sighted four probably slows the game down just a little, and he has to put the others to the trouble of calling the card as it is played, and of telling him the dummy when it is put down. In the friendly kind of bridge I play no one seems to mind.

Chess is another game ideally suited to the blind, and I count it as one of my failures that I have never been able to learn it. All that is needed for the blind player is a set of chessmen with a peg on the base of each that fits into a hole in the middle of each square on the board. R. W. Bonham, a master at Worcester College for the Blind, is one of the experts of the game, and during one of his visits to St Dunstan's he played fifteen of our men simultaneously without losing a match.

Draughtsmen are adapted in a similar way to chessmen, and dominoes are made with raised markings. We had all these at St Dunstan's in the earliest days, as well as a special board of patience, jigsaw puzzles, and various other games that men were likely to want to play after they had left. For it was always in our minds—not at the back but right at the front—that St Dunstan's was not a refuge but only an ante-room, and we would be falling down on our job if we bought present contentment at the price of future regret.

One of our men once asked Pearson if some device might be invented to enable the blind to play billiards.

"For Heaven's sake don't let us make ourselves ridiculous," he replied. "It's absurd to try to play a game like billiards, which absolutely depends on keen sight. There are so many things that we can do without making asses of ourselves."

As a matter of fact, a blind man can play billiards—not very well, of course, but if he was fond of it before he lost his sight he can still enjoy it; and, after all, that is all any game is worth playing for. Darts is a game he can both enjoy and play well. When this became a national pastime St Dunstaners took to it enthusiastically, and it has kept its popularity. Naturally, players need to be told where the board is, and some hold a cord from the bull in the left hand as a guide to direction.

I have already said enough—perhaps too much—about my own favourite hobby of wireless. In 1924, in collaboration with Oswald Carpenter, I wrote a book on it, entitled *Wireless for the Blind*. It was serialized in the *St Dunstan's Review*, and seemed to go on for ever, and then was published in braille. It was extraordinarily technical, and I should think many St Dunstaners must have been irritated as they searched in it for a clue to their sudden failure to get dance music from 2LO.

Many other hobbies have been followed, and they are too numerous even to be mentioned in full. They range from model-making, which has been practised with great skill and art, to stamp-collecting, which to a sighted person may seem a little bizarre. Vernon Mullin, one of our Australian telephonists, was already a successful builder of wireless sets and a keen gardener when he took up philately with his wife. He counted the perforations, she examined the watermarks and colours, and they valued them and put in their albums together. Mr G. J. Hutson ("Huttie") is a St Dunstaner who is nearly blind, but, although he cannot see any details in the stamps and the visual part of the work has to be done by members of his family, he is nevertheless a philatelist of international repute.

When you are blind you realize what a wonderful gift hearing is. A deaf man thanks God for his eyes. His handicap may be worse than ours. We have both got off lightly compared with those who are both blind and deaf. They have a double handicap. But you can save your pity, for it is still not an affliction. You can see this from the case of George Fallowfield, the first completely deaf man we had.

Fallowfield was wounded in 1918, and for five years he could see but not hear. By 1923 his sight had gone too, and he came to St Dunstan's. When he arrived at Brighton hardly anyone knew how to talk to him, so he was equipped with a pair of gloves with the letters of the alphabet marked on the backs. These enabled the sighted members of the staff to talk to him, but he was still out of contact with the other St Dunstaners. But it was not for long. Fallowfield had been used to this obstacle for five years, and had become adept at overcoming it. Between tea and supper on the first day he had taught the manual alphabet to half a dozen men, and soon many at Brighton knew it from Matron down.

After six months at Brighton, Fallowfield came to Regent's Park for training. A french-polisher before joining up, and a born craftsman, he had no difficulty in mastering basketry, and was soon working happily and busily in his own home. There was no end to his interests and hobbies. He made brilliant models with "Meccano," including a model railway. Making model boats was another of his favourite hobbies, and he was soon winning prizes in open competition. Often after announcing results judges of handicraft exhibitions have been amazed to learn that the winning entry was by a blind man.

Fallowfield has always been on the look-out for ways of helping others less fortunate than himself. In the Second World War, by sales and raffles of the articles he made himself, he alone raised hundreds of pounds for war charities. After the War he became a generous supporter of the Deaf-Blind Watch Fund, which supplies braille watches to the civilian deaf-blind. He celebrated the Coronation by making two beautiful baby-baskets, lined with silk and equipped with powder and soap, which he presented to the local hospital to be given to the first boy and girl born on Coronation Day.

Naturally a keen sportsman, Fallowfield literally came a nasty cropper in his first sprint at Regent's Park. We were still using guide-wires then, with a whistle to tell the runners when they had finished. Fallowfield was sent off with a tap on the shoulder, and he raced away at full speed. Too late it was realized that he would not hear the signal for the finish, and he went down with a bump. He was not a bit discouraged, and after leaving Regent's Park he took part often in St Dunstan's sports at Birmingham and Manchester as well as in London and the South. At the regatta at Putney it was a common sight to see the coxswain of the winning boat bend forward and beat a rapid tattoo on the rower's hand, and get a nod and a smile of thanks.

Fallowfield took part in the walks, and became an enthusiastic cyclist. He preferred coupled bicycles to tandems, his wife guiding but each of them at liberty to pedal when and how they wished. His deafness did not stop him from going regularly to St Dunstan's dances. Now a grandfather, a devoted family man, a keen gardener, and a sound chess-player, he is the living proof that even this grave double handicap can be overcome. Unable to enjoy the boon of talking books, he reads braille enthusiastically, and is adept at spotting authors' mistakes. He is a great letter-writer, and has many braille correspondents all over the world. Immensely sociable and talkative, he does not mind how slow people are with the manual alphabet so long as they are willing to use it. When it was suggested that the deaf-blind should be taught lip-reading by touch he protested vigorously. "In cases of necessity I have taught the manual alphabet in as little as three minutes," he said. "Anyone can learn it—why, Sergeant Alan Nichols learnt it, and talked to me fluently with his two artificial hands."

Once Fallowfield fell asleep in the lounge at St Dunstan's and was awakened violently by Bill Tovell. "We're just going to listen to the Manchester November Handicap," he explained.

"Well," snapped Fallowfield, "I can't hear it, can I?"

"No," agreed Tovell, "but you're snoring, and we can't either."

It was the sort of thing you could always say to Fallow-field, who loved a joke against himself. Wireless, of course, was another of our pleasures that was out of his reach, but being deaf and blind did not prevent him from going to football matches. Once he explained why, in a letter to *St Dunstan's Review*:

I have been asked in the past why I went to church, what pleasure could I possibly derive from dancing, and, recently, how could I enjoy a football match. In each and every case it is firstly a matter of atmosphere, whilst dancing recalls old days of hearing. But in the case of football I am forced to explain further.

When I feel like it I have a boy of fourteen take me generally to the Tottenham Hotspurs ground, and supposing the Spurs are kicking from my right, then my right hand represents that team, and my left their opponents.

The team is read out to me before the start, and sitting with my hands resting upon my knees, my thumbs and four fingers represent the five forwards of the team; thus the second finger is Hunt, the centre-forward, whilst my little finger is the outside right.

At either side of the hand and in the centre just above the fingers we find the half-backs, and two full-backs just beyond them, whilst the wrist is the goalie. My escort sits with his own hands just hovering above my own and taps each place when each player has the ball. Thus, a rapid tapping on the thumb of the right hand tells me the outside left is having a run down the wing; when a tap is made on the left hand just above the first finger, I know he has been pulled up, then a tap on the third finger of the left hand, and I know the inside-right has the ball, and so on.

As to the actual position of play, this I admit is not possible to explain, but one who has played the game can imagine the position of play within a little. A throw-in, foul, penalty, goal-kick, etc., are all told by letter code.

This idea is not my own. It was suggested whilst I was in training by an old pal, Joe Evans, of Walsall, and I hope he himself enjoys to-day a football match as well as he has enabled me to.

That was written a long time ago. For over thirty years Fallowfield went regularly to football matches with his wife, who talks to him in a very rapid code. One of their unforgettable memories is the day they went to the Cup Final.

Don't feel sorry for Fallowfield. If, with two good eyes and ears, you get as much out of life as he does, you are an exceptionally happy man.

10

Growing Up

"IN our new constitution we have been permitted to extend our operations by admitting for care and after-care members of His Majesty's Forces who have been or may be blinded in any Military Service under the Crown since the Great War. It is obvious that our organization should not confine its attention solely to men blinded in the Great War, but should extend its power of assistance to similar cases which may arise in the future."

I wrote that in 1923, when our three committees formally amalgamated, and St Dunstan's was incorporated under the Companies Act. It did not spring from any sudden doubt whether the war to end wars had really achieved its pacific aim, but from a perhaps belated realization that as long as there were Services there would be Servicemen losing their sight. Between the wars we admitted some men who had been blinded while serving in India and other parts of the Commonwealth. They were greatly outnumbered by fresh cases from the First World War.

There were more of these than we had expected, but that was our own fault. We went looking for them. In fact, we searched the country, with the help of the British Legion and the Ministry of Pensions, for eligible men. We advertised for them in our publications, at the same time appealing for money that we needed to enable us to look after the men we had already. We emphasized that the fact that a man had been rejected as ineligible for a pension did not necessarily mean that he could not come to St Dunstan's. "The difficult question of eligibility is decided by the

Council of St Dunstan's," we said. "In every case where
there is any doubt that disability is connected with Service
in the Armed Forces of the Crown, the benefit of such a
doubt is given to the man."

In practice the Council acted on the recommendation of
an Ophthalmic Advisory Board. This had three members,
of whom Lawson and Ormond were two; and very properly,
as we thought, they interpreted the question of attri-
butability to military service in the widest possible way.
So eventually we had well over a hundred men whose
claims had been turned down by both the Ministry of
Pensions and the Appeal Tribunals. They were a very
heavy liability, for they cost a great deal more than those
whose status had official blessing. They were not getting
pensions; and we made it a rule to give them half the flat-
rate pension they would have had if their claims had
succeeded. This was increased at a later date to full
pension.

This was something that only a voluntary enterprise
could have done. Had St Dunstan's been State-controlled it
would have been bound to abide by the decisions of the
impartial Appeal Tribunals, which had been set up as final
arbiters. When we came to a different conclusion we were
not criticizing the Tribunal, but just opening our door a
little wider than could be expected from the State. I would
not call it generosity; the point was that on such an
exceedingly difficult medical subject there were bound to
be differences of opinion, and we wanted to make sure that
no blind man would be denied help to which he could
conceivably be entitled through serving his country in war.

The number of these non-pensioners at St Dunstan's had
risen to 140 by 1927, when the Ministry of Health pressed
us not to take any more. The time had come, said the
Ministry, for our objects and those of charities caring for
the civilian blind to be more clearly defined, and it would be
in the general interest if in future we admitted only cases
whose claims had been officially upheld. We did not share

this view, but under pressure we gave in. We had searched intensively during the previous three years, and we did not think there were likely to be many more cases of this kind. We still did not like it, but the Ministry made it difficult for us to resist without prejudice to the interests of the two thousand or so men already on our books. While conforming generally to this ruling, we still made an exception in very special cases.

We could still expect about thirty new cases a year accepted by the Ministry of Pensions. With them came new problems in training.

No one can say whether it is better to be blinded on the battlefield at eighteen or to come out with your sight apparently undamaged and then lose it gradually over a period of years. These late arrivals had been spared the sudden shock we had had, and they had enjoyed extra seeing years. I cannot imagine what they had suffered as the light gradually failed. Some of them had many operations, and they always hoped the next one would be successful. The thought of the alternative was unbearable.

After they had left the Services they had rebuilt their whole lives on the basis of being able to see. They had gone back to their old careers or taken up new ones, married and had children, taken on all the normal responsibilities of the breadwinner. When their sight began to fail they tried to hide it at first, and fear changed to alarm when they were at last forced to give up their work. At home they became more and more dependent on others in the everyday actions of life, and when hope died it was usually succeeded by apathy and despair. With the War long past they were not the country's heroes, while their increasing dependence was accepted all too willingly by those who loved them. Pity breeds self-pity, and when they came to us most of them were resigned to their lot.

Early treatment was still the same. First there was the braille watch, then the typewriter, and bewildered hope began to break through. Then a talk, man-to-man and

M

matter-of-fact—the assurance that blindness is not a calamity but only a handicap. "But you can't understand," the
newcomer might burst out. "No one can who isn't blind."
He had said it so often at home, in hospital, to the world at
large, and no one had been able to reply. But now he was
in a world where it was normal not to be able to see.

"But I *am* blind." He heard the reply with anything
from surprise to disbelief. He was likely to hear the same
words several times in his first day or two at St Dunstan's
—from the man who showed him round, from myself, from
braille teachers and instructors in the workshops. He was
no longer able to doubt that the handicap could be
overcome.

Besides this annual intake we had to allow also for men
who had been through St Dunstan's once and wanted to
come back to be trained in a new trade.

In many cases it was a matter of physical necessity.
Wounds that cause blindness very often result in extensive
other injuries, and not many of our chaps who had their
eyes shot away got off as lightly as I did. So it would
happen, for example, that a mat-maker might find his old
wounds troubling him after a time, until he had to seek
lighter work. Then he would come back for training in a
semi-clerical occupation such as shorthand-typist or telephonist. On the other hand, a man doing an indoor job
might—again for health reasons—need to be retrained as
a poultry farmer to get him out into the open air.

There was another side to this matter of retraining, and
a much more heartening one too. Several men who had
been badly wounded came back not because their injuries
were worse but because they were better! The reason that
this could happen was that we had always tried to get our
men working as soon as possible, and they were trained in
occupations suited to their physical limitations at the time.
Often they came to us straight from convalescence, and
still had more physical progress to make. Rather than wait
for that—and expose them to the most powerful enemies

of the newly blinded, depression and loss of hope—we put them through the workshops and classrooms right away. After they had gone out and been settled several of them improved so much more physically that they were fit enough to either learn their trade more thoroughly or to learn a more profitable occupation. So they too came back for retraining.

A few others had to come back because their jobs had gone sour. F. C. S. Hilling was a striking example of this. A manager and salesman before the 1914-18 War, he learnt shorthand and typing at St Dunstan's and soon started to rise again. He was promoted to representative of his firm, and sold imported silks. Then came tariffs, the trade was ruined, and he was out of work. He came back to us and went through the two years' course in physiotherapy, and soon he was earning a good living again.

St Dunstaners were producing bigger and better baskets and mats, and costing us more and more. The deliberate paradox—the more articles they made, the greater their total indirect subsidy—made every human success a financial Pyrrhic victory even if everything was sold. In the dark years of depression, when industry was sick and economists diagnosed over-production, our stocks piled up. Widespread unemployment, the General Strike, competition by machines and by foreigners—all the pressures cried aloud for putting the men on short time, but we did not and would not until the bailiffs came in.

Fortunately, we were able to make economies of a less painful kind. By 1927 the number of men in training had dropped to seventy-six, and we were able to reduce our establishment. In the same year we moved out of St John's Lodge and some of the workshops in the grounds, and disposed of the lease. We moved our administrative offices out of the mansion into the remaining workshops, and these were all we kept in Regent's Park. We moved our stores and showrooms to a less expensive site in Raglan Street,

Kentish Town. We transferred all our training activities, including the classrooms and workshops, to our Seaside Annexe at Brighton.

To meet this influx West House expanded until it had accommodation for ninety men in addition to the resident Matron, Sisters, and Staff. With the permanent invalids and men who came for convalescence or a holiday it was sometimes a bit of a tight squeeze. However, it meant that we could put all our facilities for sport and recreation under one roof. We had our own grounds for daily use, and on Saturdays we were allowed the use of the Sports Ground at Brighton College. Dances were held regularly in the lounge, and business girls from the town joined the Sisters and V.A.D.'s as partners for the men. Good friends of St Dunstan's arranged visits to theatres and concerts and motor runs and boat trips. We had the latest thing in wireless installations, with a pair of headphones at every bed.

"How do you keep it all so neat and trim?" visitors used to ask. "With such a large family, and those all blind—how do you do it?"

The question included the answer. For the sighted, tidiness is of æsthetic rather than functional value. Except in so far as it is necessary for cleanliness, it is only a matter of appearance and convenience. For us it is as important as is electric light to those who can see. By memorizing the position of furniture and fittings we can get a clear enough picture of our surroundings to be able to move about quite easily and not too slowly without any help. This only works if the furniture and fittings are kept in exactly the same positions, and that is why precise orderliness was an inflexible rule.

"For petty squabbling and back-biting," wrote a correspondent to *St Dunstan's Review*, "ex-Servicemen are ten times worse than a pack of gin-tippling old washerwomen." The rest of his letter seemed to show that he was at least speaking for himself, but I think that on the whole the statement was a bit too sweeping. Still, blunt words were spoken when we had a slight brush with the Scottish National Institution for the War Blinded, at Newington House. The *Review* itself, normally as polite as a parish magazine, became quite thunderous. The headlines ran:

ST DUNSTANERS IN ARMS
A Scottish Attempt to Hamper Our Work
Our Men in Defence of Our Rights

The cause of all the pother was a proposal by Edinburgh delegates to a British Legion Conference in 1928 that branches in Scotland should give priority to the claims of Newington House. As we had far more Scots on our Register than they had, including 70 men actually living in Scotland, we urged our cause with such good effect that the proposal was withdrawn. Newington House had been affiliated to St Dunstan's in the very early days, but had long since gone its own way. We had the warmest regard for its work, but at that time we were not willing to give it a monopoly in appealing for funds from the Scottish public.

This little dispute was smoothed out, and our relations with Newington House became cordial again. Meanwhile our bond with the British Legion became increasingly strong. This was something I had always favoured personally. Although St Dunstan's was founded by the National Institute for the Blind, of which Pearson was President at the time, I believed that its interests lay in co-operation with organizations supporting other disabled ex-Servicemen rather than with those devoted to the civilian blind. So in 1928 we abandoned our flag days—Cameo Days, we called them—in return for 5 per cent. of the net proceeds of Poppy Day.

The public, reasonably enough, had grown tired of too many flag days, and often we had been pressed to share a day with some other body, usually a local institution for the civilian blind. But when we sought to combine it was with the British Legion, and the association was a happy one from the start. Our original agreement was for three years, and the results were so good for us that we willingly agreed to accept 4 per cent.—with a maximum of £15,000 in any one year—for the next ten years.

One of the conditions of the original agreement was that the British Legion should be represented on our Executive Council, and that a member of our Council should attend the Legion Benevolent Committee when matters affecting St Dunstan's were considered. I was nominated for this, while the Legion nominated Captain Appleby to attend our Council on behalf of the Legion. We were delighted that the Legion had actually chosen a St Dunstaner.

I had been a member of the British Legion for many years, and had taken an active interest in the House of Commons Branch; and I strongly urged all St Dunstaners who were not already members to join. I was very happy when I was elected Vice-Chairman of the Metropolitan Area of the British Legion in 1932. A strengthening of the bonds between the Legion and us could do nothing but good.

Our share of the Poppy Day collection compensated us well for the sacrifice of our own flag days, but, of course, by itself it was only a part of what was needed. We agreed to a close season for our own collections for the three weeks before November 11, but apart from that we retained the right to collect funds by all means except flag days throughout the year. In the event we voluntarily abstained for a longer period before Poppy Day—and members of the Legion and some branches helped us to make collections at other times.

As Chairman of St Dunstan's I had to make most of our appeals for funds. This was by no means as unpleasant a task as you might think. Of course, I had to be careful not to leave anyone out of the long list of people to whom we

extended our public gratitude, but it is no great hardship
to say 'thank you.' Everything that was given came freely,
no one made anything out of St Dunstan's, and in this part
of my job I saw human nature at its best.

Fortunately, when I succeeded Pearson, at the end of
1921, the foundations of St Dunstan's world-wide appeal
had been firmly laid. There was widespread sympathy for
the organization, whose name was already well known. My
task was to maintain, and if possible increase, the impact of
St Dunstan's upon public opinion. To this end I coined
such phrases as "While memory lives" and "Wars end,
wounds heal, but blindness remains" and "Please remember St Dunstan's in your will." These were widely used,
and had their effect.

Also, with the help of an old solicitor friend, A. E. N.
Ward, who died many years ago, I initiated an appeal to
solicitors to commend St Dunstan's to their clients when
bequests were being considered. This required most delicate handling, because of the highly personal relationship
between solicitor and client and the very private nature of
the disposition of testamentary bequests. Nevertheless,
many people go to their solicitors and, after making family
and other arrangements, open a discussion on "What is to
be done with the residue?" or "How can I leave some
money to charity?" I must record our deep indebtedness to
solicitors all over the land—indeed, all over the British
world—for having spoken well of St Dunstan's when
opportunities have arisen, and to hundreds of testators who
have remembered St Dunstan's in their wills.

But, of course, our debt is not only to some hundreds, or
even to thousands, but literally to millions. A great variety
of organized fund-raising—house-to-house collections,
whist drives, concerts, carol parties, and so on—had
enabled every section of the community to play its part.
There can hardly be a person in the land who had not
subscribed to St Dunstan's directly or indirectly, or a town
or village that had not helped.

If St Dunstan's itself was something new in the blind world, so was the tone of our appeals. The ragged blind beggar in the street sought alms given for pity and compassion, and our men were much too self-reliant for any charity of this kind. By publicizing their success-stories rather than their woes we made sure none would be given. We said frankly that blind men had never been treated so well before, and we admitted that St Dunstan's was now able to do more for its members than most other organizations for disabled ex-Servicemen. We showed what we had done with our money, and asked for more to enable us to carry on the good work. We were not asking for funds to relieve suffering and unhappiness; we wanted to be able to keep our men as happy as they had been so far. We thought they had earned this by their war service and sacrifice, and our many generous supporters showed that they thought so too.

It was not all sunshine, though. The story had its darker side. There were some men at St Dunstan's who would be with us till they died. They were not only blind but had suffered other injuries, often terrible ones. Broken in body or mind, some of these men lived for many years, and some are still alive. We never stressed this part of St Dunstan's, and I shall not go into it very much now. It would be too harrowing for both you and me. But it is part of the story, and cannot quite be left out.

There was a man who lay on a hydraulic bed night and day, not only blind but stone deaf, with every joint in his body, including his jaw, absolutely rigid, so that he had to be fed through the teeth. He lay there year after year, and could never see, hear, or move again. Another man, blinded by a shell-burst in Gallipoli, had lost both legs at the hip, and blood-poisoning had distorted and rendered practically useless both hands and arms. He was in almost constant pain. I could not have guessed any of this if I had not been told, for he was always wonderfully cheerful. So was another young man, blind and almost stone deaf and

paralysed from the waist down. Once a fortnight his wife
and child came to see him, and they made plans for a future
at home that we knew he would never live to enjoy. Such
men could not conquer blindness as we could, but they
were undefeated. Whatever they lacked they were not
short of courage, and they shared fully in the spirit of St
Dunstan's.

There was a General Election in 1929, and—I think for
the first time in history—there were three blind candidates.
All were St Dunstaners, but that was the only thing we had
in common. Fred Martin was standing again as a Liberal;
Thomas ap Rhys stood for Labour in Caernarvon; and I
was defending my seat for the Conservatives.

Ap Rhys had already brought so much credit to St
Dunstan's that I could forgive him his politics. He had
been studying electrical engineering at Bangor University
College when war broke out. He joined up and served in
France from 1915 until 1917, when he was badly wounded
and gassed at Vimy Ridge. At St Dunstan's he married a
V.A.D. and learnt massage. He worked in this profession
at the Alder Hey Hospital in Liverpool. The after-effects
of gas forced him to give up massage—so he re-entered
Bangor University College, studied for an Arts degree,
and graduated with first-class honours.

When he was adopted for Caernarvon I wrote and
wished him the best of luck, and said I hoped that he,
Martin, and I would all be elected. He replied most
cordially, and I doubt if a warmer public exchange of
courtesies between opponents has preceded a General
Election. In spite of this—or perhaps because of it—the
electorate turned us both down, and Martin met the same
fate. It was a pity we could not have extended our mutual
goodwill to swapping constituencies.

In view of the prevailing political wind I was not surprised at losing my seat, and about a year before the
election I had begun to eat dinners at the Inner Temple in

case I should have time to study seriously for the Bar. I passed my final examination in December 1930, and two months later I was called to the Bar. I thought seriously of practising as a barrister—I was still only thirty-four— but before the end of the year I was back in the House of Commons.

One of my first jobs on returning to politics was to try to forestall a possible cut in war pensions. The National Government was making every possible economy, and some newspapers pointed out that the review of expenditure could hardly ignore the bill for war pensions of £45,000,000. It could have been argued that the cost of living had dropped. There were several answers to this, notably the fact that disabilities did not normally improve with age. Further, in our opinion war pensions were already insufficient. We thought they ought to be the same in Britain as in the Dominions, and I had pressed both Conservative and Labour Governments to raise them to this level. Each Government had said no, and now the danger was that they might go lower still. No public suggestion of a cut had yet been made, but I thought I ought to try to make it as difficult as possible for a cut to be suggested. So at the 1932 Conservative Party Conference I moved a resolution asking the Government to maintain war pensions at their existing level. It was passed unanimously, and when the Chancellor of the Exchequer spoke later at the Conference he acknowledged the fact that he had been warned off.

About the same time, in swift succession, we lost two of the very small band who had helped Pearson to found St Dunstan's, and who had worked for it ever since. The first to leave was our Secretary, Mrs Chadwick Bates. She had been with Pearson before St Dunstan's, and she was the perfect secretary, with only one recorded lapse. That occurred when a St Dunstaner took his wife and two-year-old daughter to see Pearson, and the Chief nobly kissed the babe-in-arms. He talked to the mother for a while, and then

took the baby's face between his hands and gave it a good-
bye kiss. Mrs Bates came into the room at that moment,
and was completely unintelligible. She appeared overcome
by some emotion, and Pearson sharply told her to pull
herself together and tell him what the trouble was.

"There's no trouble," she said, "but the baby you
thought you were kissing wasn't in its mother's arms—it
was sitting on the floor."

Characteristically, Pearson told the story himself.

When Pearson first asked me to work for St Dunstan's
it was to Mrs Bates that I went for instruction. I used to
go to her office and listen to her interviewing, dictating
letters, and giving instructions, and then she would give
me packets of letters to answer for her, and afterwards she
corrected and discussed my answers with me. So I learnt
from her, and when I became Chairman she was my right
hand as she had been Pearson's, and I hated seeing her
go.

For twelve years St Dunstan's work in South Africa
had been devotedly carried on by Mr and Mrs Charles
H. Vintcent, Chairman and Organizing Secretary respectively, of our South African Committee. They had, indeed,
done this work to the exclusion of their private interests
and leisure, and to the detriment of Mr Vintcent's health.
In the summer of 1930 we reluctantly accepted their
resignations. It was necessary that an experienced member
of St Dunstan's should go to South Africa to see that there
was no break in the continuity of our work there. Mrs
Bates was invited to do this and she accepted.

Mrs Bates went to South Africa in an emergency, to help
the Committee of St Dunstan's, and we all thought she
would be back before long. We should have guessed that
they would want to keep her, and our loss was their gain.
The loss would have been irremediable but for W. G.
Askew, our General Manager, who was willing to take
over the work. So we made a presentation—which had
been planned for her completion of fifteen years' service at

St Dunstan's—and our Treasurer, Ernest Kessell, wrote an appreciation. He called her Batey, and had been her colleague from the start—and a few months later unbelievably he was sixty-five and retired. He had worked with Pearson since the early days of *Tit-Bits*, and was his right-hand man at St Dunstan's from its foundation. We felt we were losing something of the founder—until the founder's son, Sir Neville Pearson, put us still more deeply in his debt by accepting the appointment of Honorary Treasurer.

Mrs Bates was awarded the O.B.E., and Kessell was appointed C.B.E., but even these honours cannot fully express what they did. St Dunstan's inspires loyalty. It also either inspires modesty or attracts the modest, and I do not know any of our staff who have sought more appreciation than the friendship of St Dunstaners, which they have so well earned and received. When I resist the temptation to write more about them it is not through fear of boring the reader but simply because I do not want to embarrass them.

Meanwhile in 1930 I had been to New York to attend a World Conference of the Blind. Organized under the chairmanship of Robert B. Irwin, it was the first of its kind in history. The official delegates did not represent institutions as such, but we took quiet satisfaction in the fact that those from Canada and New Zealand were also St Dunstaners.

Shortly after this the National "Safety First" Association asked our opinion of a proposal that blind people should carry white walking-sticks, and all St Dunstaners were invited to state their views. Nearly all of them did, very noisily, and they were against the idea in the proportion of about twenty to one. The main objection, of course, was that we did not want any distinguishing mark that would single us out from other men, when it was already difficult enough to persuade sighted people to regard us as normal.

Opinion and practice in this matter have changed with the years, and now a good many blinded soldiers use white sticks. They have got over their early dislike and find the distinctive stick helps them to get about alone.

The use of guide dogs was a different matter, although for a long time there was a similar prejudice against them because of the old association of the blind man's dog with the street beggar. The Germans were the first to develop the idea, and by 1930 over sixteen hundred of their blinded ex-soldiers and many hundreds of civilians had been provided with trained guide dogs. I was shown over the State Schools where men and dogs were trained, and later I saw similar establishments in Switzerland and America, and I was quite keen on the idea. Back in England I proposed an experimental scheme on similar lines.

This suggestion met with a mixed and mainly adverse reception, and I was not surprised by that. My own prejudice had died hard. Even so, the list of objections raised by St Dunstaners looks rather over-comprehensive now. A dog would be ineffective in heavy traffic or crowded streets. The lead harness would be unpleasantly conspicuous. If used for going to and from work, what would be done with dogs during working hours? The Government might cease paying attendant allowance, and who would pay the cost of feeding the dog? What would happen if the dog had a fight? More important, what if the dog attacked children? Who would be responsible in the case of accident or damage by the dog? Would there not be criticism of using captive dogs for this purpose? There were laws forbidding the use of the dog for work in a harness. So it went on, and with all these objections, we decided there was nothing we could do. Later, however, the Guide Dogs for the Blind Association was started, we had a change of heart, and St Dunstaners were among the first to benefit by the provision of trained dogs. All the fears proved groundless, and the old enemy of prejudice was gradually defeated.

*   *   *

During the War, and for some time afterwards, we had our own private hospital, at Sussex Place, Regent's Park. Many eminent physicians and surgeons—led, of course, by Lawson and Ormond—gave us their services free, but it still cost a few thousands a year to run. We shut it down as soon as we could, and then the After-care took over the whole responsibility of caring for the men's health. There was no National Health Service of the kind we have to-day, and the burden was heavy, for wounds often go on giving trouble years after they have been cleared up. The fact that we were all getting older implied that there would be more sickness of other kinds. Much more alarming financially was the fact that we were all so young. Our aim was to maintain our standard of care and after-care until the last old soldier had faded away. The danger was that if we lived too long public interest and support might die first. In particular legacy income, which made up about half our revenue, was, we thought, bound to dry up. Hence our endowment scheme.

The first actuarial calculation of our combined expectations of life was based on the number of men on our register in the summer of 1922. Taking into account probable new admissions, it estimated that there would still be 1528 men alive in 1935; 1251 in 1945; and 791 in 1955. By 1927 it was clear that we were going to do better than this, for a fresh calculation gave the estimates of 1322 still living in 1947 and 445 in 1967—fifty years but one after the Armistice. These estimates were based on an assumption that a further 273 ex-Servicemen from the 1914-18 War would eventually lose their sight and come to us. "Everyone will hope that this figure may not be reached," we said when we published the actuary's estimate. Alas, it was greatly surpassed.

In the year these calculations were made our net revenue (including legacy income) for general services was a little over £145,000. Our actuary reported that if we could collect a similar sum annually for the next fifteen years we

should be able to set aside enough money each year to
endow St Dunstan's at the end of that time. We would not
have to raise our annual income, only hold it steady. In fact,
that was a tall enough order, for in 1927 we thought that
another fifteen years would make the War quite distant
history.

In the event we got off to a bad start, and after three
years our accountants reported that the Endowment Fund
was £44,000 in deficit. At the same time the Children
Fund proved inadequate—for the first time since the War
—by £118,000. Legacy windfalls came to the rescue, and
in the next two years some of the ground was made up. A
valuation and actuarial review after the first five years told
us the plan could be realized if we collected £147,000 a
year for the next ten years.

The ink was hardly dry on this when we had a rude
shock. Of nineteen new cases admitted in the year ending
March 1934, five had lost their sight through the long-
delayed effects of mustard gas. We were warned that there
might be a lot more to come.

In the Birthday Honours of 1934 I was honoured with a
knighthood. In thanking those who were so kind as to
congratulate my wife and myself I said that while we were
the fortunate ones, I regarded the award as an honour for
St Dunstan's, whose message had done so much good for
the civilian as well as the ex-Service blind, not only in the
United Kingdom but throughout the Empire, and indeed
the world.

In 1929 a St Dunstan's Empire Conference had been
held in London, attended by delegates from Canada,
Australia, New Zealand, and South Africa, who were all
old friends. In September 1934 my wife and I set off on a
world tour to meet them again and to see how their work
for the blind was prospering.

11

St Dunstan's Overseas

"I HAVE been busy on the National Association for the Blind, which we started about a year ago, and am glad to say we are doing very well. We have bought a house in Brussels, where we have our office, and attached to that house we have a big workshop, because later on we think we may be able to train some boys. . . . It is the first association of its kind in Belgium."

The letter came in 1925. It was typed and signed by Oscar Daumont, who was working as a joiner, running a shop with his wife at Courcelles. He was the first of all the St Dunstaners, the man Pearson used to visit in hospital before St Dunstan's began. Seven more Belgians came to us later. Had any repayment from our Allies been due—and, of course, it was not—this message would have been full settlement. Not much good came out of the evil of war, but at least it led to new life for the blind in many parts of the world.

Besides the Belgians we had four French, whom Pearson had met in establishments in France, and who had asked to come. All the rest were from what in those days we liked to call the British Empire. At the end of the first year there were, in fact, 14 overseas men in a total of 140. Seven were Canadians, five Australians, and two New Zealanders. The South Africans began to come in during the second year.

These early arrivals came automatically rather than out of any set policy. Wounded in France, they were sent to England because they were British, and to the 2nd General

Hospital because they were eye cases; and there they were offered St Dunstan's like the rest. This was not the intention of their own authorities, who tried to get all their disabled men home as quickly as possible; and, in fact, some of the blinded Colonials were repatriated direct from the battlefield.

Meanwhile these authorities visited their men in St Dunstan's, and quickly realized they could not hope for anything as good at home. Independently of one another and of us, they then urged all their men to stay to take advantage of St Dunstan's before returning home. They went even further than that. When these men did return home they met some of their blind comrades who had not been to St Dunstan's, and told them all about it. The difference in both abilities and morale was striking, and the men who had not been to St Dunstan's asked if they could come. With Government or voluntary help, no fewer than twenty-seven of these men made the long and war-dangerous voyage to England in order to learn to be blind.

After training, some settled in England permanently; but most went back to their old homes. In doing so they spread the gospel of St Dunstan's round the world.

Our first Canadian was Corporal A. G. Viets, and he had come and gone before I reached St Dunstan's myself. Before the War he had worked as a clerk in the Imperial Life Assurance Company of Canada. When he learnt he was blind he took it for granted that there would be no further place for him in the world of insurance. Pearson told him there was nothing to stop him from going back to his old line of business. At first Viets laughed; then, when he discovered what other St Dunstaners were doing, he thought it might not be so unreasonable as it had first seemed.

He left St Dunstan's in March 1916, when St Dunstan's was just a year old. He went back to his old home at Digby, in Nova Scotia, and stayed there for the spring and summer.

N

He met his old friends, and astonished them by his ability to enjoy life. At the same time he gave himself a private refresher course in business methods and dealing with strangers by selling subscriptions for a chain of newspapers and magazines. He made quite a lot of money, for he was a natural salesman, but the most important thing was that he gained confidence. Finally, in October, he went to Toronto.

His old employers said they would give him a trial, and they put him on their canvassing staff. He compiled a braille rate book of about forty pages, pocket size, which contained all the information he expected to need. Then he went out into the world to sell insurance; and for five weeks he sold nothing at all.

He had no connexions, for he had not worked in Toronto before; he had chosen this city because it was large and almost entirely English-speaking. He was handicapped by not being able to point his finger at a column in a prospectus, or to demonstrate with a pen and paper to a prospective client. He had to pay a boy to act as his guide, and he thought he had been in and out of all the offices in Toronto before at last he made a sale.

As a matter of fact, he had not started off any worse than the other canvassers, as he soon discovered. There were 18 of them in Toronto, and changes were frequent. Every month a list was issued showing their comparative sales, and Viets soon found his name near the top of the list. When he brought in two applications for $50,000 policies he felt his colleagues turn green with envy. The first Canadian to go home from St Dunstan's was one of our biggest successes.

Meanwhile another Canadian St Dunstaner had arrived in Toronto. He was Captain Edwin Baker, M.C., Croix de Guerre, of the Canadian Engineers, the first Canadian officer to be blinded in the War. He left St Dunstan's just about the time I arrived, and I remember he was the leading oarsman of the year.

Before the War Baker had passed through a course in electrical engineering at Queen's University, and when he returned to Canada he got a job with the Hydro-Electric Power Company of Toronto, which harnessed power from the Niagara Falls. He worked in the Trouble Department. Reports of trouble were phoned to him from different places along the line, and he had to co-ordinate them. He also had quite a lot of office correspondence, which he did mostly by "Dictaphone." He was, in fact, a typical example of a technical man doing a specialized administrative job, and doing it quite brilliantly.

With their own lives so well repaired, Viets and Baker naturally interested themselves in the rest of the blind population of Toronto. They discovered with some difficulty that there was a Free Library of braille literature in the city, and when they asked about it they were promptly invited to join the Board. They did so all the more willingly when they found that the premises consisted of a couple of rooms in the basement of an out-of-the-way school, and that the other directors thought they were lucky if they had a few hundred dollars in the bank. To two vigorous young men fresh from St Dunstan's this state of affairs was both a shock and a challenge, and they set to work to put it right. They were supported by a leading businessman in Toronto, Lewis Wood, and within eighteen months the Library had bought and furnished a large house in the grounds of Toronto University, and had quite substantial funds, with two or three women's associations working for them and collecting more.

Meanwhile other Canadians had gone through St Dunstan's and were returning home, and Viets and Baker turned themselves into an after-care department. They looked after the welfare of returning ex-Servicemen—and, at the same time, expected all St Dunstaners to help them to improve conditions for the less fortunate Canadian civilian blind.

It was mainly a matter of informing, educating, and

inspiring the public in Canada as Pearson had done in the United Kingdom. Their work received an unwanted stimulus in 1917, when 3000 tons of high explosive blew up in Halifax Harbour, with ghastly results. The tragedy was vastly deepened by a small preliminary explosion, which brought many people to their windows to see what was happening. The second explosion shattered the glass in their faces, and first reports said that 250 were totally blinded, at least 200 of them children. Many more were expected to lose their sight eventually as a result of their injuries. Early reports were greatly exaggerated. Nevertheless, this terrible accident helped the Canadian National Institute for the Blind to get on to its feet.

A month or two after this the work of Viets and Baker, supported by Lewis Wood, achieved a major victory. In March 1918 a Dominion Charter founded the Canadian National Institute for the Blind. Sir Arthur Pearson was the Honorary President, and the headquarters of the Institute in Toronto was called Pearson Hall. A training centre was established there, and all blind Canadian ex-Servicemen who had not been through St Dunstan's were given the choice of going to England immediately or training at Pearson Hall. Twelve went to St Dunstan's; the others, and all subsequent cases, were trained in Toronto. By 1918 the register of Canadian war blinded numbered 170, and a further 70 went to Pearson Hall between the wars.

The training was under the supervision of St Dunstaners, helped by some of our own V.A.D.'s. The workshops were under the charge of Q.M.S. George Eades, a champion handicraftsman who had bellowed the Canadian tug-of-war team to victory in Regent's Park. Ross Swenerton, a machine-gunner who was not hit till 1918, was induced by Pearson to go to join Eades. He went, and organized a Sales Department, and then took over After-care. He had left a clear personal mark on the Canadian version of St Dunstan's when he died, at thirty-five, in 1924.

Soon after the founding of the Canadian National Institute

for the Blind, Baker went to the United States to undertake a lecture tour to raise funds for the Third Liberty Loan. It lasted a month, during which he addressed seventy-nine meetings in various parts of the United States. When it was over the Canadian Government asked him to join the staff of the Invalided Soldiers' Commission in Ottawa and take charge of the settlement and after-care of all the Canadian blinded ex-Servicemen.

The request was a high compliment, and called for a sacrifice. It meant that Baker would have to give up his job with the Hydro-Electric Power Company, and abandon the prospect of a brilliant career. For the sake of his blinded comrades he stifled his personal ambition and accepted. He was appointed Managing Director of the Canadian National Institute for the Blind in 1920, and awarded the O.B.E. in 1935. In 1940 he was appointed President of the American Association of Workers for the Blind; he was the first Canadian to receive this honour. What he had got from St Dunstan's he gave to others a hundredfold.

Several other Canadian St Dunstaners have risen high. I have mentioned Harris Turner, who was elected to the Saskatchewan Legislature a few months after leaving us in 1917. He had been a journalist before the War, and he went back to his old profession and, with the help of two other disabled ex-Servicemen, founded a newspaper of his own which he called *Turner's Weekly*. Full of fun and high spirits, Harris Turner was undefeatable. They seem to make them like that in Saskatchewan. Another St Dunstaner, G. Foster, went back to his farm there and found his 75-h.p. engine and separator standing exactly as he had left them when he joined up. He took the machinery to pieces, cleaned and repaired it, and started up again where he had left off.

Yet another distinguished Canadian was D. J. Mac-Dougall, who was blinded in the first Battle of the Somme and came to St Dunstan's just after me, in November 1916. He was an infantry private, and before the War he had been a clerk. He learnt massage, and in the examinations he came second for all England, out of 320 entries, of whom all but a few St Dunstaners were sighted. He went to Ontario, and the Government employed him at a military establishment as an instructor to blind students. The Commandant was so impressed by his methods that he put sighted pupils under him as well.

Later he went to Toronto, and was renowned for the ease with which he went to and from his work. Once he saw a drunk home. The man stopped MacDougall as he got off the street-car, explained that he did not know the way, and gave the address. MacDougall took his arm, and off they went. Suddenly the stranger stopped and pointed. "Do you see a motor-car standing in front of the house? If there is, my dad has left it there for me to take to the garage, and I can't do it." Very gravely, and with perfect truth, MacDougall said he could not see any car. The drunk was relieved and grateful, and never guessed his escort was blind.

Later MacDougall went into private practice, with great success. A fresh ambition was born in him, and he became a student again. He graduated brilliantly at Toronto University, and became the first blind man in the world to win a Rhodes Scholarship. He went to Oxford, and we helped to supply him with books, and after a two years' course he won a first with honours in Modern History. He returned to Toronto and became a Professor of History.

Then there was Lieutenant-Colonel Perrett, who went back to his former post as Head of a large College of Teachers at Regina. There was Private Bill Dies, who bought a tobacco and stationery shop, trebled the turnover straight away, and almost immediately bought a corner site near by to put up a branch and erected a third shop for confectionery. It is true that he had his brother to help him, but it is also true that he had only one hand.

In January 1919 Pearson visited Canada, and twenty-nine St Dunstaners entertained him in Pearson Hall.

Corporal Viets was in the Chair. Bill Dies proposed the toast to St Dunstan's, and Pearson replied. Colonel Perrett, who had come over from Regina, proposed another toast. MacDougall proposed the toast to the Soldiers' Civil Re-establishment, and Captain Baker replied. "We have but carried our torches from St Dunstan's, where they were lit," he said. Four V.A.D.'s disguised as waitresses gave colour to his words.

Fifteen years later my wife and I were entertained in the same place by twenty-five St Dunstaners, with Bill Dies in the Chair. During our stay in Toronto Eddie Baker showed us how Pearson's idea had developed in Canada, and we had long exchanges of news and views. I met more St Dunstaners on the way across Canada, and at Vancouver we were entertained by Merrill C. Robinson, Superintendent of the Western Division of the C.N.I.B. A sergeant-major at eighteen, Robbie could have carved out a more profitable career for himself, but in his view none that would have been so worth while. A famous salmon-fisherman, he went to great lengths to encourage other blind people to take up the sport. Later he hit on the idea of a Salmon Derby for the blind of the area, which attracted many who had never held a rod before in their lives. It was so successful that it became an annual event, and within a few years over a hundred blind men and women were taking part.

From Canada we went to New Zealand, where a similar renaissance in the blind world had occurred. It would be untrue and unjust to say that the work of St Dunstan's in New Zealand was a one-man show at that time, and Sir Clutha Mackenzie would himself be the last person to suggest it. But he began it.

Trooper Mackenzie, of the Wellington Mounted Rifles, was blinded at Gallipoli. He wrote a remarkable book, called *The Tale of a Trooper*, in which he deliberately withheld, until the last few pages, the fact that he had lost his sight. He also introduced himself as a New Zealand shepherd, and referred to himself throughout the book as Mac. He wanted the reader to take him on his merits as a trooper, with no concessions to his disability and no respect for the fact that he was the son of Sir Thomas Mackenzie, formerly Prime Minister of New Zealand and then the High Commissioner. That was the sort of chap Mac was.

After leaving St Dunstan's he stayed with his father in London and founded, edited, and largely wrote a fortnightly magazine called *Chronicles of the New Zealand Expeditionary Force*. He paid several visits to the front to get copy, and it was a very lively journal.

Mackenzie married Miss Doris Sawyer, a V.A.D., and returned to New Zealand after the War. In 1921 he was elected to the House of Representatives, but his real public work was devoted to the interests of the blind. He not only made himself responsible for the after-care of all blinded ex-Servicemen—he wanted to help all the other blind in New Zealand.

He found at once that there was plenty to be done. New Zealand had only one organization concerned with blind welfare—the Jubilee Institute for the Blind in Auckland. Founded at the end of the nineteenth century, it did excellent work as an educational establishment of a local nature, but there were no facilities for any settlement or after-care. Mackenzie wisely decided not to found a rival organization, but joined the Jubilee Institute and proposed to extend its functions.

There was no opposition to this. Mackenzie was told he had the Institute's full support. All he had to do was to raise some money.

It was just at this time that Pearson died, and Mackenzie immediately launched an appeal for a Memorial Fund. He set a target of £45,000, and persuaded the Government to agree to give a subsidy of 24s. 6d. in the pound to turn it into £100,000. He could not have opened the fund at a worse time, for New Zealand was in the depths of the post-war slump. When he saw the money was not going to roll in of its own accord he saddled his horse and personally visited every town and nearly every village in the Dominion. He got the money, and he was appointed Director of the Jubilee Institute. Eventually it became the New Zealand National Institute for the Blind, and in 1935 the man who had developed it from a local school became Sir Clutha Mackenzie, to the delight of his many friends throughout the world.

Donald McPhee, who learnt massage at St Dunstan's, helped Mackenzie and largely ran the Auckland Social Club for the Blind. An expert oarsman with many trophies from our Putney Regattas, he founded the Jubilee Rowing Club for both sighted and blind. McPhee took charge in New Zealand when Mackenzie went to America and India on missions for St Dunstan's.

Several other New Zealanders learnt massage at St Dunstan's, including Sergeant Billy Woods, who was the first New Zealander to return home. He sailed in 1916— and the ship's surgeon gave him twelve patients to treat on the voyage. He worked in Government service until 1920, and then set up a private practice at Christchurch.

Rifleman James Chisholm could not be a masseur because the War had damaged his hands as well as his eyes. He went to the massage department as regularly as any student, but it was for treatment. No amount of trouble could be too much, for a blind man's hands are to some extent his eyes as well.

Patience was rewarded. "The happiest moment in my ten happy months at St Dunstan's took place one day at the dinner table. I had then been at St Dunstan's nearly five months. On this day I lifted a mug of milk to my lips with my right hand. The sister in charge of the table said, 'Well done, Chisholm,' and I agreed that it was well done. This was the outcome of work well done in the massage room. To a man whose left hand had only half the usual amount of feeling that was a red letter day. Two months later I reported a similar feat with a teacup."

Almost unbelievably, he learnt poultry-farming. His home was on the land, in the rough north of New Zealand, and he was determined to be of some use when he went home. He did not fear that he would disgrace himself or us, for he was a very determined man. "What I have done during the last twelve months is as follows," he wrote at the end of the first year. "I have dug one and three-quarter acres of virgin ground to a depth of from two to four feet, taking out all timber and roots. In regard to the timber, I have now at least a hundred fence posts to my credit. I have also many tons of firewood to my credit. In addition I have done about half a mile of drains. I have had my finger in a good many other pies, such as road mending, fencing, etc., but as I was not the only one at the game it is not easy to estimate my share."

From New Zealand we went to Australia, for the Conference of the British Empire Service League at Melbourne. We had our own Empire Blinded Soldiers' Conference there at the same time. I met some forty St Dunstaners at Melbourne, about the same number at Sydney, and more later at Adelaide and Perth. Here were more shining examples of the blind leading the blind. There was, first, the story of Charlie Hills.

Private Charles Henry Hills was the third man to enter St Dunstan's. He had lost his sight at Brown's Dip, Gallipoli. A teamster in Australia before the War, he had his parents in England, and was himself born at Orpington in Kent. With such a background he seemed destined for poultry-breeding, and he began to learn the job with the intention of staying in England. He was unable to finish his training as an old enemy, acute rheumatism, laid him low. He went in and out of hospital a few times, and then Pearson suggested that as Australia had done his health so much good he had better go back.

So he did, in the middle of the War, with half a dozen pullets among his luggage. He had to make his new life the hard way. There was no Settlement Department to find him a good place for his poultry farm and provide the equipment. No one in Australia seemed to have heard of a blind poultry-farmer. The people who worked for the blind did everything they could to talk him out of this crazy idea.

Charlie Hills was unmoved. He had been trained—or at least half trained—for poultry-farming, and that was what he was going to do. His only concession was to spend a few weeks on an Australian poultry farm before setting up on his own. This was simply common sense, and he had decided on it before he landed. King's Langley had a different climate from Wagga Wagga, and there could be other important local differences.

Meanwhile Hills had met some other blinded ex-soldiers who had missed St Dunstan's, and very miserable they were. The luckiest of them were those who had gone back to New South Wales and entered the Institute for the Blind at Sydney, which Hills said was easily the best in Australia. But it was still an institution, a refuge from the world to which Hills himself had been able to return. "I often shudder when I think of how near I was to missing St Dunstan's," he wrote to us, "and I shall never be tired of singing its praises wherever I am." One result of this was that some of the gloomy fellows he met were soon on their way back to England to get the training they had missed.

Hills had arrived home in April 1916, the beginning of the Australian winter. He found a site not far from Sydney, and set to work to build the farm. He did all the fencing with the help of one other man, a mechanic—who was also completely blind. They had only the corner pegs put in position to guide them. He built the first pen entirely by himself. Another ex-soldier, sighted but disabled, helped him with the other nine. The design of the farm was all his, and he developed it, bit by bit, in his spare time. It was six months before it was completed, but by then he had proved his point. No one doubted any longer whether poultry-farming was an occupation for the blind.

Meanwhile another dynamic Australian, Elmer Glew— 'Sticky' Glew, as he was inevitably called—had gone home to Melbourne as a fully trained masseur. At least, he was fully trained by British standards, but that was not considered a sufficient qualification by the Australian Massage Association. Before he could get their diploma he had to go on a further course of training, which lasted six months. Long before he finished this he and Hills, like Viets and Baker in Canada, had started a renaissance in the blind world.

Because of local conditions separate after-care committees were set up in each Australian State. Hills was the pioneer in New South Wales, and Glew in Victoria; and three of our V.A.D.'s, who went to Adelaide, helped to run the committee in South Australia. Every committee was greatly aided by the local branch of the Australian Red Cross Society. Representatives of the various committees met from time to time, each State taking its turn to play host. Glew co-ordinated their work, and he did this besides his work in Victoria for twelve years. He had to resign through ill health. A few years later his work was recognized with the award of the M.B.E. Joe Lynch took over from him both in Victoria and as President of the federal Blinded Soldiers' Association of Australia. Lynch is still President, and has been the leader and mouthpiece of Australian blinded soldiers ever since; he is a figure well-known throughout Australia. He was awarded the C.B.E. in 1936.

Another of our Victorians, Dudley Tregent, went to Melbourne University and took a first-class honours degree in political economy. He stayed on to a law degree, and after qualification he became Hon. Solicitor to the federal Association. He still has one of the best law practices in Melbourne.

Meanwhile Nobbs had arrived—Captain Gilbert Nobbs, of the London Rifle Brigade, one of our most colourful characters, who took his blindness by the scruff of the neck and shook it till it lost all its malignant power. He was extraordinarily self-confident from the start. Perhaps he got over his bad period before he came to St Dunstan's— as he was a prisoner of war in Germany for four months after being blinded, it may have been quite exceptionally bad. At any rate, at St Dunstan's his morale could not have been higher, and he seemed to take it for granted that blindness would not affect his career. Before the War he had been Foreign and Colonial Director of Holbrook's Sauce, Ltd., and he did not need Pearson to tell him he could go back. He was absolutely determined that he should. So he did, but he would have been the last person in the world to disown his debt to St Dunstan's. This came out pretty clearly in a book he wrote telling of his war experiences, called *Englishman, Kamerad!* which was pub- lished at the beginning of 1918. This was quick-fire, down- to-earth stuff, full of comradeship and high spirit and with a few hefty swipes at civilian greed and indifference; all very typical of Gilbert Nobbs.

Back in his old job in the City he was, as expected, a roaring success, although the vast foreign and colonial export business of his firm had been almost destroyed by the War. No sooner was the Armistice signed than Nobbs set off to repair it, going on a business tour of the United States, Canada, Honolulu, Fiji, Australia, and New Zealand. On the strength of his report Holbrook's decided to build a new factory in Sydney, and Nobbs set off again to supervise the building and look after the whole Australian side of the business. Taking his wife and two children, he settled in Sydney, and built up the branch until it was more important than its parent in England. His arrival added strength to the New South Wales organization for after-care, of which he eventually took charge.

* * *

We had more Australians even than Canadians, and by 1921 seventy had come and gone back home. They did not form a clique at St Dunstan's, but, like the Canadians, they kept extra ties among themselves. They all shared the triumphs of Trooper Matheson in the boat races. They provided a guard of honour for Jerry Jerome—the bee-keeping one—when he married Miss Collins, of the V.A.D. When an Australian needed a blood transfusion—a somewhat more drastic thing then than it is now—they queued up to donate.

Several men were from Tasmania. Captain Frank Marriott—Uncle Marriott to all of us—had come to St Dunstan's in 1917, when he was already an old man of forty-one. Six feet five inches tall, with a deep, resonant voice, he had showed there was plenty of life in him yet. And so there was. Back in Tasmania he farmed, brought up four boys, and fairly flung himself into public life. He entered Parliament in 1921, and he stayed there till he retired at the end of 1946. During those twenty-five years he had to fight seven general elections, and he won the lot.

As a speaker he was famous all over the island and beyond. He was brilliant in debates, and often would quote the salient clauses from a Bill word for word. They talked of his uncanny power of memorizing, but did him less than justice. He took his public life seriously. At home he would have Bills read to him, and then he would indicate the important clauses and have these read and reread; finally he would type them out himself, to impress them on his mind.

Uncle Marriott was the Chief of the Tasmania Boy Scouts, Head of Toc H, active leader of every good cause in the State—including, of course the welfare of the blind. He was created C.M.G. in 1934.

Another of our unusual Australians was Digger Scrymgeour, a name that means 'good fighter.' He fought in Palestine with the 2nd Light Horse. Shot in the eyes and the ankle, he lay helpless for fourteen hours before he was rescued. He was taken back to Brisbane, but came to St Dunstan's in 1919, and there was never any doubt about his career. He had been to an agricultural college before the War, and cattle-breeding was his future. Blindness raised obstacles that ingenuity could overcome. To find his way to the various yards in his stud farm he put up a series of overhead wires with running ropes hanging down.

Starting out with a few plain stock, he built up a select herd of shorthorns, and was soon one of the most successful breeders in the country. Eventually he had a farm of 400 acres and a stock of 80 studs, all of which he looked after himself. His dining-room was full of silver cups and bowls earned by his prize cattle and horses, but he was proudest of the trophy he had won for sculling on the Thames.

Scrymgeour judged regularly at agricultural shows, and came to be reckoned one of the best judges of stock in Australia. He could tell the fine points of a shorthorn by running his hands over it—and he had wonderful remembering hands. He would recall an animal at a touch, even after as long as a year, and as his fingers slid over it he would recall its virtues, faults, and pedigree. It was said that he could even tell the colour of an animal by the feel of its hair. I dare say he could, but I think this must have been due to some association of ideas or knowledge that certain breeds or types are of certain colours.

I have often heard it said that the blind can tell colours by feel or by some special sense. Taken literally, I think this is a physical impossibility. There was an old woman who, it was said, could tell the colours of her knitting-wool. Undoubtedly she knitted the right colours in the right places, but I expect her method was to keep the different colours in different drawers or packages; though it is just possible that the difference between white and coloured wool can be felt because of the greater softness of the white wool and the relative harshness of the coloured wool caused by the dye. It is also possible that green wool smells of arsenic or some other chemical. Colours as such cannot be distinguished by any sense except sight.

St Dunstan's South Africa Committee started in a different way from the other Dominions organizations. Charles Vintcent and his wife were living in London during the War, and as South Africans they looked after their compatriots at St Dunstan's. They offered their services to Pearson to represent St Dunstan's in South Africa and Rhodesia after the War. Pearson was only too pleased, and the Committee was formed in 1918 with Vintcent as Chairman and his wife as Hon. Secretary. It began work in conjunction with the Governor-General's Fund.

Walter Bowen, whom everyone called Mike, was a South African infantry sergeant blinded at Ypres. He had been a clerk before the War, and wanted to be a barrister. He began preliminary reading while still at St Dunstan's, and then went to Cambridge University. He passed his Bar final examination, secured the honorary degrees of B.A. and LL.D., and entered chambers in the Temple to learn to practise. At the same time he made a special study of Roman Dutch law at London University, and was first in the examination.

Blinded in 1917 and called to the Bar in 1920, Bowen married a V.A.D. at 2nd London General Hospital named Miss Gillies—a sister of Sir Harold Gillies, the plastic surgeon who did such wonders for many of our men. Bowen returned to Cape Town two years later, and became an advocate of the South African Bar. He was soon well known as a friend of the coloured people, and conducted some important cases on behalf of South African natives. In 1929 he was elected to the South African Parliament, and he held his seat until his death in 1948.

Such was the career of the talented St Dunstaner who could read braille through two pairs of cotton gloves and a handkerchief folded three times. He was an ally of the Vintcents from his arrival, and in 1925 he opened the South

African Library for the Blind at Grahamstown, with books in braille for readers of both English and Afrikaans. In his speech Bowen said he hoped it would provide an incentive to the creation of a national institute for the education and vocational training of the civilian blind of South Africa. His hope was realized when a National Council for the Blind was set up a few years later. Naturally, the first Chairman was Mike Bowen.

One of the most remarkable of the South African St Dunstaners is Hugh Stayt, who learnt massage and poultry-farming and became a distinguished anthropologist. That is hardly fair to him, for he has practised physiotherapy successfully and run a considerable poultry farm. You might think that enough for any man, but Stayt branched off on his own with a new type of anthropological research.

For three seasons running he and his wife travelled in northern Transvaal and Southern Rhodesia, living among the Bavenda tribes. They camped beside their villages, and visited all the important chiefs in their own kraals. To fill gaps in their researches they climbed rugged mountains, pushed into remote valleys, and somehow reached almost inaccessible places. They published the results of their researches in a monograph which was hailed as the first worth-while book, not only on the Bavenda but on any of the South African tribes, written during all the years in which the white and black races had been in contact.

A good speaker, always deeply interested in public affairs, Stayt took on a new job when the Second World War broke out. He became Captain Stayt, of the South African Defence Force, a Recruiting Officer for the south coast district of Natal.

My wife and I made my first post-war visit to South Africa in 1928. My father had emigrated there in the 1870's and had settled there, so that it was my childhood home. School, Sandhurst, the War, and the accident of my blindness had kept me in England for some time, and it was with particular interest and excitement that I returned

o

to South Africa at last. I went to see Fraser Street, in the town where my father had built what were said to be the first offices and house in Johannesburg, and another Fraser Street just outside the town where my sister and I had lived as children.

During this visit I met as many St Dunstaners as I could, and saw what a wonderful job the Vintcents were doing in after-care. This made it all the bigger blow when, two years later, Charles Vintcent had to retire because of ill-health. It also made me understand quite clearly why the South Africa Committee, which the Vintcents had run for twelve years, needed Mrs Chadwick Bates.

Compared with the other Dominions, we had few South African soldiers at St Dunstan's. I think it is only fair to add that South Africa was the most generous contributor of the Dominions to our funds. As the South African St Dunstaners were scattered thinly over a large country, reunions were not easy to arrange. Indeed, the very first, held in Cape Town and attended by twelve men and most of their wives, was on the occasion of the Governor-General's farewell presentations to Mr and Mrs Vintcent on their retirement.

Besides the four great Dominions, St Dunstaners were scattered in various parts of the world. Paddy Park wrote to us from Mauritius. Alec Biggs practised physiotherapy in Shanghai, and some of his clients travelled seven hundred miles for treatment. W. Gilbert Speight took the message to India, and his victory was one of the most remarkable of all.

A Territorial with the Sherwood Foresters before the War, Speight served with the Yorks and Lancs in France, and was wounded in 1915. At St Dunstan's he was trained in poultry-farming, and he was one of Captain Webber's few outstanding failures. He admitted that his heart was not in it. He also confessed that he felt a call to the ministry. In addition, he wanted to work for the blind.

The Church did not want Speight then, but he was not

going back to the chickens. He kept his ears open, and presently heard that the Church Missionary Society wanted someone to take charge of their School for the Blind at Palamcottah, in Southern India. The school was poor and remote, and it was a one-man job; and there was no rush of applicants. Speight was accepted, and given a short training course. He went out in March 1919, and we did not see him again for sixteen years.

When he arrived at the school Speight found 100 pupils of both sexes ranging in age from three to over forty years. He had no European assistance, very little equipment, less money, but immense courage and burning faith, so it is not surprising that he succeeded.

Speight decided that he could not teach men old enough to be his father together with infants who could have been their grandchildren, so he restricted admission to the young. At the same time he made it clear that the school was open to children of any race or creed. They came from a background of disease, poverty, and ignorance, and ironically most of them would have remained illiterate if they had not been blind. Speight and his Indian staff taught the children to read braille, to do sums on a special frame, to learn geography with raised maps. He also taught them to sing, play instruments, and enjoy themselves. Then he taught them to earn a living.

Weaving was the main trade, first of grass mats and then with cotton. There was also some cane-work and netting, and knitting and other handicrafts for the girls. With no sheltered work-shops or after-care, the main task was to help each child to become as useful and adaptable as possible. At the same time they were encouraged to make articles like mats, towels, sheets, and dusters that Speight could sell for funds.

The school flourished. The Bishop of Madras asked Speight to draw up a scheme for another school on the same lines. It was opened soon after, and a pattern that owed a little to St Dunstan's began to repeat itself all over India.

Speight was in early middle age when he came back to England, and he made it clear at once that he wished to return. But he had another desire, an old ambition that was as strong as ever. He wanted to enter the ministry.

There were no difficulties now, no more questions about the candidate's suitability. No ordained missionary had done more than Speight. But he had to go back to school again himself, to study for Holy Orders. He was ordained by the Archbishop of Canterbury in December 1939, over twenty-one years after he had first tried to enter the Church.

He returned to Palamcottah, and less than five years later a canonry was conferred upon him. He was awarded the Kaisar-i-Hind Medal by the Viceroy for his magnificent work. He finally came back to England in 1947 and took up a living in Worcestershire. Later he moved to Leicestershire, where he discovered in one of his churches a stained-glass window dedicated to St Dunstan. He died in 1960.

12

Ovingdean

Mr E. Bass has left Bulawayo for England to enter St Dunstan's Home for the Blind. He was gassed during the war, twenty years ago on September 5th last, and his eyes, which had been troubling him for the past few years, have lost their sight as a result.

Rhodesia Herald

NEWS items such as this appeared all too commonly from 1934 to 1939. After that they were rarer, but only because papers were smaller and human suffering more widespread. The first known case of delayed action of a splash of mustard gas came to us fifteen years after the Armistice. Nearly thirty years later cases were still coming in.

In these cases blindness had come on gradually, and nearly all the men had entered the blind world without any skilled guidance. So they had got into bad habits of thought and action, which became harder to cure as the years went on. There have been some notable exceptions, but in general the middle-aged and elderly find the going harder because they are less adaptable than the young. They are slower to learn braille, less resilient, and more easily discouraged by setbacks. They set St Dunstan's a new problem.

The unexpected new demands on St Dunstan's naturally upset our actuarial calculations. In one year towards the end of the thirties we had forty-one new cases, as against thirty deaths. Of course, we accepted the increased responsibility cheerfully, and ferreted out cases of men who had not come to us because they did not know their rights. Frederick Lavelle, for example, was found in a hospital in New York, and had long been a citizen of the United States.

Sergeant Alan Nichols visited Lavelle and heard his story, and Eddie Baker went from Toronto to offer his help. Lavelle needed help badly. For one thing the medical profession in the United States had very little experience of mustard-gas blindness; for another, Lavelle had not served in the U.S. Army, so he had no American ex-Serviceman's rights.

Lavelle had been a sergeant in the Seaforth Highlanders when he was gassed in 1917. He was blind for nine months after, but recovered his sight and went back to the front line. He fought as a fit man right up to the Armistice. In civilian life he had been a professional gymnast, performing in variety, and he went back to this career. Emigrating to the United States, he was a successful and happy family man until the darkness began to creep in.

We brought him and his wife back to England, and while he was getting expert medical treatment we succeeded in having his British citizenship restored. This gave him full pension rights, and St Dunstan's gave him a training in basket-making. His health was never good, but St Dunstan's had given him another twelve years of full life.

In 1935 the country celebrated King George V's Silver Jubilee, and the Prince of Wales came to our Jubilee Reunion in the Royal Albert Hall.

St Dunstan's was twenty years old. There were still over 1700 members of this most exclusive club. Our average age was only forty-six. Most of us had wives and children who did not need to be seen to be loved. Over 60 per cent. of us were doing and enjoying a useful job of work. We were not all in the best of health, but our spirit could not have been higher.

Over five hundred St Dunstaners attended that Albert Hall reunion, and other Jubilee reunions were held all over the country. My wife and I went to most of them. The following year we celebrated our coming of age, with more parties and reunions—and, of course, interest by the public and the Press. I have always tried to follow in Pearson's footsteps by getting St Dunstan's every bit of free publicity I could. With our new obligations as a result of the mustard-gas cases we needed it all.

We still measured our success in terms of the happiness of the ordinary man, but we also rejoiced when some specially gifted St Dunstaners stuck a new feather in our well-plumed cap. W. T. Curtis-Willson, blinded by a shell-burst in 1916, had a notable and varied career. After some years of total blindness he recovered a little sight, and was a successful political agent. Then his sight deserted him again, but this did not stop him. He became a newspaper publisher—he was Chairman and Managing Director of the *Brighton and Hove Herald*—when, in 1938, he was made a Justice of the Peace. He was one of the very few blind men to be sworn in as a magistrate since Sir John Fielding.

Justice is blind, and it is a popular fallacy that the blind are ineligible to sit on juries. They claim exemption from jury service if they like, but that is a very different thing.

Curtis-Willson sat on the Bench for many years, and in 1940 he was selected as one of the four magistrates to administer justice in Brighton in the event of a German invasion. When Curtis-Willson and I gave evidence to a Royal Commission on Justices of the Peace I suggested that it might not be a bad thing if one member of a Bench was blind—especially if the witness was a girl with a face full of sweet innocence. More seriously, we fought a determined battle to retain the right for a blind man to be a J.P. But we lost, though men who were already J.P.'s retained the dignity of the office for life, although they were not allowed to sit in court. A sergeant in the First World War, Curtis-Willson was an Hon. Wing Commander in the Second, when he raised and commanded five squadrons of the Air Training Corps. President of the Newspaper Society in 1950 and a member of the Press Council from its foundation, he was widely travelled and respected and one of Brighton's best-loved public figures until his death in 1957.

St Dunstan's began to prepare for war in the spring of 1937. At least, that was when we began to prepare for the worst while we still hoped for the best. Obviously, our rôle in a war would be so dependent on official decisions that we could at first make only tentative plans. A new war would mean more blinded Servicemen, and part of St Dunstan's would have to start at the beginning again. We could be pretty sure the authorities would be glad we were there to do the job. But we also had to think of the men blinded in the 1914-18 War whom we were pledged to help for the rest of their lives. All sorts of problems were likely to arise, from providing help in air raids to getting supplies of basket-cane.

Another question that was greatly concerning the men themselves was how they could best serve the country in another war. There was an immediate response by St Dunstaners when the Government appealed in March 1938 for a million volunteers for Air Raid Precautions, the forerunner of the present organization for Civil Defence. Telephonist Garrity at British Legion headquarters suggested that blind operators could work exchanges at hospitals, fire stations, and other vital places. The blind physiotherapists offered their services without reservation. Sergeant Alan Nichols built himself an air-raid shelter in London; his spirit evoked widespread Press interest. I doubt if any other section of the community offered a readier response.

Meanwhile St Dunstan's had been looking for a new home.

West House, the wonderful gift of the Federation of Grocers' Associations, could no longer meet all our wants.

There was not enough room for the increasing number of St Dunstaners who needed a holiday or convalescence, and the permanent residents found the building increasingly inconvenient as their disabilities worsened with the years. There were too many corners, the stairs were too difficult. For an ageing community like ours this situation was bound to become progressively worse. Something would have to be done eventually. The sooner we did it the better.

First we considered extending West House, but at best this would have been only a partial solution. Then we thought of pulling it down and putting up a new building on the site. But it was not large enough, and with the noisy traffic outside the site was not really ideal. We looked for another site in Brighton, but could not find one suitable for us.

One obvious solution would have been to go into the country, where there was ample ground at a much lower price. This might have been ideal for any other organization, but the idea was too conventual for St Dunstan's. The men liked Brighton for its amenities—the pier and the front, the entertainments and outings, and especially the hospitality and friendship of the people. These things had a greater tonic value than the sea air, and by retiring into the country we should have been losing them. Nor was there any point in looking for a place in another seaside town. The problem of finding a suitable site was likely to be just as great, and we would still have to sacrifice a great fund of local goodwill that had grown over the years.

The eventual solution was a happy compromise.

We found a site on the Sussex Downs, outside Brighton but linked with the town by a regular bus service. Between Roedean School and Rottingdean, it was on high ground a little back from the cliff, looking straight over the sea. We leased the land from Brighton Corporation, and commissioned an architect to design a building specifically for the use of the blind.

Francis Lorne was the architect, and he designed one of

the most striking examples of modern architecture put up in Britain before the War. A six-storey building of fire-proof steel and brick, our new home at Ovingdean soon became a familiar landmark on the Sussex coast. Nobody needed to ask what it was, either. We plastered our name on it in letters two and a half feet high, neon-lit at night.

When you see it first as you come along the coast road it looks like an aeroplane resting on a hill, with a rounded glass cockpit gleaming in the sun. By pre-War standards it has an astonishing amount of external glass. One of its primary aims was to catch the greatest possible amount of sunshine and air for the men inside.

Come up the drive, and the first thing you see will be the Chapel. It is Church of England, but both the building and the services are deliberately simple in design to have the widest possible appeal to other Protestant denominations. Special facilities are, of course, afforded for Roman Catholics.

Go on up the drive. If you are blind you have only to follow the hand-rail, and a rubber strip leads across to the pavement outside the main entrance. Inside, one of the first things you will see—or feel, if you are blind—is an exact scale model of the building, with ground plans of the floors. From this the newcomer can learn the size, shape, and relative positions of the rooms and corridors, so that he can visualize the building and find his way about.

One of the first things you will observe from this model is that the plan of each floor is almost identical. Functional architecture has its critics, but none of them are blind. It had even more critics in 1938 than now, but the architect could not be too severely simple and geometrical for us. The universal straight passages and rounded corners, the plain walls with the inevitable guide-rails, may strike you as monotonous if you are sighted, but if you are blind you will appreciate their gift of freedom of movement and independence.

There are lifts deep enough to take bed-cases. There are

also stairs, and when you go up them you will observe how gentle and easy they are. Let your hand slide up the banister, and as you near the top of each flight you will feel any number of steel studs from one to six. They tell you the number of the next floor. At the head of each flight you will go through waist-high self-closing swing gates, edged with thick rubber tubing, so lightly sprung that you will barely notice them. Turn round to go down again, and first you will have to pull the gates open with your hand. No one can fall down the stairs at Ovingdean. Nor can one hurt oneself badly on the edge of a door, for it is bound to be cushioned with rubber—which, incidentally, serves an additional purpose in keeping out draughts.

Every essential door is plainly marked in raised letters. In the big lounge the seats are arranged in lines so that the men can easily find their way about. This is where St Dunstaners sit and talk, play cards and dominoes, and have their concerts. There are also quiet lounges for reading aloud or reading braille, special rooms for typewriting and others for listening to talking books, a large winter garden for the sick and lame, and wonderful sun balconies for all. The blind-deaf have a special room for use when there are concerts in the lounge. There are classrooms and workshops, and a sports room equipped with everything from a punch-ball to a rowing-machine.

The dining-room, on the ground floor, holds 134 men. Tables and chairs are numbered, and easily reached with the help of guiding rubber strips down the aisles. The tables themselves, of glass-topped Australian walnut, were all made by St Dunstaners. So were the three-tiered trolleys used by the orderlies in serving meals. There are no smells of cooking—the food comes down in service hatches from the kitchen on the top floor.

Besides accommodation for the Matron and her staff there are 120 beds for the men. Each dormitory has two rubber-cushioned doors and deep wide windows with modern accordion-type Venetian blinds. The rug beside each bed is fixed to the floor by press-studs. Each man has his own fitted wardrobe, a locker with a desk-flap, and wireless earphones with the choice of three programmes.

Ovingdean was designed to meet the specific needs of the blind more completely than had been done anywhere in the world. Architecturally it was far in advance of its time, and after over twenty years it shows no sign of dating. We thought it was beautiful as well as simple when it was built, and we still think so to-day.

It was planned in 1935, and scheduled for completion by autumn of 1937. In the event it took nearly another twelve months to finish. It was to be the answer to all our prayers, the fulfilment of all our needs. It would provide a permanent home for the old or lonely, and for those who were too badly disabled to lead an ordinary life at home. It would be the training centre for new cases, who would come for a year or more. It would provide convalescence for anything from three weeks to three months to men who had been ill or had operations. Finally, it would be open to St Dunstaners who wanted a holiday among their old comrades—and whose wives, the most wonderful wives in the world, needed a holiday from them.

We hoped Ovingdean would not have to meet any greater needs than these, but we were not so blind as to feel sure about that. Originally we had intended to sell West House, but we had changed our minds by August 1938, when the men in it moved out. The Mayor of Brighton saw them off as they went to homes in various parts of the country for the next six weeks. They came to Ovingdean in the second week in October, just after the Munich Agreement had postponed the next war for a year.

During the period of crisis we had created the nucleus of a war organization that was ready to leave Regent's Park, if London was bombed, at a moment's notice. We had also sought and earmarked possible lodgings in the country for St Dunstaners living in London and other big towns. A large number of men whose homes were in the country offered hospitality to their old comrades.

After the Munich Agreement we were invited to a conference with representatives of the heads of the medical services of the Forces and the Ministry of Pensions, and the part St Dunstan's would play in a future war was hammered out. We were asked, and agreed, to be the national centre for the full care of blinded Servicemen. We accepted the responsibility for setting up and conducting a Central Hospital for all Service cases which led to or threatened blindness. This would be the equivalent of the eye wards of the 2nd General Hospital in the First World War, but it would be part of St Dunstan's, so that the surgical treatment and our training would go on hand in hand. This meant in fact that Ovingdean would be converted into a hospital and training centre for the newly blind. Our dormitories would be turned into wards, our classrooms and workshops greatly extended. In this context we would still have to look after the 1914-18 men somehow.

But all this was for a future that might never come. Meanwhile the 1914-18 men were in possession, and from the start Ovingdean was a roaring success. Although not in the heart of things, like West House, it was near enough for a full social life. F. G. Braithwaite pointed out that the distance to the White Horse was a mere ten minutes going and only half an hour coming back. Our many friends in Brighton and Hove formed a Corps of Good Companions, and came to take men on walks and car drives and escort them to dances and cinemas. Our own bus, known as Victor, did a shuttle service from the main entrance to the town, ten times a day. The regular Southdown buses stopped on the coast road a few minutes away.

That road was the scene of a dreadful tragedy for us. With its fast-moving traffic, it was clearly a potential danger to blind pedestrians and before Ovingdean opened I approached the Brighton Corporation and the Ministry of Transport about it. At our request the crossing-place by

the bus-stop was given Belisha beacons and notice-boards
warning motorists on either side. I asked for these boards
to be lighted, but there was some delay over this. A few
months after Ovingdean had opened one man was knocked
down crossing the road, and had his leg broken. A week or
so later two men were knocked down at night, and suffered
slighter injuries. The lights were installed after this, and
all went well for some more months. Then came a terrible
blow. One of our men was knocked down and killed.

After this two road wardens were put on duty, but the
real solution was a tunnel built under the road at our
request, and partly at our expense. We shared the cost of
the construction with the Corporation. It enabled men to
cross safely both to the bus stop and to the beach beyond.

Early in 1939 I congratulated T. A. Williams of Shering-
ham on being the first St Dunstaner to qualify as an Air
Raid Warden. Soon afterwards Charlie Durkin of Putney
was appointed Head Warden of the Roehampton Estate,
with fifty trained wardens under him and the responsibility
for the entire A.R.P. organization of an estate of 5500
people. Alec Biggs, back from Shanghai, was appointed
Deputy Group Controller, A.R.P., for Princes Risborough.
All over the country St Dunstaners were showing that they
had no intention of being a national liability in the event of
war.

By now nearly 2700 men had been through St Dunstan's.
The total at the time of the Armistice of 1918 had been
only 1300, so already more than half were cases of delayed
blindness. Altogether nearly a thousand of our men had
died, most of them in the first few years. Our average age
was fifty, our death-rate now normal. For some time the
roll-call had stood around the 1700 mark. Wives and
children brought the total beneficiaries up to over 7000.

No less than 95 per cent. of our men were soldiers from
the Home or Dominion or Colonial Forces. Another 3 per
cent. belonged to the Royal Navy, Royal Marines, and the

Merchant Navy. The remaining 2 per cent. were Royal
Flying Corps and Royal Naval Air Service. These per-
centages are approximate, and the total included also six
women, who were nurses, V.A.D.'s, or munition workers;
a few male munition workers; three men blinded in air
raids; and a few who had been blinded while serving in
India and other parts of the Empire during the years
between the wars.

Financially we were on an even keel. The unexpectedly
high number of late admissions—349 in the last ten years
—had thrown out our earlier actuarial calculations, but we
were confident of reaching our new target. We were half-
way towards endowment when the Second World War
broke out, and the men at Ovingdean had to prepare to
give up some of their comforts in favour of those in greater
need.

There was never any doubt about their readiness to
make sacrifices, but you can hardly be surprised at that.
After all, these were men who had sacrificed their sight.

13

War Again

AFTER twenty-three years of it I thought I had become tough about blindness. Certainly I had long since ceased to fret about not being able to see myself. Yet when war broke out my mind's eye flashed back to the Somme in 1916, and I recalled how I had felt when I first knew I was blind. The thought that a fresh generation of youngsters would have to go through the same was heartbreaking. St Dunstan's would help them to recover their nerve and spirit, they would conquer blindness as we had done—I knew that—but they wouldn't know until it had happened, and there would be the same period of shock and suffering before they laughed and lived again.

There was greater tragedy in store for some of the old St Dunstaners. Many had sons who were now of military age. They were proud of their boys, and boasted of their progress in the Services; but they were also afraid. Some of those boys would be severely wounded, perhaps blinded. Some would be killed. St Dunstan's had no answer to this.

In the First World War, under Sir Arthur Pearson, St Dunstan's had never been caught unprepared, and this was one of many traditions that we were determined to keep up. Like everyone else, we expected the war in the west to start with a bang rather than a whimper, so the first thing we did was to empty some of our beds by reducing the number of men in residence.

We did not try to send all the old St Dunstaners away, for this would have caused hardship. It would also have deprived us of a valuable element in the new men's recovery. We were not going to build a new St Dunstan's, but a continuation of the old. The first-comers especially would recover more quickly if they came into an existing community that was happy though blind.

For the same reason as many as possible of the teaching staff were St Dunstaners themselves. Most of them had entered during the First World War and become pupil teachers, and stayed in the classrooms and workshops until new admissions began to dwindle away. They came back when we asked them—and so did V.A.D.'s who had looked after us in the early days in Regent's Park. At the same time we began to train a new generation of V.A.D.'s, to balance experience with youth. Most of the new St Dunstaners would be young, and St Dunstan's could not give its best to them if they thought it middle-aged. From the start of the War I resolved that we must all be young in spirit, and as many as possible of us young in age.

The main difference in St Dunstan's was that this time it was not only a training centre but also a hospital. Dormitories became wards, and we built a new hospital wing over our garages. This wing, with an ultra-modern and perfectly equipped operating theatre, was a generous gift from Lord Nuffield. We had it fully planned in advance so that building could begin at a few days' notice. Actually we had bought some steel girders before war broke out, as we feared they might be hard to get.

As in the First World War, we had the best ophthalmic surgeons in the country. Robert C. Davenport became our medical commandant, and the greater part of the ophthalmic diagnosis and surgery was undertaken by him; he remained our principal consultant until his death in June 1961. Four Sisters also joined us from Moorfields Eye Hospital—the senior one, Miss E. A. Postlethwaite, becoming Matron of our hospital. They were helped by V.A.D.'s and unskilled juniors, one of whom was my own daughter, Jean. We were ready for casualties almost before the first shot was fired. But at first no casualties

P

came. This was the 'phoney' war, the lull before the storm, and soon we invited back the men we had sent away. Ovingdean resumed its peacetime appearance, with only one ward set aside for emergencies.

The arrival of the first casualty was almost an anti-climax, but of the happiest kind. The man was a tele-graphist in the Royal Navy, and he had damaged one eye in an accident. He was operated on, and then both his eyes were bandaged for a few weeks. I gave him a braille watch, everyone made a great fuss of him, and then the bandages were taken off and he walked out of the blind world.

St Dunstan's headquarters was still at Regent's Park, but we had moved the After-care Department to West House. At the beginning of the War it seemed reasonable to expect London to be bombed but Brighton to be left alone. We could not imagine the enemy being very inter-ested in a seaside holiday resort without any important industry and well away from the main line of fire. Indeed, we congratulated ourselves on our good luck in having such a happy situation.

Our Appeals Department stayed at headquarters, and I divided my time more or less equally between Regent's Park and West House. It was clear that we should have to appeal to the public for fresh funds before long, and we did so at once in India and the colonies and dependencies; but in Britain we decided to wait until more casualties came in. The first motto of St Dunstan's—before we adopted Pearson's slogan of "Victory over Blindness"—had been the more ironical "What the eye does not see, the heart does not grieve about." Without being sour or cynical, we thought the same saying could be applied differently to this matter of timing our appeal. It seemed likely to succeed better when the public conscience had been aroused to the tragic facts of war.

Our Sales and Trading Department remained at Raglan Street, and cursed the Germans for choosing September to start the War. As usual, they had amassed big stocks in expectation of the Christmas trade. Usually September was their busiest month, but this time they sold hardly anything at all. We were greatly overstocked, not only in finished goods but also in materials, for when war had seemed imminent I had given orders for the purchase of vast stocks of raw materials, as I feared they might become scarce. I still thought they would. I also thought that the handicraft trades would pick up before long. We would not have to compete against imported mats from India and baskets from the Continent, and competition at home would decrease as labour generally was attracted to the munition trades. Also there were possible new markets due to the War. Large numbers of camouflage nets were needed, and many of the Government departments evacuated from London would be needing waste-paper baskets and door-mats. I set about soliciting contracts right away.

More worrying was the threat to the livelihood of our poultry and pig farmers as a result of cuts in the imports of feeding-stuffs. I asked the Ministry of Agriculture to give our men special treatment because, unlike their sighted colleagues, they could not adapt themselves to other agricultural activities. The Minister conceded the point at once.

This was typical of many problems that arose out of the fact that the War brought great masses of new regulations that had, naturally enough, been designed for people who could see. We could not ask for special treatment over everything, and if we suffered only a slight inconvenience due to blindness we were inclined to let it go. Otherwise we had to ask for exceptions to be made in our favour, and invariably our requests were received with sympathy.

Another example was over the calling up of sighted assistants on poultry farms or in shops or other businesses. One or two St Dunstaners faced with this problem wanted me to ask the Ministry of Labour to exempt them from national service. I would not do this, for I thought it was quite right that everyone who could be spared should play his or her part in the War. But employers could apply for deferment of call-up, and on this basis we pressed the claims of our men. The blindness of an employer did not of itself entitle him to special consideration, but I always found Government officials willing to give some weight to this factor when the work was of national use. At the same time, deferment was only temporary—just a few months— to enable the employer to find other assistance or readjust his affairs.

We ourselves were among the employers who were affected. When members of our staff were called up they were often hard to replace because their work was specialized and skilled. However, we had two compensations. One was that many of our staff had come to us during the First World War, and of these most were either too old or unfit for service. The other compensation was the exceptional loyalty of them all. When we were a man short the others made up for it after hours. You never heard anyone protest "It's not my job."

One of those who left us to join up was A. D. Lloyds, who served with the Royal Artillery and was taken prisoner at the fall of Java. He was a chartered accountant, and soon after returning to our staff became Mr Askew's assistant, then financial secretary, and in 1955 the Secretary —that is to say, the Chief Officer of St Dunstan's—a very responsible post, which he still occupies with great ability.

When war broke out I was apprehensive, both personally and on behalf of St Dunstan's, about possible air raids. The prospect made me more conscious of my handicap than I had been since the first few weeks of blindness back in 1916. If a bomb came our way I would not be able to help women and children—my wife would have to help me. I tried to imagine what I would be able to do if the house burst into flames, and the thought made me feel helpless and anxious. As there were hardly any raids in the first six months of war I had no chance to find out how I would take it, but all of us took heart from the experience of

Captain Lindsay Caudle, whose house at Southsea caught fire one night without enemy interference.

Caudle was roused by the whining of his dog, which slept upstairs. By then the ground floor was blazing, and all chance of escape by the staircase was cut off. There were three of them in the house—Caudle, his wife, and the maid. Coolly he made a rope of several sheets, and sent the women down first. Then he threw the dog to safety. Finally he clambered over the window-sill himself—only just in time, for the flames had already reached the sheets, and the improvised rope broke asunder just before he reached the ground. It was a pretty good effort for a blind man, and again blindness was shown up as a handicap that could be overcome.

Air raids would obviously be more serious for the deaf-blind, but they too had resources of their own. George Fallowfield not only made wooden shutters for his windows and put fire buckets on the landing, but drew up suggested rules to enable the deaf-blind to receive air-raid warnings. As thoughtful and ingenious as ever, he was concerned about the accidents sighted people were having in the black-out, and suggested that I should broadcast some hints. So I gave a talk on "Getting about in the Dark," with the usual tips about counting steps, using the banister, leaning back, and protecting oneself against the edge of a door. It was much the same advice as I had been giving to the newly blind for twenty years—but this time it was the sighted who needed help.

It was nice to have something over everyone else for once, and the black-out gave us some fun. The best story was of one of our masseurs who arrived at his clinic one morning with a damaged forehead. The Sister asked him what had happened.

"That black-out," he said.

"What?" she exclaimed.

"I went out with a friend," he explained, "who unfortunately wasn't blind."

* * *

On March 26, 1940, St Dunstan's celebrated its twenty-fifth birthday, but without any of the reunions or jollification we would have liked. With over six months of the War gone, we were still apprehensive rather than hard pressed. Our total of Second War entrants was only seven. Not all of them had been blinded in action, but that made it all the harder to bear. The man who got a piece of metal in his eye in an R.A.S.C. workshop in France and the driver whose lorry crashed in Hongkong would not have been worse off with a German rifle-bullet. It made no difference to them as St Dunstaners, of course, but they naturally felt that if they had to be blinded they would have preferred it to be in action. An accidental injury seemed so unnecessary and futile.

Perhaps the most galling of all of these early cases was that of a young officer in a Highland regiment that was about to be sent to the front line in France. It was just finishing its training at home, and in a night exercise the accident happened. The young officer led his men over the top in a charge on the supposed enemy trenches, where men of another battalion had dug themselves in, and as he jumped from the parapet a rifle was shot in his face and the blank cartridge blinded him. He had been in the Territorials for years, he was splendidly brave, and the exercise could not have been more realistic; yet he was knocked out before he had even seen the enemy, and he came to us because it was doubtful if he would ever see anything again.

Happily he did recover his sight, and a few months later he went back to his regiment. This was the sort of thing that had been rare and remarkable in the First World War but that became quite common in the Second. Great advances had been made in ophthalmic surgery, and many cases that would have been quite hopeless in the old days recovered enough useful vision to go back sometimes to the armed forces, more often to civilian life.

St Dunstan's had been founded for blinded Servicemen, and when the Second War broke out it still proclaimed that it was for blinded soldiers, sailors, and airmen. It soon became clear, however, that we ought to cast our net wider in a total war. This was not a departure from our original purpose, but merely kept it up to date. War service was no longer the exclusive task of the Armed Forces. There was the Home Front, too.

This was not so easy to define, and some people thought that the line between Servicemen and civilians had become so blurred that any distinctions would be arbitrary and unfair. Although we had ourselves admitted a few civilians in the first war, we opposed this point of view. We believed that Servicemen were still entitled to special recognition. We thought the definition of war service ought to be broadened, but not to include the whole community. Our standard of individual welfare was higher than that of the blind world generally, and we believed that a line could and should be drawn. And it was.

The women's Services, of course, ranked equally with the men's. To these were added the regular police and firemen's, and all who were serving in Civil Defence. If they were blinded as a result of war-service injury—whether on or off duty—they were eligible for full membership of St Dunstan's and lifelong care.

In an earlier chapter I told how Arnold Lawson, our ophthalmic surgeon, had rejected some who wished to enter St Dunstan's, because he thought they saw too much and that their limited vision might deteriorate in St Dunstan's. It is possible that in some cases, where the degree of blindness is influenced by psychological considerations, such deterioration might take place, but in ordinary cases there is no such fear, and, indeed, during the Second War, we admitted a small number of two classes of men—one class was those who saw too much to be classified as blind but in whose case rapid deterioration was expected; and so it was better for them to come in and see what the blind world was like before entering it. The other class consisted of those who were on the border-line of eligibility and who could be helped to rehabilitate themselves, but who did not need the full care or the lifelong care devoted to the blind ex-Serviceman. These 'border-liners' came for a week or month only and did not become permanent St Dunstaners.

Admission to our hospital was a different matter. When the Ministry of Health asked us to be prepared to take in civilian air-raid casualties we agreed to give them not only medical and surgical treatment but also the early rehabilitation and adjustment to blindness that could not wait. We asked the Ministry to provide additional accommodation for such cases and to pay ordinary hospital charges, but we would give the extra comforts and the special help and guidance that all blinded patients need. After this, however, we would have to transfer them to the care of their local authorities or of the National Institute for the Blind. A voluntary organization like St Dunstan's is responsible to its supporters, and ours had not subscribed for the training and after-care of the civilian blind. We thought this was a task for other organizations, voluntary or public.

The National Institute for the Blind thought so, too, and met the challenge splendidly. Homes of Recovery were opened for war-blinded civilians to go to learn to be blind in much the same way as Service men and women at St Dunstan's. The first of these, at Goring-on-Thames, was the beautiful home of the National Institute's Chairman, Captain Sir Beachcroft Towse, V.C., who personally directed the work. By his example he inspired these air-raid victims as he had given hope to the newly blinded soldiers in France a quarter of a century before. Nearly all those soldiers had later come to St Dunstan's, and our good relations with the N.I.B. owed much to his personality. We brought ourselves closer together when, in 1940, Sir Beachcroft Towse accepted an invitation to sit on our Council.

At the same time, our strongest bond continued to be with the British Legion. When our old Poppy Day agreement expired, in 1940, a new one was made for the next ten years. As before, we agreed not to collect funds round about Poppy Day, while the Legion did not compete with our house-to-house collections.

A fresh agreement was made also with Newington House, Edinburgh, the headquarters of the Scottish National Institution for the War Blinded. In the First World War about half the Scottish war-blinded had come to St Dunstan's, and naturally we had appealed for funds in Scotland as well as the rest of Britain. So had Newington House, which looked after the other half, and this had led to overlapping, waste of effort, and mutual ill-will. When the Second World War broke out I suggested that we should co-operate rather than compete, and Newington House readily agreed.

To-day the closest and friendliest relationship exists between our two organizations, with mutual consultation and exchange of views on all matters relating to the War-blinded.

Under our new agreement we were to issue a joint appeal, sharing the proceeds according to our responsibilities. First-war Scots would remain under the care of St Dunstan's or Newington House, as the case might be. Second-war Scots would go to St Dunstan's Hospital for medical and surgical treatment and to learn to be blind during their early days. As soon as they were fit enough for serious training, those who intended to live in Scotland would be transferred to Newington House, while the others would pass into our training establishment.

There was one exception to this. Where a blinded Scot wanted to undertake some occupation that was taught at only one of the two organizations he would go to that one for training, no matter where he intended to live. This was important, because the range of occupations taught at Newington House differed from ours even more than in the First World War. The Scottish National Institution still preferred to place its men in sheltered workshops, and they were trained in the traditional handicrafts—with some additions like wire-work, bent wire-work, and wooden toy-making. We, on the other hand, were more than ever disposed to resettlement in the sighted world, and much less inclined to regard handicrafts as an ideal means of livelihood.

With this big exception—which became increasingly important as the War went on—training at St Dunstan's did not have to be greatly changed. Few other First World War organizations were able to resume so smoothly.

Partly, of course, this was due to the fact that St Dunstan's had been a going concern throughout the years of peace. Organizations that had been stood down in 1918, and tried to take up again where they had left off, found themselves in a changed world. Socially and in many other ways they were out of date. We had been forced to move with the times by the continuous intake of new admissions, adapting ourselves as we went along.

The remarkable thing was that so little adaptation had proved necessary. The greatness of Pearson's achievement was its timelessness. None of us had been able to improve on the most important things, beginning with the braille watch. The kind and quantity of help given to each new entrant had just the same balance, nicely calculated to remove awkwardness but promote independence. Pearson's amateur psychology had not been replaced by anything more professional. In the Second War ours was probably the only organization of its kind in which specialized technical psychological treatment was not included in the rehabilitation programme as a matter of course.

The original conception of St Dunstan's survived every change—even the unforeseen, unforeseeable fact that St Dunstaners would soon be divisible into two quite separate generations. Divisible, but not divided. The new men caught the spirit of St Dunstan's from the old, and it welded them together. It had to, for there was no natural bridge. All the first-war men were roughly contemporary no matter how early or late they came in, and most of the second-war men could have been their sons.

Most first-war men had sons, and those who were in the Forces were comrades of the new St Dunstaners, another link. Within a year of the outbreak of war over three hundred and fifty of them were serving—and receiving parcels paid for by the St Dunstan's Comforts Fund. Most of the money was raised by collections, concerts, and raffles of handicraft articles made by St Dunstaners. Several of our men also put their hands in pockets that were anything but well lined, giving a worthier than usual interpretation to the saying that charity begins at home. T. Thorpe, of Torrisholme, was an example. He and his wife received their first payment of their old-age pensions on the day when one of their sons joined the Forces, and they both sent their ten shillings to the Comforts Fund. Such generosity was all the more splendid because of the Government's dour attitude towards ex-Servicemen's disability pensions.

Any pensions scheme is bound to contain some anomalies, but the inequalities of the Pensions Warrant of 1939 were startlingly basic. Some of the reforms that had been so hardly won in the First World War were abolished. There were to be no independent tribunals to which an applicant for a pension could appeal against a Ministry decision; we had gone back to the days when the Ministry was both advocate and judge. A man with children under sixteen would receive allowances for only the first three. Previously there had been no limit. If he had no pensionable children, and his wife was under forty, there would be no allowance for her. Most important of all, the basic pension was to be only 32s. 6d. per week.

The Minister gave a personal promise that there would be no cut in the pensions and allowances paid to First World War men. Their basic pension remained at 40s. a week, and their allowances were correspondingly higher. The net result was that a totally disabled man with a wife and two children received 63s. 6d. if he had fought the Kaiser and 45s. 10d. if he fought Hitler. This seemed to us a poor start to the War.

It was not, of course, an exclusively or even mainly St Dunstan's concern. On behalf of all Servicemen the British Legion immediately pressed for reform, and we marched pretty well in step with the Legion. The Government and Parliament were continually reminded of our dissatisfaction by the Legion's all-party House of Commons Committee, of which I had been an active member until 1937, when I had resigned my Parliamentary seat in order to become a Governor of the B.B.C. In April 1940 I was re-elected to the House of Commons, and in May I began a series of questions about pensions that went on all through the War and for long after.

It did not take us long to root out two of the offending pieces of discrimination against the newly disabled. The limit on the number of pensionable children was abolished, and wives under forty without children were no longer denied an allowance. But on the difference in the basic rate the Government stood firm. It defended discrimination on the grounds that the cost of living was lower than it had been in 1919, when the rate had been raised to 40s.

This was true but not the whole truth. In 1919 the index figure had been 215, as compared with 100 in 1914. During the slump in the early 'thirties the figure had dropped to 136—but the basic rate had remained at 40s. While many painful cuts in Government expenditure had been made, this was left untouched in recognition of the disabled ex-Serviceman's right to a little more than mere subsistence.

In 1939 the cost-of-living index was 155 points, and after the outbreak of war it began its steady rise. It was obvious that this war, like the last, was going to be paid for partly by inflation, which meant by pensioners and other persons with fixed incomes. This was virtually admitted by the Minister of Pensions, who hinted that the lower disability rate would be raised with the cost of living. In June 1940 the first such increase was made. With a mathematical nicety that could hardly have pleased war-depleted administrative staffs, it was raised from 32s. 6d. to 34s. 2d. We were told it would go up again if the cost of living continued to rise. The 40s. rate for First World War men remained unchanged. Shortly afterwards I asked if the Government would raise the 40s. rate to meet the rise in the cost of living, and pay the same rate to the newly disabled as the old. "No, sir," replied the Minister of Pensions. "The cost of living to-day is still considerably lower than that of 1919."

This was disturbing to say the least. As inflation was continuous, there was little doubt that in time the index figure would reach that of 1919. Then, presumably, the newly disabled would receive the same basic rate as the First World War men, but in terms of real money they would be no better off than in 1939. The 1914-18 men would have suffered the equivalent of a cut of over 32 per cent.

The unfairness of this policy lay in the fact that the national standard of living had changed completely since 1919. Salaries and wages were higher, including those of employees of the Government, and they kept in step with inflation. Everyone had already had at least one rise since the outbreak of war, including Servicemen and civil servants, the unemployed and old-age pensioners. An increase for the 1914-18 disabled was overdue. It was shocking to hear that none would be granted until the cost of living had risen a great deal higher, and I took every opportunity to protest.

Meanwhile the War had come nearer home.

Our annual Sports Day had been fixed for June and the Regatta for July, but the fighting in France put paid to all that. Now we got more of the casualties we had expected at the start. A young R.A.F. officer came in with one eye gone and the other badly damaged, and a remarkable story to tell. Flying a Hurricane over enemy territory, he met two Heinkels and shot down one, but the other put a bullet through his windscreen. A splinter destroyed one eye immediately, and another splinter severely damaged the other. He blacked out and fell several thousand feet, and then flew seventy miles back to his base and somehow managed to land. By then he could hardly see at all. Happily our surgeons saved his good eye, and he was able to go back to the R.A.F. in a ground job.

Others were not so lucky. A private of the Black Watch fighting on the Belgian frontier, had been completely blinded by fragmentation from a hand-grenade. A Yorkshireman suffered the same from an exploding bomb near the Albert Canal. Grim First World War memories were revived by a Cameronian blinded by a bursting shell at Ypres. Just for a moment we thought a line might be established in France and the old style of trench warfare return, with millions of troops bombarding each other until one side or the other was worn out by the slaughter. Then the line had gone, and the Germans were just across the Channel, only eighty miles away from Ovingdean. We heard enemy reconnaissance aircraft flying over the South Coast, and then a few bombs were dropped. Events had put our peaceful sanctuary into the front line.

Seaside hotels were filling up with troops. Gun-carriers and armoured cars were rumbling in. Pill-boxes and barbed wire were going up on the beaches. There was no room for St Dunstan's in the new fortress line of Britain. We would only be in the way. And aircraft drones and bomb-whistles, siren-wails and Ack-Ack booms were the wrong sort of music for men trying to recover peace of mind.

It was time for us to move.

14

Church Stretton

EVERY chairman, director or public man must have a secretary, and he is fortunate if he has a good one. Miss Eleanor Goole had been Sir Arthur Pearson's secretary and came to work for me when he died. A blind man needs good secretarial help even more than another, for letters must be read aloud and a great many matters must be looked at through the secretary's eyes. Miss Goole is a very remarkable wcman, and I owe her more for her great ability and loyal help than I am able to record. She stayed with me until she retired in 1955, having worked for St Dunstan's for forty years.

"I'm sorry I'm late," Miss Goole told me one morning, "but a bomb dropped on us during the night, and I couldn't get out."

She sounded perfectly composed as she told me how the bomb had blown all the windows and window-frames over her bed, blocking the door. She emphasized her good fortune, as the bomb had destroyed half the house. The incident had nothing to do with St Dunstan's, and it was by no means the first stray bomb that had dropped near by. I knew I ought to look at things from a broad and general point of view, and not be over-influenced by individual experiences. Yet this incident impressed me because it made what I knew so much more vivid and real. We began to look for a new home.

It was not easy to find. There had to be certain natural features and amenities, and it was most important that there should be room for rapid expansion if necessary. It would have to be quiet and well away from bomb-targets, yet it ought to be on a main railway line so that the men could easily travel home. We made several journeys through England and Wales before we hit on Church Stretton, in the Shropshire Hills. My wife and the St Dunstan's secretary, W. G. Askew, went and stayed at the famous Longmynd Hotel, set amid trees high up on a hill. Their enthusiasm could not have been very gratifying to the management, for they were inspecting it to see if it was suitable for requisitioning. They were especially impressed by the hard tennis courts, which would be an ideal site for temporary huts.

No one put down a red carpet for us when we said this was just what we wanted. The Army told us to keep out. The people of the locality were doubtful and apprehensive. Their "Caution—Blinded Soldiers" notices seemed to put us in the same class as dangerous dogs. We went in as gate-crashers—but that did not last long. Once we had proved that we were human after all, Church Stretton, Shrewsbury, and the whole of Shropshire made us wonderfully welcome.

At first only our training centre moved to Church Stretton, taking from Ovingdean the First World War men who had recently gone blind and the convalescent casualties from the new war. Our After-care Department was split up between London and Blackpool. St Dunstan's Hospital remained at Ovingdean, but we took over another hotel, the Concord in Blackpool, as a convalescent home. We also had to find a new home for our permanent invalids, mostly bed-ridden cases, and this problem was solved by the generosity of American friends of mine, Mr and Mrs W. V. C. Ruxton, who lent us Melplash Court, their Dorsetshire country house, for the duration of the War. As President of the British-American Ambulance Corps, William Ruxton later presented us with an ambulance. Another wonderful gift St Dunstan's received from the United States, when we were still fighting alone, was a cheque for £25,000 from the British War Relief Society. The generous Americans had no reason to think then that we should be able to help some of their men before the end of the War.

The separation of hospital from training centre did not last long. Within only a month or two the hospital also moved to the Longmynd Hotel. For a while we kept Ovingdean going on a full care and maintenance basis, so that it could be reopened at short notice, but in the end we had to give up our beautiful house. The Admiralty took it over, and it became H.M.S. *Vernon*, a naval school for instruction in under-water weapons. The Admiralty also took over West House, and incidentally, our next-door neighbour, the famous Roedean School.

Our headquarters remained in London, in spite of several German attempts to blast us out. Early in September 1940 they dropped a bomb just outside our gate. None of us was hurt, and the damage was soon tidied up.

I felt a bit better about air raids after that. The bombs announced themselves with the same whistling sound as long-distance shells, and in the same way a swift increase in noise told you when one was coming near. Because of his greater use of his sense of hearing, a blind man could also soon learn to tell the difference between the noise of the bombs and of the anti-aircraft guns. Air raids lost some of their worst terrors for me that night.

A month later we were bombed again, and this time it was a direct hit. The bomb fell on our Talking Book studios and workshop, destroying them completely. The whole building was badly damaged, and would have taken several months and a lot of money to repair. As further knocks were at least possible, we moved our offices out to Tyttenhanger Park, near St Albans.

My own house, next door to the old headquarters building, was also badly damaged, and I had to give it up as a residence. However, when the roof had been patched

Q

up it was sufficiently weatherproof to be used as an office, and I lent it to St Dunstan's for the duration for the use of our Appeals Department. "St Dunstan's, Regent's Park" was the address familiar to our friends all over the world, and I thought it important to keep this if we could.

My wife and I moved into a small house north of London with a large kitchen garden in which we became greatly interested. I had always favoured gardening as a hobby for the blind, in a theoretical way, and I knew it was popular from the letters that came in from those who accepted our standing offer of free packets of seeds. Now we joined the ranks of those who boasted that no vegetables tasted as good as those they grew themselves.

We had got off lightly compared with some, and St Dunstaners generally suffered more than their proportionate share of bombing. Many were blown out of their houses. Some were killed. All bore their misfortunes with typical courage and cheerfulness. A man who can crack jokes about being blind can see the funny side of anything. Frank Griffee, an Irish St Dunstaner in the Midlands, told me one of the best bomb stories I ever heard. He was awakened one night by a tremendous crash in the attic above his bedroom. There was no explosion, so it was presumed to be a time-bomb, and he and his family were rushed out of the house. Further investigation showed that it was not a bomb but two hundredweight of railway line that had been blown half a mile. The railway company solemnly wrote to our Irishman demanding the return of their property.

The Blitz showed that if people disliked being bombed they hated being bombed out, and there were many pathetic instances of families going back to the uninhabitable ruins of what had been their homes. Blind persons were even less inclined to be uprooted than the rest, for if they were moved away they had to learn the new local and domestic geography, and that meant a temporary reduction in their independence. So complete resettlement was only a last resort. But the first shock made most people want to go and stay with friends or relations for a few weeks, and this was something we had to arrange. When there was nowhere for them to stay we would take the St Dunstaner into one of our convalescent homes, either at Blackpool or at Melplash Court, and the Matron would take rooms near by to put the family up. Individual St Dunstaners, led by George Fallowfield, helped with offers of temporary accommodation for bombed-out comrades.

Many St Dunstaners, besides those already in A.R.P., were busy showing that they were national assets rather than liabilities. As well as digging for victory, several did a stint of roof-spotting, a job with unexpected scope for the blind. When visibility was poor enemy aircraft could only be detected by the spotter's sense of hearing; and some of our men built up local reputations for their uncanny ability to spot by sound. Others worked as fire-watchers, manning stirrup pumps when the incendiaries began to fall. A. Hayes of Nottingham teamed up with a very deaf friend, who had reduced his handicap by developing his sense of sight as we develop our hearing. Between them they had the sharpest ears and the sharpest eyes in the section, so no wonder the Chief Warden said they were the best couple he had.

Several first-war St Dunstaners enrolled in the Home Guard. They did guard-room duty, taking and sending messages, looked after armouries, and carried out a variety of other essential jobs. Sergeant-Major Lowings served for two years, mainly instructing recruits. He did not leave willingly but was discharged when physical standards were tightened up and the blind excluded. He did not qualify for a Defence Medal, as he had not served three years. One of our South Africans, James Crawford, even rejoined the Army. He enlisted in the Medical Corps as a physiotherapist, and became the first blind soldier on active service in the world.

We had indeed come a long way since the First World

War. Whenever I had to ask the Government to make special provision for the blind over some matter—there were so many new wartime regulations for civilians that I had to ask rather often—I was fortified by the thought that we were not entirely dead weight.

Many civilians came to our hospital during the 1940-41 Blitz. E.N.T., facial injuries, and minor medical and surgical conditions were treated as well as eye injuries, but most of our cases were of the kind that could draw the most benefit from the special atmosphere and facilities of our hospital. Some of the air-raid casualties we saw saved us from becoming too self-centred and concerned about the inconveniences we had suffered ourselves. To me nothing could equal the tragedy of a factory-worker in the Midlands and his family, the Lawsons, who had been enjoying themselves at a works tea-party and social one Saturday afternoon when a lone raider dropped a bomb. Many people were killed, including this man's younger child. His wife, his other child, and he himself were all blinded.

He was in the Home Guard, so he came to St Dunstan's as a Serviceman. His wife and child came with him. Sylvia Lawson, five years old, was bewildered and frightened. The mother, bereaved of one child and unable to see the other, clung to the blind daughter she could no longer look after, but who needed looking after as never before. The father was dazed and stunned. I had never seen such human misery. I doubt if St Dunstan's had been put to such a test.

When the mother had been calmed down our nurses taught her to bath her child, and that was the beginning of recovery for both of them. Within a few weeks the mother was dressing herself and the girl, knitting clothes, and learning to cook and make beds. Meanwhile the father, his mind more at rest now, was going through the normal course of training. He passed out as a telephone operator, and went back to his old firm. But the happy ending was still deferred.

An ordinary home is not the best place for bringing up a blind child. Parental love is not an adequate substitute for the skilled care the child needs. In this case, with both parents blind, it was obvious from the start that they would have to be separated from their dearly loved child. Naturally, we said nothing of this until the mother was well on the way to recovery, but as soon as humanly possible we persuaded the Lawsons to send their daughter to one of the National Institute for the Blind "Sunshine Homes." These homes for blind children had been running since 1918.

With some natural reluctance, they took our advice and sent her to the Sunshine Home at Southport, after we had assured them that their daughter could not go to a better place. We were immediately proved wrong. In the whole war only one of the Sunshine Homes was hit by a bomb, and that only once—the home at Southport, just after Sylvia Lawson had arrived. This time she escaped injury, but three nurses were killed, and the child was nervously upset. So were her parents, only much more, and they took their daughter away from the home and sent her to live with her grandmother.

The Lawsons' action was understandable, but living with Granny could not be good for the child. So I used my best efforts to get her to Chorleywood College for Girls, which she entered in 1942. Five years later she went to Henshaw's Institution for the Blind in Manchester. Trained as a telephone operator by the N.I.B., she took up a post in Warrington. After a number of operations she recovered a certain amount of sight. Now she is married and has two children, and a dreadful tragedy has an almost incredible happy ending.

Sylvia Lawson was the youngest we had at St Dunstan's. The oldest 'new boy' was Charles Edwin Beaufoy, O.B.E., who had been Mayor of Dover at the end of the First World War. He was Chief Special Constable of Britain's front-line town in 1940, when he was blinded by a cross-

Channel shell. Over seventy years old, he shook his fist at the Germans and announced that he would stay where he was. "Not until hell freezes will any Jerry keep me out of Dover," he announced. "I've promised the boys that I'll lead them in the Victory March." Before he could keep that promise he suffered a greater blow than blindness in the death of his wife. That was when he came to Church Stretton.

He came first to look round, and he did not expect to want to stay. "I'm only seventy-two," he explained. "I'm still too active to go into an institution." There was no boasting in this. Both physically and mentally, he was a good twenty-five years younger than his age.

Matron Pain took him into the lounge to meet some of the men. He went, as he admitted afterwards, expecting to find an atmosphere of gloom and depression, with everyone sitting round nursing grievances. Instead he found two men wrestling on a sofa, a group discussing horses, another man singing, and some more telling the singer to pipe down.

"This will suit me," he said, and Grandpa Beaufoy, as he was promptly christened, suited St Dunstan's. He learnt braille and typewriting, threw himself into all our activities with great enthusiasm, and capped it all by getting married again. His bride, Kathleen Perry, worked at Church Stretton Food Office, and the wedding was in the parish church. They had twelve happy years together before he died at the grand old age of eighty-six.

Grandpa Beaufoy was an exception. Most newcomers to St Dunstan's were again young men from the Forces, with a leavening of delayed-action cases from the First World War. We were less rigorously exclusive about the degree of blindness than we had been in the first war. Men who came into our hospital and—usually thanks to improved surgery—regained a limited amount of vision, were still given a modified service. These border-line cases were not blind enough to be trained as blind men, but they could not see well enough to get an ordinary sighted job. We took them under our care, gave them what special training they needed, and helped them to find suitable jobs. We thought the nation ought to look after men whose eyes had been so hurt while serving the nation that they were handicapped in the race of life. There was another point. Often the man's recovered sight was precarious, and we knew that some of these men would eventually come back blind. It would be easier for them if they already knew what St Dunstan's could do.

Church Stretton had been chosen as our wartime home with an eye on possible expansion, and it proved a good choice. Though small, the place had a marvellous talent for producing houses and sites at the right moment.

At first we grew quite slowly. Huts were put up in the grounds of Longmynd Hotel, on the lawn and the tennis courts, and the garages were converted into workshops. Our hospital was transferred to another building, Tiger Hall. A separate house was found for the V.A.D.'s, another for the teaching staff. We took over Brockhurst, a preparatory school with accommodation for about fifty, and put up more huts in the grounds. By then Longmynd Hotel had become purely residential.

Then we had to tackle the War Office, which had already requisitioned hotels and other buildings in Church Stretton that we wanted to use. At first they turned us down flat, but after some months of negotiation, and a bit of luck in cutting through red tape, we persuaded them to hand over their holdings to us. With two more hotels and several other buildings at our disposal, we carried out a complete reorganization. We put a single training school and recreation centre in the middle of the village, and used our buildings all round it purely for residence.

As in the First World War, we always tried to anticipate events. Every extension was made before it was necessary, to be ready for the casualties when they came. During the

War we had many difficulties, and doubtless made a lot of mistakes, but we never had to say "Sorry, full up," or "House full," and we never had to rush anyone through to make room for the next.

We watched closely as the first of the new generation of St Dunstaners went through the training programme that had stood us first-war men in such good stead. The first thing we discovered about these youngsters was that they were much quicker to learn. The St Dunstan's braille test had seemed a big hurdle to most of us; some of these new chaps took it in their stride.

Partly this was because the teaching was better. I do not mean that we had better teachers—far from it. Matron Dorothy Pain was Head of the Braille Room in the First World War and again in the Second. She had old St Dunstaners working under her, like Tommy Rogers and Rupert Graves. The teaching was better because the teachers were more experienced.

That was only part of the story. The other reason for the superior achievements of the new men was that most of them were better educated. They had been at school longer and learned more, they had been keener and quicker readers before they lost their sight. So they made our old braille reading test look very elementary, and we introduced an advanced test and encouraged them to go on practising until they could pass this.

I was stirred into further study myself. I had always been lucky enough to have people to read to me, and had been too busy to keep my braille up. I realized that I had never really mastered it, and now that I was even busier I set myself the task of relearning it. During the war years I raised my speed of reading three or four times, and for the first time I was able to read in braille for pleasure. I decided that I should have done this long ago, but there had been no one to urge and persuade me to go on. Most old St Dunstaners had let their braille go in the same way.

So we encouraged the new generation to keep at it, tempting them with prizes, and they became really keen. Altogether 90 per cent. tried to learn braille, 70 per cent. passed the ordinary reading test, and as many as 30 per cent. the stiff advanced test.

Although they were generally better educated than the older generation, many had left school at fourteen when they would have benefited if they had been able to stay longer—not only in earning their living, but also in using their leisure. We did what we could to provide further general education for these men, for they were going to need greater resources now for both work and play. Besides, it seemed to us reasonable that a blinded Serviceman should come out of it with at least a better education.

Early in the War a boy in the Home Guard, W. H. Cowing, was blinded by an incendiary bomb while on patrol in the street. He was seventeen when he came to St Dunstan's. The youngest of a family of fourteen, he had been earning his living as a shop assistant for three years. We continued his schooling from where it had been broken off. So through being blinded he got a secondary education that he would not have had otherwise. That does not entitle anyone to call him lucky. He is still vastly more handicapped than a sighted person who never went to school. Happily, he has overcome his handicap and is a hard-working, cheerful telephone operator in Barclays Bank.

Cowing was not the youngest man we had. Michael Oliver, of West Wickham, was blinded while on manœuvres with the A.T.C. at the age of thirteen. He went to Worcester College and the N.I.B. College at Bridgnorth, and at twenty he was earning his living as a shorthand-typist.

Cowing and Oliver were exceptional cases, and even men in their early twenties could not easily be put back into the schoolroom. But we provided general instruction in subjects like English, history, geography, and current affairs, and special individual courses were arranged in anything from Latin to economics. Blinded servicewomen took their full part, and in addition were trained in domestic work, including cooking, washing, ironing, and sewing.

With typewriting and braille, all this general instruction was part of the preliminary training. Handiwork was mixed in with brainwork, and plenty of time was allowed for the traditional crafts. The range was larger than in the First World War, and included weaving and leather-work, metal and plastic model-making, and "Meccano" as well as basketry, carpentry, rug-making, and string-netting. But the main innovation was that instruction in handicrafts was no longer regarded as vocational.

This was the main difference in our training in the Second World War. Home handicrafts had always needed to be subsidized, and they had become increasingly uneconomical in the years between the wars. They had been nearly knocked out of our list of trades by the competition of the machine. They had become merely paying hobbies rather than jobs.

Paradoxically, they boomed during the War. As we had expected, they benefited from the shortages of labour and goods, and for the first time they actually paid their way. The men also had the satisfaction of doing their bit in the War. Instead of fancy baskets for West End shops they were making mats for anti-aircraft guns. The demand was tremendous, and most of the civilian blind workshops in the country were doing overtime.

Even purchase tax proved a blessing in disguise. Manufacturers with a turnover of less than £2000 a year were exempted from this, so that our home workers did not have to collect any tax on the goods they sold themselves. Of course, St Dunstan's itself had a big turnover, so goods sold from Raglan Street had to carry tax. So had the same sort of goods sold in ordinary shops, and this gave our men a big trading advantage in local sales. We encouraged them to work for local orders, which not only helped themselves but saved us the cost of carriage and handling the finished goods.

Another thing that stimulated sales was the growing shortage of raw materials, although this boomeranged on us as the War went on. We bought wherever we could, but quite soon many materials were unobtainable through normal channels. This reduced competition still further, but it also meant that we had to start running down our stocks. We had to ration some materials to eke them out.

The handicraft boom was a bubble that would burst with the end of the War, and with more mechanization in industry we expected that when it reverted to a paying hobby it would pay less than before. So we did not encourage new men to become home workers. Hardly any of them wanted to be, except a few who were too severely disabled for any kind of outside work—and a St Dunstaner had to be really hard hit for that.

Other hospitals taught handicrafts as occupational therapy, but their function for our men was more important. They taught the men to use their hands as eyes, to see with their finger-tips.

The 'chippy' shop, where Frank Ralph taught carpentry, was one of the most popular workshops, and the most generally useful. St Dunstaners going home for a break in their training loved to astonish their families by taking a hammer and chisel and doing some odd job about the house. The cobbler's shop, under Sidney Kitson, was also a busy place, although boot-repairing was no longer the popular trade it had been in the old days.

A special portion of the workshops was set aside for the building of models using the well-known children's "Meccano" apparatus and mechanisms. Bridges, models of the Eiffel Tower, cranes, trolleys, and all kinds of familiar objects were put together, and this formed a most excellent way of teaching young blinded men how to use their fingers and simple tools.

The "Meccano" shop also served a less obvious but very

important purpose. It helped us to advise a man on a suitable job.

First there had to be jobs, and the growing shortage of labour opened up new possibilities. This seemed to be our chance for getting a foothold in open industry. If we were to stay there permanently, after the War, we needed to make sure the jobs were right for our men. With these thoughts I approached leaders of industry, commerce, and the Press, and we met in June 1940 and set up the St Dunstan's Research Advisory Committee under the Chairmanship of Major the Hon. J. J. Astor, M.P., now Lord Astor of Hever. The chemical industry was represented by Lord McGowan and the engineering industry by Lord Nuffield, and everyone showed the utmost goodwill. The newly formed research committee at once set up a smaller executive committee of which I was chairman, to carry out investigations in a variety of factories all over the country.

While this research was going on the first of the new men were already undergoing vocational training.

As in the 1914-18 War, the first question was always whether a man could go back to his old job, either as it was or in a modified form. There was no difficulty in the case of Lieutenant Esmond Knight, R.N.V.R., who was blinded on the *Prince of Wales* in the famous action against the *Bismarck*. The only problem he set us was the impossible one of finding someone to take his place in our Dramatic Society when he left. A well-known stage and film actor before he was blinded, he has won still greater fame since. The first blind man to play sighted parts on the stage or screen, he took part recently in a film that really rolled back the years. It was *Sink the Bismarck*, and he had the uncanny experience of reliving the action in which he was blinded.

Private K. B. Sleigh, A.T.S. (F.A.N.Y.), came in at the same time, blinded in an air raid. A professional singer before the War, Beryl Sleigh lifted our Musical Society right out of the amateur class before she went back to her former career.

Captain R. W. Slatter was the first blind Army Welfare Officer. Another St Dunstaner who went back to his arm of the Service was Lieutenant-Commander Robin Buckley, the first naval officer to lose his sight in the War. A torpedo officer with fourteen years' service—part of it with H.M.S. *Vernon* at Portsmouth—Buckley was in the battle of Crete. He was decorated with the George Medal for his coolness and courage in dismantling an enemy explosive of a novel type. After training at St Dunstan's he went back to the Navy as a lecturer and instructor. He again served with H.M.S. *Vernon* at Portsmouth, and became Command School Liaison Officer on the staff of the C.I.C. After many more years of valuable service he joined the staff of St Dunstan's as Assistant Appeals Organizer, later taking over the joint duties of Appeals and Publicity Officer. Buckley had the very good fortune to follow Mr E. Stanford, C.B.E., who for nearly twenty years had been head of our Appeals Department, where he had been extremely successful. Mr Stanford continues to sit on our Appeals Committee and our debt to him is a great one.

Another to join our staff was Lieutenant Peter Matthews who took charge of our Estate Department, a post in which he, too, was following his pre-war profession as a chartered surveyor.

Our first R.A.F. officer, Flying Officer E. K. Kitson, was the first of the new generation of St Dunstaners to go in for a professional career. Blinded in action in 1940, he undertook preliminary economics and law, reading at Church Stretton before going to Corpus Christi College at Cambridge University. He graduated brilliantly in 1944 with a first-class Honours degree, and is now a legal officer in the Civil Service.

Rifleman H. Preedy and Fusilier Ernest Russell were the first two men of the new generation to go out and earn their living, both as telephone operators. Preedy, a London Scot, went on the exchange of a large public utility company, and Russell to Leeds Civic Hall.

Russell had spoken the commentary in a documentary film on St Dunstan's, and he never lived it down. Still, when it was shown in Leeds he agreed to a request to make a personal appearance at the cinema—with the result that the Mayor sent us a cheque for nearly £3000. Russell quickly became one of the leading lights in the Leeds Group of the British Legion, and I doubt if any St Dunstaner has worked harder for the benefit of all ex-Servicemen.

It was no accident that Preedy and Russell were both trained in telephone-operating, for none of our first-war careers had worked out better. The hundred-odd men we had trained in this job had earned a great reputation, and big firms like Shell-Mex and Barclays Bank kept asking for more. The drop-shutter system was still holding its own against the light-flashing method. It was actually suitable for men and women, and it was an adequately paid job for life.

Another outstandingly successful occupation taken up by St Dunstaners was massage, or physiotherapy as it is now called. The course had become much longer, the examinations much stiffer; but the rewards were higher, and the fact that our men were generally better educated meant that more of them could go in for this cultured profession.

Our first man to qualify, Douglas Calder, began his course before Preedy and Russell started to learn telephone-operating, but his training took much longer than theirs. A Scot from Edinburgh, he stayed with us under our agreement with Newington House. With Edmund Toft teaching, he did the first year of his massage course—including anatomy, with the help of a skeleton affectionately known as Clarence—at Church Stretton. He went through his preliminary training in typewriting and braille at the same time. He had to pass both reading and writing tests in braille before he could be admitted to the N.I.B. School of Massage, where he went for the remaining two years of the course.

A long training for a man impatient to earn his living, but well worth it. When Edmund Toft died another first-war St Dunstaner, Jock Steel, took over, and by the end of the War we had fifty men and women either trained or under training.

Barbara Bell, our first woman physiotherapist, passed her finals early in 1946.

Calder set them all a brilliant example, and was elected to the Council of the Chartered Society of Physiotherapy only a few years after qualifying. He used to go regularly to Wimbledon to massage the leading tennis players, and has played a big part in raising the reputation of War-blinded physiotherapists even higher than it was in Edmund Toft's day.

Shopkeeping had proved another success. As in the First World War, we gave special consideration to men with additional handicaps, like the loss of a limb. We helped others who seemed to have the necessary qualities, setting them up in business under a special trustee scheme.

It worked like this. Firstly, we gave the man a special course of training at St Dunstan's, including book-keeping and economics, buying and selling, and human relation-ships. Then we bought a shop and put his name on it, but we did not give it to him. For the first few years he worked as manager, paying a modest interest on the sum we had spent but being credited with the whole of the profits after this was paid. These profits were not all handed over to him, part of them being held in reserve. An expert on our staff visited him monthly to take stock, examine his books, and give him advice. After a few years he could begin to buy the business from us out of his accumulated reserve, on easy terms. This thoroughly businesslike arrangement has worked extraordinarily well, and we have seventy-two successful shopkeepers to-day.

The fourth highly successful occupation for St Dunstaners of the First World War was poultry-farming, but in the second war this was nothing like as popular. Partly this was because it was much more difficult to start a smallholding, owing to the rationing of animal feeding-stuffs and the Government restrictions on new entrants into the profession. But that was not the whole story—if there had been any great desire for this healthy outdoor life I imagine I would have campaigned for our men.

After the War we ran a training farm at South Mimms for a while. The course included instruction in keeping pigs and other small livestock besides poultry, and growing fruit and vegetables. A few men were enthusiastic and became highly successful, but we closed the farm early in 1949 for lack of recruits. After that individuals who wanted the training were sent to Plumpton Agricultural College, and this arrangement worked very well.

I suppose the main reason for the decline of interest in poultry-farming was that there were more attractive alternatives. You have to work jolly hard before you get much out of it. It is easier to go into a factory and earn good money right away.

The factory gates began to open to us in 1941. The Research Committee set up the previous year met with few of the objections that had foiled our attempts to break in before the War, and many jobs for which sight had previously been considered essential were now thought to be well within the scope of the blind. Industry generally was ready and even eager to give the blind a chance.

We in our turn were determined that the chance should not be muffed. Employers' requirements are naturally lowered when labour is scarce. Our task was to find our men jobs for life, not just for the duration of the War. We were delighted to have them employed in sighted men's jobs, but in the long run they would be better off out of it unless they could work equally well.

So we did not rush into industry, but entered carefully.

We investigated each possible job very thoroughly before we approved it, and the first men we proposed for factory work were all hand-picked. They had to be fit and strong, able to do a full day's work on the bench without continually going sick. They had to be hard-working, cheerful, and congenial—sociable chaps, good mixers, who would be happy and popular in the community life of a factory.

These were the main qualifications, but there were two other important points. One was that the job generally had to be within daily reach of the man's home, for it was already almost impossible to find new houses in strange towns. The other was that we would not encourage any man to give up an adequate permanent job, even if factory work was better paid. The whole thing was experimental. We hoped it would open up tremendous new possibilities of employment for St Dunstaners and the blind world at large, but we could not ignore the fact that it might be an utter flop.

Craftsmen from the First World War who were still in their early forties seemed the right men to invite into the pilot scheme. Basketry and mat-making were not adequate jobs, and they could always go back to them anyway. In some cases craftsmen were being forced on to short time through lack of material. Timber was scarce, like everything else, and our joiners had to curtail their work considerably. One of these, T. W. Chamberlain, was our first man to go into an aircraft factory. That was in June 1941. He was employed in the Inspection Department, where all the parts of the aircraft were examined for faults before assembly. First he was put on inspecting bolts and nuts and spar plates. He soon got the feel of it, although he had never seen a snap gauge or plug gauge in his life. Then he was trusted with the examination of other parts, such as castings and tubes. Soon he had enough variety of work to avoid any danger of boredom.

Chamberlain was a success, both at his work and among his work-mates. Paddy Ashe, another first-war man, soon

R

joined him, and he was followed by two men from the Second World War. One was W. N. Stephenson, a Petty Officer Sailmaker already in his forties, who had served twenty-six years in the Navy when he was blinded in the battle of Narvik. The other was Paddy Campbell, of the Royal Irish Fusiliers, the first Irishman of the War to come to St Dunstan's. These two were put on assembly, and worked on the same bench. You can imagine how we all felt when Paddy was asked in a broadcast how he managed to fit the most delicate instruments into aircraft panels at a faster rate than that of the sighted worker whose place he had taken.

Soon there were eight St Dunstaners working at this aircraft factory, all on equal terms with the sighted workers and at least as quick and efficient. It was not our policy to concentrate our men in a single factory, however—on the contrary, we thought it better if there was just one blind man among hundreds of sighted workers. The reason for this exception was that the employers, the Miles brothers, were exceptionally keen on helping the disabled to do factory work.

The goodwill of enlightened employers was vital to us, for at first the men had to be trained on the job. Once the scheme had proved successful we put up a new and bigger machine shop at Church Stretton to train the men ourselves. Our first industrial hut included a capstan lathe, a router, and an outfit for upholstery. Men whose aptitudes had been noted in the "Meccano" shop, while they were doing their preliminary training, came in and learnt to operate lathes, drills, and presses with something of the normal factory atmosphere and background noise. Often a job was found for a man before he had finished training, and then he could receive instruction in the precise operation he would have to do at the factory.

Some men had the advantage of previous experience. Stoker Petty Officer Richard Dufton, for example, had been blinded in action just as he was completing a special two-year Mechanicians' Course. A man with high engineering attainments, he was soon doing the responsible work of progress-chaser, following special jobs through, dealing with hold-ups, and keeping production moving. He did not have to worry about his job after the War was over. He became Chief Designer to the Miles Martin Pen Company, and produced the "Biro" ball-point-pen. Later he supervised the mechanical and physical testing side of the business. He worked with a braille dictionary of metals and other reference books in braille, and a set of special precision instruments that St Dunstan's supplied. In 1960 he gained his Associate Membership of the Institution of Mechanical Engineers. Shortly before this St Dunstan's had lost the services of its adviser on research matters. Dick Dufton's professional qualifications and his valuable years of industrial experience in research and production suggested him to us as an ideal person to continue this work, and in March 1961, he was appointed Director of Research at St Dunstan's. He also acts as the executive officer of our Scientific Committee and of our Development Workshops Committee, under the Chairmanship of Air Commodore Dacre, and advises us on aids for use in the technical training and employment of St Dunstaners.

Dufton was not our first A.M.I.Mech.E., but the case of Tufnell was slightly different. He had already passed the equivalent of the intermediate examination before he joined the R.A.F. One eye was destroyed when he was shot down, and the other emerged with a pin-point of sight so limited that he could read only one letter at a time. At St Dunstan's he was coached for his finals. With the co-operation of the Institution he was provided with a special desk and light and a special copy of the book of logarithms, photographed up to pages a yard square so he could 'look up a log.' (In fact, the examination paper did not contain a question involving a logarithm.) He passed, and found employment with the Bristol Aircraft Company, rising to principal P.R.O. engineer.

Ray Benson of Farnborough, who came to us long after the War, followed the same trail. Blinded while on research work at Guided Weapons Experimental Range, in Australia, in 1953, he came to St Dunstan's for the usual training, and then returned to the Royal Aircraft Establishment to continue research work. Eventually he also gained his A.M.I.Mech.E.

Dufton, Tufnell, and Benson each had the advantage of a good start before being blinded, but most men had to learn from scratch. Our confidence in them was high to start with, yet sometimes they surprised even us. The question Paddy Campbell had been asked could have been put to many more. Why was their output rate so often higher than that of the sighted men?

Partly the reason was that they had undergone a more thorough training. Like our telephone operators, they took their work more seriously. Even simple repetitive jobs demanded—and received—great attention and care. Then there was the feeling of helping to win the War. Most men went into aircraft or munitions factories, and it was a great moment for them when they were given a part in preparing the weapons that were going to defeat the enemy. When the War was still to be won, "You've done your bit" was the last kind of compliment a St Dunstaner liked to hear. Finally there was the fact that they liked the life.

The factory experiment was a success in more than economic terms. The men were not only earning a good wage, sharing the work of sighted men and getting the rate for the job. They were also thoroughly enjoying it. A blind man is essentially a companionable person, and the community life of a factory could have been made for him. The camaraderie of the workers and the social activities that go on in any big firm gave the blind man something he was bound to miss while making mats or baskets in his own home. By the home-handicraft system Pearson had emancipated the blind from sheltered workshops, islands of sightlessness set apart from the world. With their entry into open industry their return to the community was complete.

We were still conservative in our placements. The men had too much trust in our advice and judgments for us to gamble with their future. However successful our men were during the War, there was still the possibility that the whole scheme would collapse with the return of normal labour after demobilization. So our placing officers continued to apply strict standards in selection, both for the sake of individuals and for the reputation as factory workers of St Dunstaners in general.

In spite of our caution in placement, we had over a hundred men working in factories by the end of 1942. The number increased steadily as the War went on, and so did the range of jobs taken on. We kept a small but good research team looking for possible new activities all the time.

We were not alone in all this. The National Institute for the Blind had been seeking similar opportunities, and factories began to take in the civilian as well as the ex-Service blind. We welcomed this, and it was to our benefit as well as theirs. If we had blazed a trail for the rest of the blind world, it was in our interests to encourage others to follow. With those who looked after the civilian blind, and who were equally concerned about securing permanent factory employment after the War, we had a good measure of common cause.

We were both affected, therefore, by the Disabled Persons (Employment) Bill, 1944, which compelled every employer of more than twenty workers to employ a quota or percentage of persons who were disabled. In the House of Commons I called this humane piece of legislation a milestone in our social history, and said it was probably the greatest single action that had ever been taken to give security and happiness to disabled persons. It covered all disabled persons, not only the blind, but it was bound to be a powerful aid to our men in factories when the labour shortage ended. If there were again more men than jobs an employer might discharge a blind worker in favour of a sighted man—but he would think twice before replacing him with another disabled worker of unknown worth. If their work was satisfactory blind men in factories would probably be kept on as part of the firm's disabled persons quota.

While we shared with the N.I.B. in rejoicing over the new Bill, we also shared the British Legion's disappointment over its failure to give any preference to disabled ex-Servicemen. At the Second Reading I asked the Minister of Labour, Ernest Bevin, to write a preference into the Bill, but he refused. He said that employers would be entitled to engage ex-Servicemen as a preference if they wished, but that was as far as he would go.

We then had a council of war with the British Legion, and agreed to use all possible pressure to make the Minister change his mind. I wrote to all the Members of the House of Commons branch of the Legion, and set about organizing a body of opinion in the House. We went into action on the Committee Stage of the Bill. Mr Bevin promised that the Ministry of Labour would give ex-Servicemen an administrative preference. Lady Apsley, Chairman of the Women's Section of the Legion, exclaimed that ever since the days of Agincourt people had had short memories of the war-disabled when the fighting was over, and demanded a guarantee. When Mr Bevin said he hoped priority for the ex-Serviceman would always be the policy of the Ministry of Labour, I said that this could only be ensured by changing the Bill. The Minister tried to placate the House, but we kept up the pressure until at last he gave way and agreed to put the preference in the Bill. It was a victory for us and, I think, for the British kind of democracy.

Sport played as big a part in training at Church Stretton as it had twenty-five years before in Regent's Park, and again the older generation helped the new to find their feet. We had all the same games as in the first war, and a few new ones. Only in one thing were the new men worse off, and that was in rowing. There was no lake at Church Stretton, and by comparison the River Severn was a long way away. Rowing there had to be limited to one afternoon a week. The men were coxed by boys from Shrewsbury School, all splendid youngsters who gladly gave up their free time.

The facilities for swimming, on the other hand, were better. From the summer of 1942, when we took over Brockhurst Preparatory School, we had our own pool. So while we had no regatta, water events—including diving for plates—became part of our annual sports day.

The other events were much as before—sprints, standing long jump, throwing the discus and cricket ball, and the rest. There were a few additional novelty events, such as lighting the candle and pillow-fighting on the greasy pole, but in general the picture was hardly changed. The tug-of-war was again a house competition, a form that was peculiarly suited to St Dunstan's. Because of their desire for companionship, blind men like team sports best. And while everyone pays at least lip-service to the ideal of the game being more important than the result, for us this is literally true. Winning and losing are unimportant beside the exercise, the comradeship, and the sociability of it all. Of course, we puffed our chests out a bit harder when our relay team beat the Army and the R.A.F. on equal terms—but that was a victory for St Dunstan's, yet one more proof to the world that the blind can do anything but see.

Tandem cycling was as popular as ever. We had several machines, and a tandem club was formed. Again sociability was the keynote, with rides to Ludlow and picnics on the way. This did not stop individual men from going off alone with their escorts, the traditional start to a St Dunstan's romance. Other men preferred a horse. A newer form of exercise was climbing, with Tommy Rogers the moving spirit of the brightly named Salopian Alpine Club.

Individuals took up bowls, golf, and fishing, and later fencing was added to the list. Almost everyone played our brand of football, kicking for goal. In the gym we had a punchball, wall-bars, a rowing machine and a wrestling mat. It was all done for fun, and it was just as valuable as the classroom and workshop.

There were many outings, like weekly trips to Shrewsbury to the cinema, and visits to Wolverhampton and Birmingham for a show or a play. Another popular outdoor entertainment was the organized treasure-hunt.

Indoor entertainments were on a much bigger scale than in the first war. Edmund Toft started off a new debating society, and the standard of speaking was far higher than ours had been. Darts was wildly popular, and so was dominoes; while of card games cribbage became all the rage. There were also many new recruits to our Bridge Club, which was invited to Harrogate in February 1941, and more than held its own in a series of matches and drives. Yorkshire hospitality being what it is, this led to the institution of the annual Harrogate Bridge Week.

Our Dramatic Society flourished under the guidance of Lady Buckmaster, who taught braille. A member of the British Drama League, "Lady B," as everyone called her, had an uncanny flair for spotting dramatic talent. Most of the plays we did were thrillers, with at least one murder on the stage.

Dancing was again the most popular indoor entertainment of all. Our men were invited to dances at near-by Army and R.A.F. units and in the village hall, and we gave regular dances ourselves. We had our own band, of course. Trumpets were blaring and drums crashing before anyone had passed the first braille test. It has been said that if you put eleven Britons on a desert island their first action would be to form a football team. That's nothing: you only need two St Dunstaners for a jazz band to be formed.

Leslie White, a first-war St Dunstaner teaching braille, organized our first breaking-up concert, and, of course, it became an annual event. The men were so keen on music, of one sort and another, that at the end of 1943 I decided we needed a professional to take charge. I conferred with Henry Hall, our Honorary Musical Adviser for many years, and as a result Claude Bampton was appointed Director of Music. A truck-load of instruments arrived at the same time. The theory of music, the piano, and almost every other instrument were taught.

New bands soon sprang up all over the place. We had our own saxophone quintet and an accordion band. There were the St Dunstan's Hawaiian Serenaders and the St Dunstan's Rumba Band—very popular, this, for the instruments were light and quickly learnt. There were countless St Dunstan's Dance Bands. We also had a very fine quartet, an all-steel outfit—I mean Jock Steel, the head instructor of St Dunstan's Massage School. Jock was nearly as expert on counterpoint as on anatomy and his wife and two daughters shared his interest. The four of them put on eighteenth-century clothes and wigs and played us into an eighteenth-century drawing-room.

All this musical activity led to bigger and better concerts, and soon the St Dunstan's Fol de Rols took the stage. Ambitious shows like big revues were put on. One of our masseurs, Jeff Bond, became a first-class conjurer and also wrote many of the topical numbers with Claude Bampton. We had several good comedians, and for cross-talk acts they nearly all paired off old-war men with new. These comic acts bridged the gap between the two generations by laughing at it.

We were nearly always short of girls, for the happy reason that very few were blinded. Even to-day, when the toll must be complete, there are only twenty-eight from the Women's Services. Our matchless contralto, Beryl Sleigh, came very early in the War, and was followed by a lovely Welsh soprano, Gwen Obern, who was injured in an ordnance factory. So was Violet Formstone, of Liverpool, who played accordion solos. These three girls were not lost to us when they left St Dunstan's, but came back to take part in every concert. Violet missed one, but it was not her fault. The doctors insisted on taking her appendix out. At first she refused to let them, on the grounds that the concert could not be postponed for her appendix, but an operation could be done any time. She had, perhaps, an over-casual attitude to operations, but then she had already had twenty-eight. That was four more than Gwen Obern had had at the time. These brave girls were too cheerful to deserve sympathy. Their proper due was admiration.

Church Stretton could not be another Ovingdean, which had been designed and built specially for the blind. It could be, and was, another Regent's Park.

We had to improvise and adapt as we went along. The beautiful grounds of the Longmynd Hotel would do the men no good if they had to clutch a girl's arm when they went for a walk, so we put guiding wires along the footpaths, with projections to give warning of roads and gateways ahead. We had a relief map made of the surrounding countryside, and a model of the buildings of the Training Centre on the same lines as the model of Ovingdean. Of course, there were a few stumbles and tumbles, but a fit man could not be called St Dunstan's-trained until he had learnt to get about on his own.

As I walked through the grounds I would hear sounds—the occasional tap of a stick on a wire, the snatch of a song, a brief whistle—that evoked memories of the original St Dunstan's Lodge. It was still the same motor-horn business, the warning of one's approach to the other chap coming along the wire. History repeated itself in all sorts of other little ways. There were the same jokes about braille and bones and V.A.D.'s, the same anecdotes about well-meaning but foolish strangers who thought we had lost our brains as well as our sight. There were the same arguments about dark glasses and white sticks—although I found that fewer St Dunstaners shared my dislike of these things than in the past. Richard King Huskinson re-appeared, parked his caravan in the grounds, and helped many newcomers to learn the ropes. "Mr H," as they called him, was as popular at Church Stretton as he had been at Regent's Park. It was good to hear the voice of my former co-editor of the *St Dunstan's Review* again.

The value of having old St Dunstaners as instructors proved itself completely, not only in the classroom and workshops but also in games and entertainments, in our whole social and community life. To take further advantage of this feeling of kinship between the two generations I arranged for two beds to be set aside each week-end for distinguished old St Dunstaners to come and visit us and mix with the new men. By distinguished I did not mean merely men who had received honours or decorations, or who had gained professional or academic qualifications. I meant any old St Dunstaner who had distinguished him-self by going back into the world and leading a happy and successful life. I wanted the new men to meet physio-therapists and masseurs, shopkeepers and the more recently started factory workers, men who had been quite ordinary until the challenge of blindness had stirred them to call up reserves of strength and character that perhaps most ordi-nary people have but rarely need to use.

Not all the new St Dunstaners were second-generation men. Men who had fought in the First World War were still going blind through the delayed effects of mustard gas. They had just the same treatment as their juniors, and this helped to keep the single-community spirit. I have said before that St Dunstaners are not saints, but have normal individual likes and dislikes. This did not matter so long as the antipathies remained individual, and did not coalesce into two age-groups. Much of our strength lay in our unity, in our feeling that we all belonged to the same family.

When we first pitched camp in Church Stretton Miss Dorothy Pain was our Matron-Commandant and in charge of pretty well everything. In the summer of 1941, when we were really getting under way, we appointed a Director of Training. The man who took on the job was I. M. Bankes-Williams, an old soldier and a former science master at Harrow School with experience in games and dramatics and a weakness for carpentry. His brilliant scholastic record was not held against him. "Oh," said the first St Dunstaner he interviewed, "you're D.T.'s, aren't you?" Bankes-Williams dined out on this story for years.

He ran the whole of our extensive programme for three years. Then the job was split, and he became Director of Education. Air Commodore G. B. Dacre, C.B.E., D.S.O., took over as Commandant, leaving Dorothy Pain free to give all her time to the demanding work of Matron. Dacre had had a distinguished career in the Air Force, which included a three-year appointment as Air Officer Commanding R.A.F. Halton, the principal function of which was training R.A.F. apprentices, so that he was accustomed to the organization, training, and handling of young Service-men. Bankes-Williams left us a few months later, much in his debt. He became Headmaster of Wellington School, Somerset. Shortly after Dacre's arrival we were discussing indoor and outdoor sports when he suggested rifle-shooting. This interested me keenly. I had often wondered about the possibilities of rifle-shooting for the blind, but the practical difficulties had seemed too great.

"How would you aim?" I asked.

"By hearing. You have an ordinary standard target to shoot at," Dacre explained, "and at an angle from the line of fire is a photo-electric target, which is excited by a beam of light projected at an angle from the rifle. The marksman

wears a pair of earphones and hears a difference of intensity
of noise, or a different kind of noise, according to the part
of the target he is aiming at."

A week or two later I had a letter from an old St
Dunstaner, Charles Temperton, which gave us further
food for thought. "I must tell you that I am a first-class
shot with an air rifle, with someone knocking the object
which I have to hit," he wrote. "It is not so dangerous as
you think. I use potatoes for pellets—not whole ones,
of course. I asked my boy, Dennis, to fire at my hand to
see if it hurt much. It didn't, so I asked him if he would put
his hand up and let me try to hit his left hand, making a
noise with his thumb and finger. I am pleased to say I hit
his hand every time."

I could not help wondering if Dennis was equally
pleased. Meanwhile I asked our Research Engineer to
look into Dacre's idea.

We had a Chaplain before we had a Chapel, and he was
another link between the new men and the old. After
twenty years' parish work the Rev. Andrew Nugee came
back to St Dunstan's, not to learn but to teach; or, as he
put it the first time he preached, to serve. If his first
sermon went down well, we were even more impressed by
the way he read the Lessons. There was not one slip, not
an unnecessary pause, and we only felt ashamed that our
own braille reading was still so bad.

The first St Dunstaner to be ordained in the Second War
was, rather oddly, a first-war man. Dennis Pettit, blinded
soon after his twenty-first birthday, had left St Dunstan's
as a shorthand-typist in 1918. He worked at this job—
contentedly, as I thought—for seventeen years, and then
came and told me he was not contented at all. His discontent was of the kind that has been called divine. He
wanted to do something more useful and valuable in the
world.

He already had a splendid record of voluntary service.

He had been an active member of Toc H for many years, and for most of the time he had been both Branch and District Chairman. "Have you thought of the Church?" I asked. If he had he had thought it beyond his reach, for he had received only an elementary education as a boy. But he had the vocation all right, and the next step was to find out if he had the ability. I suggested that he should study in the evenings with a view to taking the London Matriculation, keeping on at his job during the day. So he got the necessary braille text-books, his wife and friends read to him in the evenings, and finally he had a little help from a coach. Two years after seeing me he took the examination and passed.

After this remarkable feat there was no room for any doubt of his talent or industry. A sympathetic bishop told me he would ordain Pettit if he passed the examinations, so he gave up his job and entered a Theological College. He was ordained in 1943, a quarter of a century after he was blinded, a very valuable if unexpected addition to the Church of England.

Not long after this a newly blinded man asked me to advise him whether or not to enter the Church. It was our first meeting. He had just come into our hospital, and I was giving him the usual braille watch. A South African by birth, Michael Norman had been training to be a land agent, and his blindness was not likely to be any greater handicap to that than to the work of a priest. But he had the vocation, like Dennis Pettit and Andrew Nugee, whom he soon met. After training at St Dunstan's Norman went to Cambridge University, where he took a B.A. Honours degree, and then entered Westcott House Theological College. After ordination in Canterbury Cathedral he worked in an English parish for two or three years, and then returned to South Africa with his Canadian wife. He started a new parish outside Cape Town, where he and his parishioners have built and paid for their own church. Norman tells me that his one handicap, which annoys him greatly, is the Colour legislation in South Africa, which forbids marriage between whites and 'coloureds' or Africans—thus rendering it impossible for him to conduct any marriage service without the help of another priest, because he cannot himself see the colour of the bride and bridegroom. Representations from the Archbishop of Cape Town and from me have been unavailing.

I have said that we delayed launching a fresh appeal for funds in Britain until the first casualties came. From then on we appealed vigorously, and the public response was wonderfully generous. Our world-wide collections reached a record figure, and the record was broken regularly each year of the War. In spite of our great new expenditure and heavy new commitments, our financial position became strong enough for us to achieve one of my oldest ambitions. On April 17, 1944, we were able to write 220 letters, one each to all the first-war St Dunstaners who did not receive the full 100 per cent. Government disability pension, to tell them that for the rest of their lives St Dunstan's would make up their money in full. Some of these men were getting a 70 per cent. or 60 per cent. disability pension, and some none at all. We had always given the latter an allowance equal to a 50 per cent. pension, which was all we felt we could afford without taking some risk on our existing commitments. We were overjoyed when we were at last able to make up every man's pension to the level of 100 per cent. I do not think any organization for ex-Servicemen had ever done anything like it.

However diffident they were about accepting help themselves, St Dunstaners were ruthlessly efficient in extracting money for any other cause. Some of our greatest achievements were the annual summer fêtes held to support the big national money-raising campaigns—War Weapons Week in 1941, Warships Week in 1942, Wings for Victory in 1943, Salute the Soldier in 1944.

These were preceded by house-to-house canvassing of the village and advance sales of raffle tickets. Church

Stretton was a small place, but the people were big-hearted, and this got us off to a good start. On the day of the fête St Dunstan's was thrown open to the public, who came with open pockets and left with empty ones. "It's sheer robbery!" one of our smartest salesmen assured his customers cheerfully—but it wasn't, for they had a good time. We gave them home-grown variety concerts in the afternoon, and dancing and cabaret in the evening. There were side-shows and competitions, games and amusements, fortune-tellers and refreshments, and the whole thing was run by St Dunstaners and the staff. We showed them round the hospital and the training centre, and they could dictate a slogan to a shorthand pupil and carry away half a yard or so of braille—at sixpence a time. Altogether we raised several hundreds of pounds. Thousands of pounds were raked in at the mock auction, the high-spot of the show, where the highest bidder received not only the object auctioned but also Savings Certificates to the amount of his bid. It was all great fun, and we went to bed happy in the thought that we had done another little bit towards finishing off the War. St Dunstaners have no monopoly of patriotism, but they like to feel they have done right by the nation—even when, perhaps, the nation has not always done quite right by them. It is worth remembering that St Dunstaners were still going all out in the war effort at a time when they had every reason to feel aggrieved. The Government was still not being exactly profligate over the matter of pensions.

Between June 1940 and February 1942 nothing went up except the cost of living. The basic rates were still 34s. 2d. for the newly disabled and 40s. for the old. I continued to urge that they should be paid the same, and that this should be substantially more than 40s. The British Legion, at its Annual Conference in 1941, resolved that they should all be paid 40s. A Resolution that the Legion should seek to increase this basic rate was unaccountably lost. This was a comfort to the Government and a great setback to us. I immediately urged all St Dunstaners who were also members of the Legion to use their influence to change this opinion before the next Annual Conference, but meanwhile I could hardly hope for an early increase for the 1914-18 men.

So for the time being I concentrated on two things. One was to get the newly disabled put on the same basis as the 1914-18 men. The other was to seek family allowances for men who married and had children after they were wounded. As in the First World War, the State paid allowances for wives only if they were married, and for children only if they were born or at least conceived before the man was disabled. Therefore if a man married afterwards—as we rightly encouraged him to—he had to keep his wife and children on a single man's pension. In the case of St Dunstaners our Children Fund had gone some way to remedying this defect in the Pensions Warrant, but that only underlined the injustice of the regulation.

I felt very strongly about this, and considered it an even more important matter than a general rise in the pension itself. Eventually I was able to persuade the Legion to the same opinion. The Government was harder to convince, so once again we issued children's allowances from our own funds. At the same time we introduced educational allowances, to help St Dunstaners with children who could profit from secondary or advanced education.

In February 1942 the basic rate for the newly disabled was raised to 37s. 6d. per week. This was merely catching up with inflation. The First World War men, still on 40s., continued to fall behind. After twelve months of further inflation neither rate had changed. Meanwhile the Beveridge Report had been published. It did not concern us directly, but we found it interesting. It put the minimum subsistence level for a married couple at £2 a week.

In the meantime I had been elected Chairman of the Committee of the House of Commons branch of the British

S

Legion, and we were getting increasing support from members of all parties. In March 1943 there was a full-dress debate on pensions in the Commons, with the Government very much on the defensive. We demanded the higher rate for all, wives' and children's allowances for all, and more and larger attendant allowances. We had a very good Press, and public opinion was now running in our favour. The Government was forced to hint at future concessions. As nothing was promised I issued a call for action to St Dunstaners, urging them to whip up other ex-Servicemen and bring pressure on their local M.P.s. I was well aware that Members of Parliament were greatly occupied with wartime matters, but they still had a duty to their constituents.

Ten weeks after the debate the Government still seemed insensitive, so I put down a motion calling for a Select Committee. Over 160 other Members added their names. We were offered another debate instead, but I replied that this would only waste the Government's time unless they were prepared to make concessions.

The Annual Conference of the British Legion was held as usual, at Whitsun, and I was elected National Vice-Chairman with a place in the National Executive Council. The mood of the conference was militant, and the Legion and St Dunstan's were now completely in step. Our campaign became more intense. In the Commons I pressed the Government at every opportunity. Then at last, in July, new proposals were announced. We did not get all we had asked for, but it was a big advance.

After four years of pressure (and inflation) the basic rate for the newly disabled was raised to that of the old. It stayed at 40s., but there were attendant allowances and supplementary pensions for the most seriously disabled, and wives' and children's allowances were extended to some (though not all) post-injury marriages.

One other victory was gained at the same time. Until 1943 a man claiming a pension had to prove that his disability was caused or aggravated by war service. Now the boot was put on the other foot. If he was fit when he enlisted and unfit when discharged it was assumed that his disability was attributed to service unless the State could prove it was not.

This very important reform was accompanied by the setting up, at long last, of independent appeal tribunals, for which we had been pressing since the War began. The Minister of Pensions had resisted the demand on the ground that there were not enough doctors available to staff the tribunals. I was sure enough could be found, and asked the Government to call for volunteers. In the end the Minister yielded, and the first of the tribunals began work just over four years after the outbreak of war.

All these reforms removed many major grievances but left others. I thanked the Government for what it had done, promised to go on pressing for what it had not, and asked it in future to be more sensitive to opinion in the country and in the House.

To be effective, pressing the Government is a more subtle operation than it sounds. Concessions are commonly refused on the grounds that they would create precedence or administrative difficulties, so you should try to prove that they will do neither at the first time of asking. Progress is slower if the Minister digs his toes in, and something depends on his character and on your personal relations with him. If you are always making a nuisance of yourself, and are unreasonable, Ministers become prejudiced against you, and you get very little. On the other hand, if you are too sweet and reasonable they ignore you. You must find the happy medium. My motto is this: make sure your case is a good one, then prepare the ground thoroughly, get as many allies as possible, and finally attack as vigorously as you can and keep the pressure on until you succeed.

15

Home and Away

ON the outbreak of war we had at once thrown St
Dunstan's open to all blinded Servicemen from the
Dominions, free of cost to their Governments.
This was not an impulsive act of generosity, but some-
thing we had taken into account when we worked out our
plans for the War.

In the First World War by far the greater part of the
blinded Dominions Servicemen had received full training
at St Dunstan's. We did not expect to be used as much in
the second war, because of the great missionary activities
of some of these Dominion St Dunstaners. In 1914–18
there was nothing like St Dunstan's in the Commonwealth
—indeed, in the world. By 1939 the cuttings planted by
Eddie Baker in Canada and Clutha Mackenzie in New
Zealand had grown into sturdy plants. How far the
Dominions could cope with their own blind was something
for each of them to decide. St Dunstan's was there for
them if they wanted it, either for preliminary training or
for the full course.

Because of the needs of their own work in the same field,
we did not encourage the people of Canada, Australia, or
New Zealand to support the parent organization in Britain,
but they rallied to help us when we needed them most. At
Christmas, especially, the bonds of St Dunstan's throughout the Commonwealth were strengthened by the arrival
of gifts, food parcels, and thousands of plum puddings.

We did not anticipate having to care for blinded
Allied Servicemen as well, but here history repeated

itself with exaggerations. Pearson had willingly taken in blinded Belgian soldiers when their country was over-run by the Germans, and we extended similar hospitality to men from Poland, France, Holland, Belgium, Yugo-slavia, and Estonia. The gruesome parallel ends there, for we were cut off from many casualties by the closing of the Mediterranean.

The name of First World War is something of a misnomer, for nearly all the fighting was in Europe and the Near and Middle East. With the Mediterranean open, it was natural that casualties were brought home to Britain from the Dardanelles and the Levant. For most of the Second World War our only line of communication with the Middle East was the long journey round the Cape of Good Hope.

Obviously some kind of staging was going to be neces-sary, and the first step was the establishment of a St Dunstan's Committee in Cairo. The Chairman was Mrs R. G. (now Lady) Casey, wife of the Minister of State, Middle East. This Committee made contact with the blinded men as soon as they reached base hospitals, took them the message of St Dunstan's, and looked after their evacuation.

The first stop for most of them was South Africa, and there were bound to be some delays there while they waited for a ship. So a preliminary training centre was set up at Wynberg, Cape Province, where they could start learning to be blind. Mr Norman Kennedy generously lent us his house, standing in three acres of grounds. Its name, Tembani, could have been chosen for us, for it means 'to hope and go on hoping.' We ourselves had every reason to hope that this new branch of St Dunstan's would be successful, for it began and continued life under the expert guidance of Mrs Chadwick Bates. We reluctantly spared Miss Hester Pease, who went out as Matron, after being with us for over eleven years.

Tembani was officially opened on February 18, 1942,

and it stayed open until September 30, 1945. It was far more than a mere staging-post. Huts were at once put in the ground for classrooms and workshops, and Mrs Bates began to engage her staff. Two of her first recruits were South African St Dunstaners from the first war—W. A. Helm, who taught braille and basket-making, and J. Crawford, instructor in massage. Before long the first men took their tests in typewriting and in reading and writing braille. Advocate Bowen went and gave a talk on "Victory over Blindness." I was able to arrange for the men to broadcast messages to their relatives through the B.B.C.

Corporal James Ellis of the 10th Hussars, one of the first men in, accepted the job of Tembani Correspondent for the *St Dunstan's Review*. His first dispatch had a familiar ring. "I am learning to read braille, and I have typed this article myself," he wrote, and apologized for his mistakes. "If you could see the result of our dancing lessons when we go to a dance, or some of our boys out rowing on the lake, you would begin to realize the wonderful work St Dunstan's is doing. Yes, we are all very happy here, and although I speak for myself I know I voice the opinion of all us boys. St Dunstan's has given us a new lease of life."

Batey told us more about Corporal Ellis. "Jimmy is making splendid progress with braille and typewriting, although he can type only with two fingers of his right hand (his left has been amputated) and can use only one finger for braille. He can, and does, make weird and wonderful noises with a trumpet. As he was a musician before he became a St Dunstaner we are hoping for a great deal of help from him in forming our band."

The next time we heard from Jimmy Ellis he had been to the Military Hospital at Johannesburg to be fitted with an artificial hand. "These people were not used to dealing with a St Dunstaner; they insisted on handling me gingerly, like a piece of delicate china. They soon learned differently when I began taking jaunts of my own, having made myself familiar with the various landmarks in the ward. They had many surprises to come. I was the centre of interest when I brought out one of John Buchan's novels, written in braille, and began reading. They had another little shock when I requested the loan of an ordinary type-writer, in order to keep up with my correspondence. . . . Among my unusual experiences in Johannesburg was an elephant ride at the Zoo. Another great thrill I had was a ten-mile horseback ride across the open veldt."

Before long Jimmy graduated from journalism to the editor's chair, founding a lively magazine called the *Tembani Times*. The men produced it entirely themselves, cutting their own stencils, duplicating on a hand-operated machine, and assembling and clipping the sheets. Somehow this magazine survived the loss of Jimmy Ellis when he was able to say good-bye to Tembani and come back home.

Tembani was not intended to be more than a pre-liminary training school, and it achieved that aim with plenty to spare. Most of the men who went through it came on to Church Stretton, including all the South African Servicemen blinded in the Second World War.

St Dunstan's Training Centre in India came about in a different way and for a different purpose. Its doors were always open to British Servicemen who had been blinded in South-east Asia, and a few stopped there before going on to Tembani and Church Stretton. But its main function was to look after our blinded Indian comrades in arms.

You do not need to know much about India and its peoples to realize what an enormous task this was. In the First World War it had not been attempted. Instead St Dunstan's had handed a lump sum over to the Indian Soldiers Board, which in exchange had paid special allow-ances, additional to pension, of five rupees a month to every war-blinded man for life. It had been far from an ideal arrangement, but not even Pearson had been able to overcome the difficulties in the way of giving more practical help. Most of those difficulties were still there in the Second World War, and I do not think they could have been overcome but for a single factor. A human factor.

Sir Clutha Mackenzie happened to be on holiday in India in September 1939. I invited him to stay five or six months to take charge of our new appeal, and he stayed the whole War; but not just raising funds. He created, almost single-handed, a St Dunstan's for blinded Indian Servicemen. And not only this. Towards the end of 1942, when his work was still at the planning stage, the Government of India cabled me a request for half his time. They were so impressed by his work that they wanted him to carry out a review of the Indian blind world as a whole, and draw up plans for the post-war welfare of the Indian civilian blind. As their number was estimated at about a million, this was hardly a spare-time job, but Mackenzie was happy to take it on, and I gladly agreed to the Indian Government's request. The two tasks were closely allied, for whatever Mackenzie was able to create for blinded Indian Servicemen was bound to blaze a new trail for the Indian civilian blind.

Their vast number was not the greatest difficulty. A much greater obstacle was the traditionally fatalistic attitude towards blindness. Its cause was ascribed either to bad luck or to a misspent life in a previous incarnation, and it was accepted with little complaint but with total resignation. A few of the blind were employed in reciting passages from the sacred works or singing in temples and mosques, but in general it was accepted that a blind person could do nothing except beg. Because of the St Dunstan's grant most of the Indian soldiers blinded in the first war were spared this, but Mackenzie found no difference in their outlook. They had gone back to their villages and lived with their own people, drawing their pensions and allowances and doing nothing all day. When Mackenzie spoke to them of an alternative they were incredulous.

So were some of the British in India to whom Mackenzie

went for advice. "But that's all these fellows want," he was told. "They've no desire to do anything else, and it's a waste of time to try. They crumple up, too, under such a heavy physical blow—you won't find it easy."

Mackenzie did not find it easy. Nor did he find the life of the blinded Indian soldier living on his pension and doing nothing as easy and happy an existence as it sounded. The attitude of the man's relatives and neighbours was a mixture of kindness, callousness, and exploitation. There was no general feeling that it was the duty of a blind man's family and his community to support him. Mackenzie might still have hesitated to interfere if the men had been contented as well as resigned, but without exception he found them dejected and miserable. So he went ahead.

The Army authorities provided quarters in the United Provinces, in the former P.O.W. and internment camp at Dehra Dun. They inherited these bungalows and a handful of other buildings in various states of repair. The five acres of ground were already half-way back to jungle.

"To get a training centre equipped in the days of peace would take time," Mackenzie wrote. "Now that there are rations, control permits, and shortages ever ready to justify delay we don't take too seriously the breezy assurances that this, that and the other thing will be completed, delivered or installed to-day, to-morrow, or next week. Somewhere in India, tradition says, is the grave of a young I.C.S. man, the stone bearing the epitaph: 'He tried to bustle the East.' But we can point to one grand sign of progress. This morning a large Army truck emerged from the mangoes, guns, and date palms bowering our drive. It carried four men, two lengths of 'four by two,' and a notice board six feet by one. Before an admiring audience of babus, hawkers, coolies, children, buffaloes, goats and a brahmini bull, we supervised its erection at our gate, to be certain it was not put upside down. It bears the brief but potent words 'St Dunstan's.'

"Next day. Yes, and to-day there is another very

definite sign of headway. Returning from telephoning at a neighbouring bungalow, we found two orderlies and a blinded soldier. Havildar Abdul Karim has arrived, our first trainee: so we really have started, this tenth day of June, 1943."

One of Mackenzie's first tasks was persuading men to come. They were shy of the unknown, and so sure that blindness was an irreparable catastrophe that they suspected a trick. And even if they were willing to go to the Training Centre, their womenfolk produced all sorts of reasons to make them change their minds. The most effective of these was that the scheme was a Government plot to get them working in order to stop their pensions. To make Mackenzie's task still harder, some of them had already been discharged from the Forces and were difficult to find.

In spite of all these problems, twenty men arrived for training during the first six months. One was an English soldier, who went on to Church Stretton. The others came from all over the sub-continent, were of different races and religions, and represented six separate language groups. One spoke only Tamil, and no one else could understand him. Another spoke Karen, Burman, and a little English. The others spoke Mahratti, Punjabi, Hindi, or Gurkhali, but most of them had a greater or lesser smattering of Urdu, which they had learnt in the Army. Some had been able to read and write in their mother script before they were blinded. About one-third had learnt in Army classes to write elementary Urdu in roman script. The rest were completely illiterate.

This was only one of the special problems at Dehra Dun. Mackenzie, undaunted, using Urdu as the *lingua franca*, set to work to teach them to typewrite and read and write braille. He thought that the general illiteracy in India might even be turned to their advantage. "It may give them a little occupation in their villages as letter writers, in addition to adding to their status as possessors of

typewriters." Meanwhile he was handicapped by the lack
of braille literature in Urdu and the fact that few of the
men could write letters in a script that anyone in the
village would be able to read.

They not only learnt, but several of them passed typewriting and braille tests. When it was organized the classroom routine was the least of Mackenzie's worries. One of
the worst was the problem of finding suitable trades. An
after-care system on the English pattern was clearly not
feasible, so a trade was only suitable if the raw materials
were produced in the immediate neighbourhood of the
man's village, and if the finished articles could maintain a
market in the village itself. But this was only part of the
problem. Even less easy to overcome was the influence of
the traditional caste system, with the collateral custom that
the son followed the father's trade. Leather work of any
kind belonged to the lowest caste, practically outcast.
Basketry was also low-caste, and weaving not much higher.
Many simple kinds of work that could easily be done by
blind men—the jobs of sweeper and dhobi, water-carrier
and coolie—were beneath those of all but the lowest caste.
Religious differences created further difficulties. When
Mackenzie organized music lessons one man, an orthodox
Muslim, said his faith barred him from taking part.
Happily it did not stop him from taking part in the camp
concert, at which he sang a religious poem without
accompaniment.

They had their first concert a few months after opening,
and the success of it was Clutha Mackenzie's first reward.
"Memraj Ram gives us a solo, accompanying himself on
the accordion. He has lost his right hand, but uses the
forearm to work the bellows and plays the keys with the
three good fingers of his left hand. . . . Krischinagar, due
to his wounds, is, like Memraj, also a three-fingered, left-
handed artist. . . . Everyone is jolly and happy. Each
performer signals the end of his piece by heartily applaud-
ing himself, and we all join in. . . . Sweet tea is passed

round, we eat sugary Indian cakes, we smoke cigarettes
and come to the end of a happy and friendly hour."

Their happiness was Mackenzie's triumph. Teaching
braille to illiterates, welding men of different races and
religions into a single community, even overcoming the
obstacles created by the caste-system—tremendous achievements as these were, the real victory was over the fatalism
of the East. Mackenzie proved for ever that these men
belonged to our blind brotherhood after all. Given the
chance, they would conquer blindness like anyone else.

After two years over seventy men had gone to Dehra
Dun, and a few had completed their training and gone out.
"Four Maharattas have left us to go back to their county
in Southern Bombay, a thousand miles away. They have
each gone off equipped with a piano-accordion, a braille
watch, a small loom for the weaving of newar—a webbing
which takes the place of wire springs in Indian beds—and
a supply of cotton yarn. We are solving for them, too,
problems of housing, marriage and land." Another man
who had graduated was a Gurkha named Dal Behadur Raj.
"He came here eighteen months ago, rebellious, scorning
the idea he could do anything again, and sadly wounded.
He had lost several fingers, and his face, despite months of
plastic surgery, still shows too clearly the effects of a shell
burst. But he came round and soon gained a prize for the
best achievement against difficult circumstances." A devout
Hindu, dedicated to service, he left to take up a post as an
instructor in weaving newar and in braille at a Home for
Blind Hillmen in the Himalayas.

No longer did the men have to be cajoled quite so much
into coming to Dehra Dun. "Among the new arrivals,"
Mackenzie wrote early in 1945, "is Lance-Naik Karam
Singh, a sprightly old Sikh, blinded in Gallipoli in 1915. I
was in the battle in which he was wounded, and must have
been close to him at the time. He was with an Indian
Mountain Battery, which, dug in immediately behind our
front trench, gave us magnificent support, undeterred by a

hail of short-range machine-gun and musketry fire which lashed about them. He arrived in cheerful mood, with spotless turban above his snowy, flowing beard, and quite unwearied by three days in grilling heat in overcrowded trains. He won an Indian Order of Merit for his gallantry at Anzac, and the Government gave him twenty-five acres of land, then newly irrigated desert, now converted to rich crops and pleasant shade trees. He heard of St Dunstan's and wrote to know if he might come. Aged sixty, he is quite undefeated, and he set himself a programme of weaving, music and braille."

By then the problem of settlement was Mackenzie's main concern. Nearly all the men came from villages, and one had to think back several centuries in England to picture the conditions they would face. Perhaps, thought Mackenzie, something on the lines of the sheltered workshop would be a better solution for them. He worked out plans for a substantial permanent colony, with a model village and workshop, where they could live together. He put the project to the men, and they discussed it for four days. Deliberately Mackenzie refrained from trying to talk them into it. He wanted them to decide freely and independently, and in the end they decided against his plan. They told him they appreciated the difficulties they would face in their villages, but they could not resist the call to go back.

Another problem was marriage, in one case probably remarriage; for a wife had taken one look at her husband in hospital and gone back home, regarding his blindness as good grounds for a divorce. This attitude was not uncommon. The Gurkhas were especially concerned about marriage. They said it was difficult enough for an active sighted man to get a wife in Nepal, for a blind man impossible. They represented to Mackenzie that the only solution was for St Dunstan's to prevail upon His Highness the Maharajah to give an order that so many wives must be supplied.

Some problems had to remain unsolved, for Mackenzie could not drive a horse and cart through the social structure of India. Like Speight in Palamcottah—who spent a busman's leave at Dehra Dun, sharing ideas and experiences with him—Mackenzie had to adapt St Dunstan's to India. Through all his difficulties he never faltered in confidence, guts, enthusiasm, and optimism, although for a long period he lived in the shadow of personal tragedy. His son, Ian, was reported missing from a commando operation against the Japanese. There was no news of him till the end of the War, when he was found alive and fit in a P.O.W. Camp.

Meanwhile Mackenzie had left the war-blind in New Zealand in good hands. Donald McPhee, who had been sharing his work for many years, was perfectly equipped to tackle the new problems that arose. When the closing of the Mediterranean was followed by the spread of the War to the Pacific our offer of hospitality to New Zealanders could hardly be taken up. It was not practicable to bring them half-way round the world in the middle of a global war. McPhee then decided that as the men could not go to St Dunstan's, St Dunstan's would have to be taken to them, and a 'little St Dunstan's' was set up at Auckland where newly blinded men received the same kind of training as we were providing at Church Stretton. McPhee and I corresponded frequently, and our feeling of kinship was strengthened by this extension of St Dunstan's overseas. After the War McPhee was awarded the O.B.E.

Gilbert Nobbs was awarded the same honour for similar work in Australia. We did in fact have two Australians at Church Stretton before the end of the War, and others came later, but all the rest had to be trained in their home country. Geography alone made this a much more difficult task than it was in New Zealand. There was, it is true, a federal Blinded Soldiers' Association, under the energetic presidency of Joe Lynch, but for purely practical reasons after-care work had been done by the various State Associations. In such a vast country centralization was extraordinarily difficult. When Sir Neville Pearson was in Melbourne in October 1943, and the federal Association gave a dinner in his honour, it was announced that an institution similar to St Dunstan's would be established in Australia. Plans for appealing for funds had already been made. But the practical difficulties proved too great for a centre like the 'little St Dunstan's' in New Zealand, and Australians were trained individually in hospitals or civilian institutions or by firms that had given them employment. The responsibility for the training lay with the Repatriation Department, and the organization was done largely by Gilbert Nobbs, who had been invited, at the outbreak of the Second War, to become chairman of the Repatriation War-blinded Welfare Committee in New South Wales. He told his second-war story in a second book, *Blinded but Unbeaten*, another lively but moving contribution to the literature of St Dunstan's.

War-blinded Canadians were in quite a different position. On the one hand they were engaged mostly in Europe, and therefore were almost bound to come through Britain on their way home. On the other hand, their need of our help was probably less than that of any other Dominion troops, for a training-centre on St Dunstan's lines awaited them in Toronto.

In an earlier chapter I told the story of how Eddie Baker and A. G. Viets founded the Canadian National Institute for the Blind. When I visited Canada in the summer of 1942 I found it one of the best voluntary agencies for the blind in the world. Eddie Baker was still managing director, and full of plans for training and resettling the new-war blind. I told him what we were doing at Church Stretton, and especially of our successful invasion of open industry. I also repeated our earlier offer to provide blinded Canadian Servicemen in Britain with whatever help was needed.

As in the First World War, Eddie Baker opened a training centre for blinded Servicemen at Pearson House,

Toronto. Again he was helped by other first-war Canadian St Dunstaners, notably A. G. Viets and Bill Dies. But nearly all the new men—over sixty altogether—came to Church Stretton before returning home, for preliminary training, for learning the first vital lessons in the art of being blind. If any of them needed to stay longer—for example, to take some training course not available in Canada—we made it clear that they would be very welcome. If they benefited from St Dunstan's it is also true that St Dunstan's gained much from them.

Several of these men went back to Canada to carry on the tradition of service to their comrades begun by Baker and Viets.

My wartime visit to Canada was followed by a tour of the United States, as the American authorities also had invited me to confer about their war-blinded Servicemen. All the facilities of St Dunstan's were at their disposal, and I tried to explain what we had to offer. Besides conferring with the authorities I had a day's discussion in New York with the Blinded Soldiers' Committee of the American Association of Workers for the Blind, under the chairmanship of Robert B. Irwin. Also there was Frank Smith, a Canadian St Dunstaner who had learnt massage and osteopathy when he was at Regent's Park. He had settled in Philadelphia, and was Dean of the School of Osteopathy and Lecturer in Psychiatry. I was happy to see a living proof of the success of St Dunstan's, but I need not have worried about our reputation. "No name," said one American blinded veteran, "sounds so sweet in the blind world as the name of St Dunstan's." No music sounded so sweet to my ears as the roar of applause that greeted this remark.

I found that there was a tendency on the part of the various States and local institutions to wish to have individual blinded soldiers under their care. It was no business of mine, but the Americans had paid me the compliment of asking my advice; I therefore gave it, earnestly and emphatically, and persuaded the meeting to pass resolutions calling for a single centre for the nation's blinded Servicemen. This was what they eventually got, although not in the form I had hoped. Avon Old Farms Convalescent Hospital—it was not a hospital, but the misnomer was required by U.S. Army regulations—was established at Valley Forge, Pennsylvania, in 1944 to provide "social adjustment training" to all Servicemen blinded in the war. Meanwhile we in Church Stretton had the honour and pleasure of giving seventeen American Servicemen their first leg-up on the road to recovery.

We were also very happy to welcome visiting American ophthalmologists and others interested in the welfare of the blind, who came to study our methods. I was therefore all the more disappointed when I visited the United States again in 1947 and found how little had been done. Blinded ex-Servicemen received about three months' training in getting about alone, and a few learnt typewriting and braille. Then they went home, the great majority to live on their pensions and do no active work. Their pensions were higher than ours, their lives much poorer. A group of them formed the Blinded Veterans Association, for mutual help, and this was their only link after the brief training at the Government centre at Valley Forge. A minority found jobs for themselves, and rehabilitated themselves in quite a remarkable way. Heartening in itself, this also showed how much better off the majority would have been with a private-enterprise organization on the lines of St Dunstan's.

All through the War we made every effort to bring help to blinded men as early as possible and this was now needed in Italy in 1944. Serious eye cases were concentrated in the Military Hospital at Naples, and had to stay there until they were fit to travel home. One of our V.A.D.'s, Bridget Beckwith—Becky to everyone at

T

Church Stretton—went out armed with braille and handicraft materials and the message of St Dunstan's. Becky
taught them to play draughts, wrote their letters home,
took them on picnics, guided their unskilful fingers as they
made a first crude hat or handbag for Mother—listened to
them and joked with them, and ticked them off; for few
things are more reassuring to a newly blinded man than
an ordinary unsympathetic rebuke.

There was one group of men that we could not reach,
and they caused me more concern than any others. There
were men who had been blinded and taken prisoner by the
enemy. At first it was difficult to find out their names, and
even how many there were, let alone try to give them any
help. Naturally, we hoped that they would soon be repatriated, and I reminded the Foreign Secretary regularly
of the importance of this. Although some of our most
successful first war men, like Captain Gilbert Nobbs, had
survived imprisonment with their spirit unscathed, it was
obviously a very poor environment for a man who had just
lost his sight. It was urgently necessary for us to do all we
could to break the monotony and probable despondency of
these men.

I asked the War Office to get their particulars, and I
sought the help also of the British Red Cross. The Invalid
Comforts Section of its P.O.W. Department had special
facilities that we wanted to use. We worked out an agreed
scheme, under which St Dunstan's were to pay for the
sending of all ordinary and special comforts, and also
apparatus for blind British and Allied prisoners of war.

To begin with we sent them literature about St Dunstan's that could be read to them, and a pamphlet I had just
written for the newly blind. We sent special ridged paper
for them to use when writing home, and at the same time
we provided them with material for learning braille. I
thought we would have to try to teach them by a correspondence course, with the help of any sighted prisoners

of war who might be willing and competent to act as teachers. I wrote to each man as soon as we got his particulars, telling him of the future that awaited him when he came home, and sending him a braille watch. I also got into touch with his family in Britain, by letter and through after-care visitors.

Until the first replies came in I pictured these men as dejected and resigned, hopeless and helpless, just sitting around cursing their luck. In this I underrated both them and their fellow prisoners of war. Before they had even heard of us, four men in one camp in Germany had their own school. Their self-appointed teacher was a fellow-prisoner, Lieutenant the Marquis of Normanby, who was also badly wounded, but not in the eyes.

Neither Lord Normanby nor any of his pupils knew anything about braille, but he found a braille alphabet in an encyclopædia in the camp library. He taught himself, and then taught the men. They had to learn the hard way, pricking out letters on cardboard with glass-headed pins. Lord Normanby later started lessons in other subjects as well, including geography, book-keeping, and economics. He also pulled some strings and acquired two Kepel typewriters, which the men used for writing home.

At the same time Lord Normanby helped them to invent or adapt recreations that were within their scope. They had few facilities but unlimited enthusiasm, and put on plays to entertain the rest of the camp. They had their own debating society, and it could have been a copy of ours. When I learnt they had been discussing whether women should use cosmetics I knew they had already caught the St Dunstan's spirit.

They had, in fact, started a branch of St Dunstan's in the heart of enemy territory, and we recognized this by sending them St Dunstan's badges. We also appointed Lord Normanby an honorary member of our teaching staff. It was not until long after, when the men came home, that we realized how much he had done for them. He was their representative, schoolmaster, guide, and comrade. They had one other piece of good luck after all the bad. Another fellow-prisoner was Major David Charters, a well-known Liverpool ophthalmic surgeon before the war. They could not have had a better medical officer, and he was much more to them than that.

We sent them typewriters and braille writers, and plenty of braille books and magazines. They were fast learners, and their first letters soon began to come in. At Church Stretton we formed a P.O.W. Correspondence Club, and many braille-pen friendships were formed. Lord Normanby held tests in both typewriting and braille, and their general standard was high. But they were still normal St Dunstaners. "The Red Cross is asking us how we like braille," one of them wrote in their house organ, the *Dotty Mag*. "Why hasn't someone got the courage to tell them?"

We sent them braille playing-cards and handicraft materials, and carpentry and boot-repairing tools for them to learn to be handy and enjoy making things for the camp. We sent them musical instruments, and they soon had their own jazz band. Their signature tune was *Smile, Darn You, Smile*.

Their captors allowed them to go for walks outside the camp, and sometimes to go swimming. Another good thing the Germans did was to concentrate all blind prisoners in one camp, and soon Lord Normanby had a class of between twenty and thirty men. When the blind were moved to a new camp, at Haina Kloster, Lord Normanby and Major Charters were allowed to go with them.

Their thirst for information about St Dunstan's was insatiable. I invited their families to come to Church Stretton and look round, so that they could write letters about what they had seen. We also sent their families presents and plum puddings at Christmas, and encouraged them to tell us all they could about these St Dunstaners whom we had not yet seen. In this way, and with the help of Lord Normanby's reports, we were able to organize some vocational training. We found out all we could about each man's history, aptitude, and inclination, and provided special courses of reading.

We were not able to do so much for the blind in Italian P.O.W. Camps, but the Red Cross took them braille watches and reading matter, typewriters and games. They were the first to be repatriated, and we welcomed five of them to St Dunstan's in May 1943. Five months later we were excited to hear that twenty-seven of our men from Haina Kloster were on their way home.

My wife and I went to Liverpool to meet them, and Church Stretton turned out to give them a proper heroes' welcome. The main street was gay with flags and streamers and lined with cheering crowds, and a military band marched them in. We greeted them as old friends rather than new entrants, and many of them had been St Dunstaners for years.

Lord Normanby was repatriated with them. He accepted a seat on our Council, and went to the House of Lords to make a maiden speech pleading the cause of returning Servicemen after the war. The Editor of *The Times* asked him to write an article on the Haina Kloster braille school. Somehow he contrived to make it so impersonal that one of his pupils had to write a letter pointing out that Lord Normanby had been the originator and mainstay of the school throughout. For his work at the camp he was awarded the Military M.B.E. Perhaps his greatest honour was given by the men he had worked for so hard and so well. When they arrived at Church Stretton we put them together in a big ward, and, with their aptitude for recognizing these matters in their own way, they named it Normanby.

There was one man missing from the celebrations. Major Charters had refused repatriation because he was the only British ophthalmologist in Germany and there were still seven blind prisoners of war. Three of these were repatriated six months later, and Major Charters was again given the chance to come. He had been in captivity for over four years, but again refused, and he stayed with the men until the end of the War. He also received the Military M.B.E. and the lasting gratitude of St Dunstan's.

Geoffrey Treglown was a young Methodist Army Chaplain, and the incident that cost his sight won him the M.B.E. During a battle inoculation course he was crawling through a ditch with some other officers when a stick of gelignite fell near by. Realizing the danger to the combatant officers, he deliberately picked the stick up to throw it clear. The others were unscathed because of his brave action, which lost him his sight and his right hand. His ears were also badly injured, resulting in partial deafness, but nothing on earth would have stopped him from going back to his calling. For many years he continued his work as a Methodist, and then, in 1960, he entered the Anglican priesthood.

Treglown is a well-known religious broadcaster, one of the very best I ever heard. Once in a B.B.C. *Silver Lining* programme I heard him give a Christian's answer to blindness that impressed me deeply by its quiet courage and common-sense:

"Some listeners have told me that for years they've been praying for divine healing," he said. "They try to generate more and more faith; sometimes they visit faith-healers. Yet healing doesn't come. Why? Well, I don't know, for I too believe in the power of God to heal. I also know from personal experience the strain and anxiety of years spent in praying for healing, and in seeking it from doctors and less orthodox healers. In the end, I saw that this constant search was making me very self-centred, and was delaying a real acceptance of my disability. Because I went on praying for sight, I wasn't able to accept blindness, or adjust myself to it, or overcome it. In the end, I decided to copy St Paul, who prayed just three times that his thorn in the flesh might be removed, and then accepted the divine assurance, 'My grace is sufficient for thee.' I prayed once and for all for healing, and when it didn't come I accepted God's help and got on with the job of living. I want to commend Paul's way to you. Let me say emphatically that I believe in God's healing power which comes to us through prayer, through the surgeon's knife, and through the laying-on of hands. But the fact is that not everybody is healed, however deep their faith and long their prayers. Some have to accept a cross, as Jesus did. I know the Bible teaches the value of prayer, but I don't believe that God wants you to go on all your life centring your thoughts on your own troubles. I believe He may want you to take your burden to Him, once and for all, and leave it there. Then, if you're healed, well, give thanks to God. And if you're not, accept the position, and get on in His strength with the adjustment and the victory."

A man of Geoffrey Treglown's faith and ability would have overcome any handicap, and whatever he got out of St Dunstan's he put back many times. Men with double handicaps naturally needed more help than those who had only lost their sight, and Treglown was a living example of what could be done by a blind man with only one hand. Another fine example was Harry Wainman, a private in the East Yorks Regiment, who was wounded early in the War. Blinded and deprived of one arm by machine-gun bullets, he was already forty-five years old when he came to Church Stretton. We revived a first-war tradition by helping him to start shopkeeping, and he was soon doing well.

By no means all one-handed St Dunstaners went in for shopkeeping. Before the end of the War they were doing quite a variety of jobs, including poultry-farming and lift-operating, teaching and lecturing, wool-rug making and joinery, and some kinds of office work. One man was working as a telephone operator, writing shorthand with his only hand. Another was in a factory successfully operating a lathe. With one hand and no sight these men were doing work at which others with all their faculties often failed.

If their achievement was remarkable it is hard to describe the triumph of the men who had lost both hands as well as their sight. There was a depressingly and unexpectedly large number of these. Only three men had survived such multiple injuries in the First World War. In the Second war, although casualties generally were halved, there were thirteen, and there were nine others, whose hands were so badly damaged that St Dunstan's treated them as within the handless category. Probably the increase was due partly to landmines and more shattering explosives, but also, I think, to better medical care and the use of the new antibiotic drugs in battle areas that saved badly wounded men's lives.

Sergeant Alan Nichols, a handless St Dunstaner from the First War, had not only made an excellent recovery but had a naturally inspiring personality with a sense of humour, and the new men with similar disabilities could not have had a better example on their journey—so much more difficult than ours—back to life and happiness.

Another wonderfully inspiring example to the men of the Second War was Drummer N. Downs. Blinded at the age of sixteen, his injuries included as well amputation of his lower right arm and almost complete loss of his left hand; but if ever a man embodied the spirit of St Dunstan's that man was "Drummer," as he was universally known. I suppose he should also have been classified as handless, but no one ever thought of him as such. To see him lighting a cigarette, playing cards, making tea, or typing his letters was a revelation.

To those of us who were running St Dunstan's these new handless men were a challenge. The conquest of blindness alone by large numbers of ordinary men had been startling, yet here we were, only twenty-five years later, regarding men who were both blind and handless with precisely the same outlook.

Of course, we knew the difficulties would be much greater, but we had the same positive approach. We tackled the problem not from the point of view of what the man had lost, but by finding out what he had left and going on from there. A perfect example of the application of this empirical method was the case of Geoffrey Preston, who was blown up in India. He sustained very severe head wounds causing blindness, lost his right hand, and was practically paralysed in the left arm, leg, and foot.

He was the first English blinded soldier to go through Dehra Dun, and our first knowledge of him came in a letter from Clutha Mackenzie. "Just before Christmas, Geoff Preston left us at a few hours' notice to join a hospital ship for England, and perhaps Church Stretton will see him soon. Though he was heavily handicapped by not having the use of either hand, he was always full of jokes, and ready for banter or argument. He is a wizard at crossword-puzzles."

By the time he reached Church Stretton, Geoff Preston had developed his aptitude for solving crossword-puzzles still further, and the idea occurred to him that he might compile them professionally. We encouraged him because we thought he had all the things he needed for success. These were an independent spirit, a good clear brain, and one handless arm that could operate a metal finger. For a man with Preston's mental gifts and physical handicaps it was an ideal occupation, involving much thinking and little writing. He would compose the whole puzzle in his head in perhaps a couple of hours, and then spend five or ten minutes setting it down on a specially designed typewriter which he operated with a metal finger strapped to what remained of his right arm. It may sound like a stunt, but pretty soon Preston was selling his efforts on their merits, not only to newspapers and magazines at home but all over the English-speaking world, except the U.S.A. Far from being a liability to the country, he earned us much-needed hard currency by securing a contract to supply one puzzle a week to a Canadian paper.

Preston's success is a personal triumph for which St Dunstan's claims little credit except for the specially adapted typewriter, which I described in an earlier chapter. This was one of the first products of our Research Department, which was set up in 1943 specifically to devise aids for St Dunstaners who had lost not only their sight but also their sense of touch.

It was one thing to set up a new department, another to find a man to run it. Not surprisingly, at that time it was impossible to get a skilled tool-maker or mechanic or engineer. They were all either in the Services or employed in munitions. I was at a loss until I had the idea of going to the Hospital at Roehampton to see if I could find a wounded or slightly disabled man who would come and work for us.

I struck lucky, although I had no idea how lucky at the time. They took me to a bed-patient who had set up a kind of repair workshop in the ward. He was surrounded by radio sets, watches, bracelets, and all kinds of objects belonging to patients, nurses, and even the hospital itself.

"Are you a watch-maker by trade?" I asked him.

"No," he said, "but I'm getting along all right with them."

I knew at once that this was the man I wanted—a technical man, keen and ingenious and inventive, who could turn his hand to anything.

Peter Nye came to work at St Dunstan's as soon as he was well enough to leave hospital, and stayed for sixteen years. Only at the end of 1959, after passing his finals for the A.M.I.Mech.E., did he leave for the commercial world. It would not be easy to measure his contribution to the art and science of beating blindness. St Dunstaners remember him as the man who listened to their ideas for gadgets and always said "Right, we'll try that," never "No, it cannot be done."

He began his research work by studying Sergeant Alan Nichols and learning what one blind and handless man had been able to do on his own. Then Nye appointed himself

valet-companion to one of the new-war men with the same
disabilities, and refused to be shaken off for a whole week.
By the end of that time he had plenty of ideas on the kind
of gadgets that were needed, and he returned to his back-
room to try to invent them. More assistants were engaged
later to help him, but our Research Department started as
a one-man show.

I have said that the first two milestones on the St
Dunstaner's way to recovery are the braille watch and the
typewriter, and adaptations of these for the handless were
the first two gadgets that our back-room produced. Only
the watch did not have a braille dial, but was an ordinary
repeater with a plunger which the wearer pressed to hear
the chimes. The time was rung on two bells incorporated
in the repeater movement, and could be told to the minute.
If the wearer had the misfortune to be deaf as well as blind
and handless the watch could be further adapted by
removing the bells, so that the hammers beat on the
watch-case and transmitted the vibrations of the ringing
code to the body.

The watch was shaped to fit comfortably into the breast
pocket and to remain in position when operated. The inside
of the housing was hollowed out partly to reduce the weight
and partly to reverberate the sound of the chimes. The
plunger, made of ebonite, was shaped like a fountain-pen
top so as not to look conspicuous in the pocket. It proved
the perfect answer for the blind-handless man. It was not
so suitable for similarly handicapped women because of its
dependence on a pocket, but their problem was at least
partly solved by a repeater mantelpiece clock for the home.
Designed to look good as well as work well, it was
operated by a plunger surmounted by a large metal button
which was pressed with the stump of the arm.

Another quite early gadget enabled the blind-handless
to use a telephone without any help. Again a plunger was
involved, but he did most of the work with his feet. An
ordinary hand microphone was fixed to an adjustable

mounting with the dial mechanism inside the base. A plunger was fixed to the base, and a two-pedal foot unit on the floor below. The user pressed the left pedal to answer the phone and the right pedal to ring off. To make a call he pressed the left pedal and waited for the dialling-tone, and then pressed the plunger with his stump. This automatically dialled O, calling the attention of the exchange.

So far, so good: but why shouldn't the disabled man dial his own calls? One man almost could—he had a surviving very short stump of thumb which enabled him to get some grip on the microphone set but which was too big to go into the holes of the dial. The answer in his case was simple—a specially large dial was made. Another man had a badly damaged hand, and could use an ordinary dial with some finger-slipping, but only by kneeling on the floor. For him the dial was built up to a horizontal position, and a shroud was fitted round it to eliminate the finger-slipping.

These were special cases. The blind-handless in general, the man who had nothing more than arm-stumps, used a mechanical key-sender. A special guide-plate was devised to enable him to select and dial his number on the ten keys by pressing them with his metal finger.

Might it be possible, I asked in 1943, for a blind-handless man to operate a switchboard? Might not some of these doubly handicapped men join the many other St Dunstaners who earned their living at this job?

I asked the G.P.O. if there was any telephone system in existence that could be operated by the blind-handless, and after a thorough exploration they came back and said there was not. Then could one of the G.P.O. systems be adapted for the purpose? The answer came back after two and a half years of research and experiment by Peter Nye and J. H. Combridge, an Executive Engineer of the G.P.O., with the indispensable help of some of the handless St Dunstaners.

The answer was yes. An automatic G.P.O. system was supplemented by a pedal platform and a cabinet containing forty push buttons that the operator could work with a metal striker fitted into his artificial arm. With this equipment he could handle a board with the capacity of ten exchange lines and fifty extensions. One of the first places where the system was installed was at the headquarters of our own Research and Experiment Department, where Tommy Gaygan took charge.

When Gaygan shaves himself—and he does every day—he occasionally comes up against a metal splinter. "Thank goodness they got most of the stuff out with a mine-detector," he quips, and carries on giving himself a nice clean shave. Gaygan helps his wife tidy and polish the house, and boasts that he never breaks anything when he washes up. He is a first-class road-walker, a 7 m.p.h. man at his best, and was St Dunstan's champion for some time. He likes dancing, and plays the drums and the trombone. He has a full-time job as a telephone-operator, and he does the lot without eyes or hands. To put it down to virtuosity would be to miss the point. Sheer courage, laced with a Cockney sense of humour, is the secret of Tommy Gaygan's success.

He was an Eighth Army trooper, and was a victim of a booby-trap during the fighting in Tunisia. A moment's violent explosion changed him from a healthy young soldier to a helpless invalid, maimed and disfigured and only alive at all because he refused to die. That same determination carried him through the many shocks and trials that lay ahead. "We aim to take out your left eye to try and save the right," a surgeon told him when at last he reached a base hospital. Both eyes were still bandaged when Tommy came round after the operation, and he pestered the nurses to take them off his right eye; but when they did he still could not see.

Plastic surgeons performed skin grafting operations on his arms, and between grafts he had more operations on his remaining eye. Skilled surgeons worked wonders for him, but they could not give him back his hands or his sight. He came to Church Stretton, and began to learn to live with his handicaps. Fitted with artificial hands at Roehampton, he soon learnt to type. Eating was more difficult, dressing harder still. Dancing seemed out of the question, but he went with a friend one night just to listen to the music and the laughter. He sat there with his gloved hands well out of sight until the band struck up the last waltz and a girl named Audrey went up to him and said, "Come on, let's do this one." He told her he couldn't. "I wouldn't let it beat you, you know," she said, and that stung him as she had hoped. Tommy made the running after that, and many dances later they married.

"Number, please." Tommy rattles his metal finger down the bars across his box to find the right row of holes between them. Almost in the same movement he runs the metal rod along the grooves to find the correct hole. He dials by plunging the rod into the various holes in turn, and links up his extensions by playing an organ concerto with his feet on a couple of pedals and half a dozen buttons. It is a brilliantly ingenious switchboard, and Tommy will tell you it is dead easy to work. But it was not dead easy to learn. Nothing was, for Tommy Gaygan. His success in overcoming his physical handicap was a victory for his spirit.

That goes too for Bert Baldwin, another Desert Rat who was blown up in the Middle East. He was the first of our blind-handless telephone operators, working the switchboard at headquarters. He learnt to play the vibraphone, bred budgerigars, and was the first handless St Dunstaner to play darts. He gripped the dart with a pair of automatic tweezers tipped with rubber attached to his artificial arm. The only help he needed was to be led to the board. He took three paces back and then made the normal throw with uncanny skill, and beat many good players with eyes and hands.

After a while Baldwin left the switchboard to take up weaving, and our engineers constructed a brilliantly inge-

nious loom for a blind-handless man. He used his feet to
operate the heddles and beater, and fired the shuttle with
the stump of his arm. All he had to do was to move a lever
which operated a spring-loaded plunger, and when the
shuttle was fired from one side the plunger on the opposite
side was automatically cocked. Each loom had two magazines containing bobbins, and when one shuttle had
exhausted its supply of twill a bell rang. Then the operator
moved a vertical lever with his stump, and the shuttle was
automatically fed with more twill. Once the loom had been
set up the blind-handless operator could weave about sixty
yards before he needed any more real help. One of our
handless Australians, who came to St Dunstan's in 1948,
took one of these specially adapted looms back home with
him and used it with great success.

Joinery proved another manual job that could be done
without hands. Dickie Brett, once a lance-corporal in the
Pioneer Corps, suffered multiple injuries in Italy, including
the loss of his sight and both hands. After he left St
Dunstan's we helped him run a private car-hire business
for a while, and then he came back for a course in the
chippy shop. He had always been a handyman, and one of
our industrial staff applied his inventive mind to the adaptation of a carpenter's tools. Each tool was fitted with a
ring through which Dickie inserted the stump of his arm.
Many ingenious jigs were made, not least the saw, and
even a plane was well within his scope. No special use
could be made of his feet, but his mouth came in handy for
securing wooden sections with panel pins. He used it to
feed a spring-loaded tool which he then pressed with his
stump to drive the pin hard home. Brett specialized in
magazine and letter-racks and cheese trays. His big
moment came at a war-disabled exhibition in London when
the Queen asked him to make her a letter-rack. He did it on
the spot—in twenty minutes.

Brett became an enthusiastic darts-player when our
back-room boys improved on Bert Baldwin's tweezers by

inventing a spring-loaded clamp attached to the stump of the arm.

Tommy McKay is another skilful craftsman with a double handicap (and besides that he has lost a leg). He enters annually the International Handicrafts Exhibition at Olympia, and just as regularly wins awards although he declines to enter the Heavily Disabled Class. In the last three years he has won a hat-trick of prizes with a grandfather clock, a nest of oak coffee-tables, and a combined coffee-bed-table.

Shopkeeping was an obvious occupation for the blind-handless. A large number of our successful shopkeepers had some kind of double handicap, and men like Harry Wainman showed how the loss of one arm could be overcome. The blind-handless needed more help in the way of equipment, and our engineers produced a number of useful devices.

Their first task was to enable the shopkeeper to identify coins proffered by customers, and to give them change. A change-giving machine was easily adapted from the standard automatic cashier used by the railways, but the coin-identification machine had to be invented from scratch. Obviously if the shopkeeper could neither see nor handle the coins he would have to identify them with his ears, and our engineers went on from there. The final article was a bit too intricate to be easily described in words. Two specially shaped guides prevented any particular coin from passing beyond its appropriate position. There were nine positions, one for each of the English coins, and a buzzer sounded as the coin passed each position. The shopkeeper identified it by the number of buzzes he heard. Then he touched a couple of levers, and the coin was automatically slid into a rack and stacked.

Another mechanical aid produced for the blind shopkeeper was a cigarette cabinet, similar in construction to the ordinary type of cigarette slot-machine. The drawers were designed specially to allow the shopkeeper to open them and remove a packet of cigarettes. The cabinet could hold fifty packets of each of eleven different brands, and there was a compartment for matches.

David Bell was a shopkeeper. A sapper in the War, he had been blown up by a booby-trap while clearing a mine-field in the Libyan desert. When he recovered conscious-ness it was to learn that he would never see or feel again. He had his first training at Tembani, and then went on to Church Stretton, where he met and married a girl named Sybil before taking over a tobacconist's business in Edin-burgh. Within a few years he had become one of our most successful shopkeepers, and there the story would have ended but for some demon inside Bell that kept driving him on. He became interested in politics, and then had the ambition to take a Master of Arts degree at Edinburgh University. Unable to use braille text-books, he had to study entirely with his ears. Fellow-students went through their notes with him, and his wife read aloud to him. "When examination time came along," he said afterwards, "my spoonfuls of breakfast were mixed with spoonfuls of Plato and Adam Smith." He took Second Class Honours in Social Anthropology, completing a three-year course in two years—in his spare time. This done, he went on to read for the degree of Bachelor of Commerce. "All I had to do was to go and sit the examinations," he said after being capped a B.Com. "My wife and the students who came and read to me did all the work." He had a first-class distinction in Banking and a second-class distinction in Industrial Commerce.

After holding many public appointments, Bell was asked by the Ministry of Labour to sit on the Edinburgh Disable-ment Advisory Committee in 1956. Two years later he accepted an invitation to serve on the Appeals Committee of the B.B.C. Advisory Council (Scotland). He also appeared on television, to his surprise, as the subject of a programme in the series *This is Your Life*. This feature, often criticized for maudlin sentimentality, was never so wholesomely free

U

from emotional overtones as when David Bell appeared, sightless and handless but completely at ease.

Bell will tell you that he has acquired a great gift. "The eyes are only messengers of the brain," he says. "They miss a lot and often are deceived. Without them I can see with my brain, right into people." John Proctor is another man who has found positive happiness in the dark. "There is no dust, no dirt, no shabbiness now," he says. "Nobody is ugly. Friends have lost the defects that marred their looks. The touch of their hand and the sound of their voice are what I know them by now." He means the touch of his friends' hands, of course, for he has none himself; and their voices only reach him through a hearing-aid.

Proctor was knocked out of the War on his twenty-seventh birthday, when he was bombed in the Aegean islands. Like Gaygan and Bell, he has a wonderful wife, who helps him to run a highly successful travel agency in Rottingdean. He arranges holidays for people all over the world, including the isles of Greece where he looked for the last time. "Don't you wish you could go and see all these beautiful places?" a client sometimes asks. "But I do go," he replied in surprise. John and May Proctor travel abroad a lot, for both pleasure and business. He likes recreation as much as he enjoys work. "The rustle of papers, the clamour of the phone, the talking of clients, the feel of my desk; these are the things I could not do without. They are the noises and shapes that complete the sunny world around me." Beauty? "If people were to go about blindfold for a month," he says earnestly, "they would realize what beauty they miss every day of their lives."

One of the simpler gadgets for the handless invented by our engineers is a device for switching radio sets on and off and tuning-in. It was left to Proctor to look for a means to operate a transmitter. I think I may have been the first blind radio ham in the world, as long ago as the 1920's, but the record is of no great moment. Certainly it does not come anywhere near Proctor's achievement in becoming the world's first blind-handless qualified radio operator. The Radio Club of Brighton and St Dunstan's engineers helped him with his equipment, but John alone had to tap out Morse with the stub of his wrist to pass the tests required by the G.P.O. for the issue of an amateur's wireless transmitting licence.

Warwick Castle, with its magnificent Chapel with Italian paintings and superb stained glass, attracts large numbers of visitors, who shower questions on the official guide as he takes them round. If they are observant they see that he has no hands. They may leave still unaware that he cannot see the beautiful things he describes. Ted Miller lost his sight and his hands in the battle of the Ardennes in 1944, and he had to have special training for his unusual job. He learnt the layout of the castle and its surroundings while he was at our Training Centre, from a specially constructed model on which all the buildings and special features could be distinguished by feeling them with his elbow. Trees were represented by pieces of sponge, lawns by cloth, the River Avon by a strip of bicycle-tyre rubber. Meanwhile two tutors gave him a three months' intensive course on the history of the 900-year-old castle. "Even if I cannot see the Chapel and its beauties, I know so much about them that I can appreciate them as much as anyone," he says. One should not underestimate the vision of an intelligent blind man's mind's eye.

More than one blind-handless man has been able to work as a lift-operator, thanks to another piece of ingenuity on the part of our Engineers' Department. The combined call-and-switch system has been adapted for the operator's ears and stump. When the call button is pressed at any floor a buzzer sounds in the lift and the corresponding switch button on the operating panel is automatically ejected an inch. The operator draws the stump of his forearm across the surface of the buttons—which have been made to the dimensions and spacing needed for easy selection and operation—finds the ejected one, and presses it in. The lift automatically moves to the required floor, and when the button is released it returns to its normal position. Special quick-release handles fitted to the lift-doors allow the operator to open and shut them with his stump. There is a push-button fixed below the hand-rail in the lift which enables the operator to sound the alarm in an emergency.

Winnie Edwards set our engineers a whole series of problems when she said she wanted to go back to looking after her husband and children. An explosion had taken away her sight and both hands, and we had no experience of providing mechanical aids for a blind-handless housewife. Our back-room got to work with a vacuum cleaner, and attached specially adapted leather-lined brackets to the cleaner tube into which she could put her forearm stumps. She was able to vacuum-clean the carpets with freedom and comfort, and other gadgets enabled her to do more of the jobs of running a house. But Mrs Edwards was not only a housewife. Her husband was running a private car-hire business, with his home as his office, and when he was out she took charge. Pretty soon she was receiving and transmitting telephone messages as well as anyone else, and noting the times of calls by the mantelpiece repeater clock.

Not all our engineers' inventive efforts were devoted to helping the blind-handless to work. They needed special help also in enjoying many of the greatest pleasures of the blind. There was the talking book, for example, which other blind men could operate alone. To make the blind-handless almost equally independent we combined the ordinary reproducing machine with an automatic record-changer and fitted control pedals for operation by the feet and knobs that could be moved by a stump.

"How nice it would be to pick up a cigarette and light it yourself!" The blind-handless man who smoked a lot naturally chafed at having to keep asking someone to put a cigarette in his lips and light it. This limitation of independence was important enough to require another gadget, an oblong box with room for twenty-five cigarettes and a plunger at one end. Press the plunger, and up pops a cigarette. Hold it in your lips, take a couple of draws—and you are smoking. The secret is a lighting element operated by two small batteries which is automatically switched on when the plunger goes down.

What about games? Our Research Department accepted the challenge and produced the Domino Player. A vertical contact plate, twelve inches square, is clamped in an upright position to the table, and dominoes are inserted in a rack in the back of the plate. Grooves or shallow ruts run both vertically and horizontally across the face of the plate, dividing it into segments each of which represents a domino. The player scans the plate by running a metal finger attached to his forearms along these grooves, and buzzing signals tell him the values and positions of the individual pieces in the rack. Having selected the domino he wishes to play, he runs his finger downward and inserts it in one of the series of holes. The domino then flies out from its position in the rack on to the table. As the dominoes have raised dots, like those used by other blind men, the player can enjoy a game with both blind and sighted comrades. But there is one important difference between these and the normal dominoes for the blind. In each number combination one dot is made of metal and spring-loaded so as to make the appropriate electrical connexion with the contact plate.

For blind men with one hand our engineers devised the Card Player, a crescent-shaped card-holder with clips for holding the cards, leaving the sound hand free to select and play them. It is a simple device by comparison with gadgets for the handless like the Domino Player, but it has given tremendous pleasure to the one-armed blind.

Our Research Department was not confined to devising aids for the doubly handicapped, and it has produced a variety of useful gadgets for the ordinarily blind. Housey Housey, or Lotto, was always popular in the Forces, and it caught on at once at St Dunstan's when special cards and disks were supplied. Instead of being thin pieces of cardboard the cards were made of bakelite with the numbers brailled in recesses, which held the white ivorine disks in position when they covered the numbers.

One of our men had been a maintenance electrician before the War, and he wanted to go back to his old job. Our engineers designed a voltmeter, an ammeter, and a megohm meter calibrated with braille characters. With these he was able to do practically everything. Then there was the farmer for whom a spring balance was adapted, complete with a braille reading scale, to enable him to weigh the quantity of milk produced by his cows each day. Maureen Lees, formerly an A.T.S. sergeant-major and latterly our champion weaver, wanted to set up her own loom, and, on her suggestion, a new threading device was produced. In such ways many individual St Dunstaners were able to push the frontiers of the blind world farther.

The blind-handless needed the help of our engineers most, and it was given in all sorts of ways. Drinking tubes were devised—one for drinking beer, lemonade, or any long cold drink, and one for hot drinks like tea or coffee. The man who could neither see nor feel was even enabled to make his own tea by the adaptation of an electric kettle which was fitted to a stand with a swivelling spout and automatic cut-off. Car-type door-handles and lever-type water-taps, gauntlet fitting sponges and fixed soap-bowls for washing, sanitary appliances and electric razors—the full list of St Dunstan's gadgets for the blind-handless is long. They range from a horse-riding appliance to a universal spoon-holder, a pipe-holding device to a rowing attachment, a skipping appliance to a specially adapted dictaphone. They include several musical instruments.

Thomas Floyd, a one-handed St Dunstaner from the First World War, had become an extremely able pianist. Beginning with the surprisingly large number of pieces written for the left hand only, by composers who included

Saint-Saëns and Scriabin, he continued with one-handed arrangements of other classical works, and finally learnt to arrange popular songs and pieces himself. Padre Treglown devoted his surviving hand to a sixteenth-century instrument called a whittle, or three-hole pipe. Not unlike a recorder, it could have been made for a player with only one hand.

For those with no hands the problem was harder, but not insoluble. At one concert we gave at Church Stretton—in aid of the Shropshire Red Cross—no fewer than five men with this double handicap gave solo performances, each on a different instrument. Jimmie Ellis, our trumpeter, still had a few fingers, but each of the other four had lost both hands. Bert Baldwin played the vibraphone, Freddie Higgs the xylophone, David Bell the trombone, and Tommy Gaygan the drums. Our Research Department had adapted the trombone by fixing an adjustable attachment to the frame which fitted into the artificial arm or gauntlet of the left stump, giving the instrument the necessary support, while a swivelling lever connected his right artificial arm with the slide. Several handless men learnt the instrument well enough to play in the St Dunstan's Band. "The only thing wrong with it," said Tommy Gaygan, "is that if you get fed up with playing you can't get rid of the thing until somebody takes it off."

For their artificial hands our men went to Queen Mary's Hospital, Roehampton, the centre for limbless ex-Servicemen. In July 1944 our Hospital Unit parted from the Training Centre and moved to Stoke Mandeville, becoming two or three or more wards in a big thousand-bedded hospital. Against the disadvantages of the separation was the fact that new admissions could now receive almost every kind of specialist treatment on the spot. Also the departure of the Hospital Unit gave us more room for the Training Centre at Church Stretton, which was badly needed. The number of second-war men on our books jumped from 394 at the beginning of 1944 to 656 at the end.

The revival of air raids embarrassed a number of us, although happily no bombs fell on Church Stretton. Several St Dunstaners were bombed out of their homes, and my own house in London was burnt to the ground. We were dining out, but when the raid started drove home to find our house ablaze. We could not get into the doors because of the smoke, but I climbed through a window at the end farthest from the fire and telephoned for help. The Fire Service and willing neighbours eventually got the fire under control, but by then the whole of the house was a heap of ashes. Three St Dunstaners who were staying with us and were fortunately in our air-raid shelter helped my wife to pull a few things out, but we did not get much.

St Dunstan's had a bad fire at the end of 1944, when the Raglan Street stores were gutted. This was not due to enemy action but possibly to an electrical defect. It was bitterly ironical after getting through the Blitz and the later bombing unscathed. Fortunately, we had taken the precaution of dispersing our stocks in other buildings, but we had still suffered a heavy loss of materials that could not be replaced.

Three months later the war in Europe ended, and soon afterwards the Admiralty handed Ovingdean back to us. Mr Askew and his staff at once began to get the place ready for our return. It had suffered no war damage—but when the fighting was over we had another ironical slap in the face. In a great storm that swept the South Coast our building was damaged twice—by mines that were washed up on the shore.

16

Victory over Blindness

WHEN the fighting stopped just over 1000 new war-blinded had come to St Dunstan's. Of these 300 had regained a useful degree of vision and 100 had transferred to other institutions after treatment at our hospital. The remaining 600 would be St Dunstaners for the rest of their lives. From first-war experience we could expect about as many more in the years to come.

Happily, we could not expect as many as had come from the First World War, when British Empire casualties generally had been so much higher—over 1,000,000 killed and about 2,400,000 wounded, as against about 390,000 killed and 480,000 wounded in the second war. In its three and a half years of life up to the 1918 armistice St Dunstan's had admitted 1300 for training, and a further 1500 had come afterwards. At the end of 1945 the number of 1914-18 men in our care was still 1700.

As in 1918, after the end of the fighting new admissions did not immediately decrease but increased, and when Ovingdean was handed back to us we could not just pack up at Church Stretton and return to our old home. It had been designed and built for the use of the blind, but not as a large training centre. It had neither the accommodation nor the equipment and facilities needed for the large number of new men we had under training. We would have had to spend a large sum of money on putting up temporary huts and workshops if we had returned at the end of the War.

There was no need, anyway. Much as we looked forward

to renewing our old happy association with the people of Brighton, we had all we wanted at Church Stretton, including generous hospitality and local goodwill. New entries were going to continue for some time after the War. It would have been silly to move our training centre before the peak was reached. Our Hospital Unit similarly remained at Stoke Mandeville.

Other parts of St Dunstan's could not be moved quickly enough. We did not want to outstay our welcome at Melplash Court, which Mr and Mrs Ruxton had lent us for the duration. Their generosity had enabled our permanent residents to live through the War in peace and quiet, and there was nothing to stop them from returning to Brighton. We congratulated ourselves anew on not having sold West House, which was soon got into shape again. The permanent residents were moved back in July 1945, before the workmen had finished. As the rest of the building was prepared, other men were able to go there on holiday or convalescence. Christmas was something like old times at Brighton, with seventy-five St Dunstaners in West House. Our many friends of pre-war days had evidently been lying in wait for us, for we had a wonderful welcome from the Good Companions.

We decided to keep our smaller northern holiday and convalescent home, at Blackpool, for the next few years, leaving Ovingdean clear to take in our Training Centre when we eventually left Church Stretton.

Our migration from the Shropshire hills back to the Sussex Downs was made in 1946, according to schedule, in two waves. The preliminary training departments were transferred during Easter, and industrial and massage in the August holidays. "Operation Seaside," as it was called, was carried out with military precision—if Air Commodore Dacre will permit the term, for the move was his show. We had a civic welcome, the Mayor of Brighton coming up on our roof to hoist our blue-and-gold flag again after nearly six years. The men under training came in batches so that they did not all have to learn the geography of the place together.

There were many lumpy throats and misty eyes in Church Stretton as St Dunstan's left. We had become part of the village, and our roots proved deeper than we had realized when the time came to pull them up. At the last leave-takings many St Dunstaners had madly racing thoughts and fears of not having shown their gratitude for all the villagers had done—but it was too late for graceful compliments; nobody could do much more than blurt out gruff thanks. Several years later, when I stayed at the Longmynd Hotel and suffered acute nostalgia, I met many old friends and found we had done no lasting damage to the lovely village. Indeed, we had modernized some of its hotels and given it a splendid new building, our Training Centre, which is now its County School. What Church Stretton had given us is not so easily set down, but immeasurably more valuable.

We were sorry also to lose some of our staff. Many came with us to Brighton, of course, but others left. Among these was Padre Nugee, our Chaplain, who went back to his work as parish priest. Happily he remained an Honorary Chaplain to St Dunstan's, and he has continued to give his services whenever the opportunity arose. Altogether there are five Church of England clergy; all of them are Honorary Chaplains to St Dunstan's and take a service at our chapel from time to time.

We found Brighton, with its much greater range of amenities, as hospitable as ever. There were free seats for St Dunstaners at the Grand Theatre and the Palace Pier Theatre, and at most cinemas, free entry with escorts to the Follies' Concert Party and to the Princes and Regent Dance Halls any evening. Captain Knight gave free trips on the *Martha Gunn* motor launch, and the Rottingdean Bathing Pool was reserved for us on Saturday mornings. The Shoreham Rowing Club made all our men honorary members, and took parties rowing in the evenings and at

week-ends. Sussex County Cricket Club invited St Dunstaners to all matches played at Hove, and there was free
admission to the Greyhound Track. All this, and much
private hospitality and universal friendship, made Ovingdean as good a place after the War as it had been before.

At first we were packed out. Since the last shot of the
War was fired, and military hospitals were cleared, the flow
of new entries had been swollen by the return of former
prisoners of war from the Far East. Most of those who came
to us had not been wounded, but lost their sight through
malnutrition while in captivity. Altogether we had about
fifty former prisoners of war of this sort, and some of them
had additional handicaps as well as blindness to overcome.

This kind of blindness was the result of the deficiency
diseases of beri-beri, or pellagra, which caused atrophy of
most or all of the fibres of the optic nerve. Most cases also
developed peripheral neuritis, and impairment of sensibility
of the hands and feet was very common. In many cases this
cleared up with treatment, but in some it persisted, and we
have a number of men with a diminished sense of touch.
Many cannot learn braille, and some cannot use their hands
effectively for machine-work or telephone operating; on
the other hand, some have made a remarkable recovery
and are doing very well.

When we moved from Church Stretton, then, the peak
had been reached but not yet passed. With almost two
hundred men under training or nearly ready to begin, we
had to take an extra house as a dormitory, and reserve a
few beds at West House and at Blackpool for men under
training who could do with a short convalescence. After
going through two wars without having to form queues,
we were not going to put up any 'house full' notices now.
We had nothing to spare, but with a little bit of transfer
and juggling we were able to fit everyone in so that each
man got the attention he needed.

We had, of course, put up a few temporary huts for

classrooms and workshops before the transfer took place,
and we took a small house near by as a hostel for the girls.
If a few things were not quite ready no one minded about
that. Heating would be fully installed by the winter, and
no one could have known that the summer would start with
howling gales. Not that anyone complained. "It's wonderfully airy," the new arrivals said of the braille hut, with
undeniable truth. Only when the hut was nearly blown
away did the braille class move into the Winter Garden.
But it was not long before M. Clements, in West House,
decided the time had come for him to write a little booklet
called "How to dress on the beach in three easy stages."

December 9, 1946, was the twenty-fifth anniversary of
Sir Arthur Pearson's death. As had been our custom every
year, we held a memorial service in our Chapel and laid a
wreath on our Founder's grave. If time had softened the
poignancy of his death, it had allowed us to place a more
accurate value on his work. "I measure his achievement in
the blind world as the greatest in our generation and
probably of all time," I wrote then and repeat unchanged
now, "for he revolutionized our outlook and the view of
the outside world about us, and his gospel has spread all
over the Empire and to many foreign lands."

It was twenty-five years since I had succeeded him as
Chairman, and tried to follow his ideas and ideals. St
Dunstaners all over the world presented me with a walking-
stick at our New Year's Dance, a token of a gift of table
silver to replace some that we had lost when our house was
burned down. Mr (as he was then) Winston Churchill
handed me the stick. "This is a symbol of your gratitude to
him and a crutch to aid him," he told the gathering, "not
only in finding his way about, but in disposing of anybody
who stands between him and the high purpose he serves."

The walking-stick is the oldest of aids to the blind. As
an extension of the arm it discovers steps and obstacles,

enabling the user to feel his way along without having to grope about. It guides him also through his sense of hearing, on which he mainly depends for getting about. It is not easy for a blind man to get his bearings in a busy street where there is a confused jumble of noises made up of direct sounds from the traffic and the footsteps of passersby and of the echoes from all these sounds. By tapping his stick he gets a clear sound from a fixed point in relation to himself, causing its own echo to tell him where the obstacles are. It brings an echo from the neighbouring wall, which may be close at hand, or from the wall on the other side of the street, which is farther away, or from the house opposite. It tells him where he is.

Personally I do not favour constant stick-tapping, which both sounds and looks pathetic, and I began to think of a possible alternative when I first heard about radar, the new method by which enemy aircraft were located when out of sight. Science had enabled men to 'see' objects that were invisible and to determine their direction and distance. This was the blind man's problem when finding his way about alone. I wondered if radar might provide a more efficient portable obstacle-locator than the stick, a device that would serve the blind man in the same way as sighted travellers in the dark used a pocket-torch.

I was not the only one to have this idea. Captain H. G. Round, M.C., an inventor, had already been making experiments on similar lines. Air Commodore Dacre, newly arrived at Church Stretton and with more knowledge of radar than he was allowed to divulge, suggested that I should get in touch with Air Ministry scientists. My old friend Professor E. D. (now Lord) Adrian, whom I had consulted years before as to the possibility of applying television for the production of artificial sight, wrote and told me he had heard of similar thoughts and experiments in the United States. I learnt of other wartime advances in electronics that might conceivably be of use to us. The upshot was the setting up in 1944 of a Scientific Advisory

Committee, under the Chairmanship of Professor Adrian, to carry out a thorough study—I think the first of its kind in the world—of the use of the remaining senses of hearing, touch, and smell, and their substitution for sight, more particularly in the matter of reading and walking.

After some six years' effort R. L. Beurle, who also undertook to experiment on a possible obstacle-locator, reported negative results. The wavelength of the radar beam made it unsuitable for locating small objects at ranges of a few feet. Light beams, sound beams, and ultrasonic energy had been tried instead. An acoustic 'clicker' device offered the best possibilities, and a number of blind 'guinea-pigs' were trained in its use. The first tests were encouraging, mainly because the clicker taught some of those using it to appreciate the significance of echoes they had not noticed before. More experienced walkers found that the extra information provided by the clicker did not make much difference on familiar routes.

Another big drawback to these guiding devices was that they were too bulky and heavy to be carried with convenience. Although Professor Adrian's Committee was before its time and did not succeed in finding a way of reading print, or a guiding device, they nevertheless— under the technical direction of R. L. Beurle and basing themselves on L. S. Pinder's earlier work—devised the prototype of a tape talking-book machine, which some years later was adopted. Earlier objections seemed likely to disappear with the development of the electronic art, transistor radios, and other inventions, and in the early summer of 1959 we set up another committee to study the problem afresh. This new Committee comprises Dr A. M. Uttley, of the National Physical Laboratory, Dr H. B. Barlow, of Kings College, Cambridge, Dr R. L. Beurle, Dr D. E. Broadbent, of the Medical Research Council, Cambridge, Dr M. Clowes, of the National Physical Laboratory, and myself, with Air Commodore Dacre as first Chairman. Dr Uttley succeeded to the

Chair in 1961, Dacre joining our Council and remaining lay representative on the Committee. Its terms of reference were, "to investigate guiding and reading devices, having regard to recent developments in electronics and sound-recording techniques." This Committee is quite apart from the Development Workshops Committee, under Air Commodore Dacre's chairmanship, which deals with inventions and gadgets to overcome the handicap of blindness, and, in particular, to help the doubly handicapped men. We were not the first, for in 1912 Dr Fournier d'Albe of London invented the "exploring optophone," a clever device that exploited the influence of light on the electrical resistance of selenium. It detected obstacles by distinguishing between light and shade. The user wore earphones and was informed by a buzzing tone. Because it could not give any indication of range, the device failed as a guiding aid, but d'Albe had more success when he applied it to the task of translating ink-print into recognizable sounds.

A practical means of reading the printed word has long been the philosopher's stone of the blind world, and d'Albe's optophone was the first instrument to come within reach of it. Developed by Messrs Barr and Stroud of Glasgow, it scanned ordinary type with a selenium cell and, by rotating disks, broke the letters down into five ranges of sound. The highest note was sounded when the upper portion of a letter like 'h' or 'l' was scanned; the lowest note when the selenium bridge passed over the bottom portion of 'p' or 'j.' The three intermediate musical notes responded to the portions of letters between. A remarkable blind woman, Miss Mary Jameson, learnt to use the instrument, though others who tried to learn it did not have anything like her success. Most blind people found it very hard indeed to read anything at all.

When we set up our Scientific Advisory Committee in 1944 research was started to see if the recent strides in electronic knowledge could be used to improve on the optophone, and in the United States similar experiments were undertaken by Vladimir Zworykin, the inventor of the television iconoscope. Very little progress was made on either side of the Atlantic, and Miss Jameson and two students of hers are still the only persons in the world who know how to use it. It is a wonderful invention, but the warbling sounds it gives out are not sufficiently readable for the average blind person, and production at present would be far too costly unless a large number could be made at once. However, the possibilities of a simpler, and therefore cheaper, optophone are constantly under consideration by our new Scientific Committee.

One of our men once asked if a machine could be produced to enable a sighted person with no knowledge of braille to write braille letters, so that a wife could write confidentially to her husband. Yes, it could, in a number of different ways. Peter Nye estimated that a prototype would cost at least £100. It was unlikely to be wanted by enough St Dunstaners' wives and others to bring the price of each machine down to a reasonable sum, so no experiments were made.

An improved braille writer was a different matter, for this was something in general use. "Stainless Stephen," as the old Stainsby-Wayne was sometimes called, had stood us in good stead for many years, and still had a lot in its favour. It was light and inexpensive, and wrote on both sides. But it was very noisy, and it wrote downward, so that you could not read what you had written without turning the paper over. Also it was extremely difficult for a one-handed man to use. Other machines had been designed which wrote upward, but they were heavy and expensive. I asked the Research Department to look into the matter, and in 1949 they came up with the St Dunstan's Braille Writer, writing upward like a typewriter and designed for easy operation by one hand.

After the war interest in reading braille quickened rather than slackened. The publication of *St Dunstan's Review* in

W

braille as well as ink-print was a great success. A further stimulus was an anonymous gift of £500 for the encouragement of braille reading. We drew on this money and the Arthur Pearson Memorial Fund for what I called postgraduate courses of competition. We had already been awarding £1 prizes to all who passed the Advanced Braille Reading Test, and now we raised the sum to £3. We intended also to hold an annual championship competition, but our return to Ovingdean created practical difficulties. So many St Dunstaners—including a large number of first-war men—entered and took the Advanced Test that we instituted an even stiffer one, the Senior Braille Reading Test, with a prize of £5 for a pass and a consolation prize of £2 for a very near miss. Later we increased the prizes to £8 for the Senior Test, £5 for the Advanced, and £2 for the Preliminary. Some men achieved a really striking standard, and eventually we added a second Advanced, stiffer still. Yet I doubt if anyone deserved his reward more than Alec Craigie when he received his £2 prize for passing the Preliminary. For Craigie was seventy-five. An Australian first-war man living near Brighton, I expect that he had, like me, learnt braille at Regent's Park and then promptly forgotten it. He was not too late to draw dividends of pleasure in what Tommy Rogers once happily called "investing in braille."

The recreations and entertainments at Ovingdean after the War were mostly the same as before only rather better. In November 1947 we opened our rifle range, the result of Peter Nye's experiments on the suggestion Air Commodore Dacre had made three years before. Instead of a photo-electric target excited by a beam of light, as Dacre had proposed, Nye used an electronic sighting device; but the aiming was done by hearing just the same.

The principle was simple enough even to the layman. Surrounding the barrel of a ·22 Service-pattern rifle, slightly behind the foresight, a screened circular metal ring was placed. The ring and the rifle barrel were wired into a twin-beat frequency oscillator, whose tuning was varied as the position of the barrel was moved relative to the ring. When the barrel was in the centre of the ring—and in line with the bull's-eye—the oscillator was tuned to zero so that there was no sound. The farther the rifle was moved from this central position the higher the oscillator rose in tone. The rifleman heard the note either over a loudspeaker or by earphones.

I had the honour of firing the first shot and got a bull. Lieutenant-Colonel Sir Lionel Fletcher, Chairman of the National Small Bore Rifle Association, was present at the opening ceremony and, shooting blindfold, also scored a bull. He also testified that rifle-shooting by the blind was not just a stunt. All the pleasures of the sighted marksman are enjoyed by the rifleman who shoots by hearing, and success depends on the same concentration, muscular control, and steady nerve. No wonder the rifle range became hugely popular, twenty thousand rounds of ammunition being fired in the first eighteen months.

A few months after the successful birth of this brain-child Air Commodore Dacre retired as Commandant. He had originally joined us for three years, to see the training through, but we had managed to persuade him to stay four. He had reorganized and modernized our training system, reopened Ovingdean, planned our career and settlement services, and supervised our special work for the doubly handicapped and our department of inventions and research. More largely responsible than anyone else for our re-education and training, he left us with a smoothly running organization and a sense of immense gratitude.

Dacre, continuing as Chairman of Technical Committees, was succeeded as Commandant by Lawrence Fawcett, a pre-war civil servant and wartime naval officer, who had held the same position at West House for eighteen months. He has been in charge at Ovingdean ever since.

We were still full up with men under training when
Fawcett took over from Dacre. We had begun to shed our
annexes, but it was not until October 1949 that we were
able to invite a few St Dunstaners to stay at Ovingdean for
a week's holiday, for the first time for just over ten years.
The offer went to those who we thought needed a break
most—the Muffled Drums, as our deaf-blind called themselves. They had held their first reunion as far back as
1932, and in 1948 we squeezed them into West House for a
long week-end. In October 1949 we welcomed them at
Ovingdean, where they have held their reunions ever since.

It is sad to think that there are enough deaf-blind St
Dunstaners to hold a reunion of their own, but it is heartening to be with them and see what they get out of life. On
coach trips or fishing off the pier, speaking at dinners or
dancing at dances, playing dominoes or housey-housey or
just swapping jokes and yarns, they stop any single-
handicapped man from getting a swelled head about his
own success. The Muffled Drums do not talk much about
themselves, but one of them, Wally Thomas, told his story
in a book called *Life in My Hands*, which was published in
1960, and had a well-deserved success. It has also been
broadcast in "Woman's Hour" on the B.B.C.

Something had to be done about West House, the
building we would have sold as redundant but for the
outbreak of the Second World War. It had served us well
and faithfully for nearly thirty years, and the permanent
residents loved every step and corner of it—and there were
plenty of both. But whatever they might say about it, it
was blatantly sub-standard compared with Ovingdean. Old
and old-fashioned, with no lift, rambling passages, and
inadequate accommodation and ventilation, it looked at
first sight as if the best thing would be to find somewhere
else. Easier said than done in post-war Britain; and,
besides, there was a case for keeping it. It was structurally
sound. With our great new increase in numbers it looked

as if we would need it for quite some time. The permanent residents did not want to move. So in 1949 we decided to rebuild the inside, and what was virtually a new home rose within its walls. The residents were put up temporarily at Ovingdean and at Blackpool. The reconstruction took nine months, and we were very careful to see that the modernization did not destroy the intangible character of the house. I think we succeeded in this, for when the men moved back they said it was nearly as good as it had been before.

Although the accommodation was increased, the re-modelled West House was mainly for the old and sick and lonely who needed a permanent home. Their number was increasing, and obviously would continue to rise. About a dozen beds were set aside for other men needing extended convalescence. For holidays and short convalescence we now had enough room at Ovingdean. There was a little heart-burning over this, for some of the first-war St Dunstaners preferred West House—not only for senti-mental reasons, but because they knew their way about. This quickly faded when they found how easy it was to master Ovingdean's much simpler geography.

In 1957 West House was renamed Pearson House in memory of our Founder. I cannot imagine that any other memorial would have pleased him as much as this. It was also an expression of the widespread feeling among St Dunstaners of affection and regard for their President, Sir Neville Pearson, the son of the Founder, who had throughout his adult life been a most active officer and member of the Council.

Like all other ex-Servicemen, second-war St Dunstaners had at least one big advantage over first-war men in their passage back to civilian life. There was no large-scale unemployment after the War. On the contrary, the labour-shortage continued. Men no longer needed in war indus-tries were quickly snapped up. Our men in the factories held their jobs or got new ones. Others joined them as they finished their training. There were no accidents, and the insurance companies did not charge extra premiums to cover industrial risks. Our conquest of open industry had at least outlived the War.

About 80 per cent. of our second-war men were successfully placed in positions to earn their living. Jobs were easier to find than homes, and our Housing Department had a heavy task. There was little reluctance by employers to include St Dunstaners in their 3 per cent. quota of disabled persons, although severe and light cases counted equally. In the House of Commons I suggested that where an employer took in men disabled in the severest degree they should be allowed to count as two in the percentage, but my idea was not taken up.

I made this suggestion in a debate on conditions in one of the Remploy factories, which provided employment for all classes of disabled persons who were so severely handicapped that they could not obtain other employment. I supported the idea of these sheltered factories, which proved suitable for one or two more severely disabled St Dunstaners who were unable to do the harder full-time work of a normal factory. At the same time I thought their importance had been exaggerated. Whenever it was possible—and often it was, even for doubly handicapped St Dunstaners—a disabled man was generally happier working in an open competitive factory alongside normal workmen.

A few St Dunstaners were employed by St Dunstan's itself. It had long been our policy to bring into the organization a small number of our own, and there was nothing of charity in this. We could not afford to carry passengers on the staff any more than any other employer. No jobs were made for St Dunstaners, and those we engaged had to have the necessary ability and experience. Because we regarded them in this unsentimental way, those that we took on invariably proved good investments for us.

Pat Owens was an example. A former regular soldier, he had worked his way up from sapper to R.S.M. before being commissioned in the War, so he knew Service life at every level, besides having the technical experience he had gained in the Royal Engineers. Since coming to St Dunstan's he had regained a little bit of vision, and he made light of his additional handicap of an artificial leg. At thirty-five he had a good experience of life without having lost his youth. He was ideally suited to come and take charge of the placement and after-care of shopkeepers, telephone operators, and men employed in factories and similar jobs, when the sighted man who had been doing this job moved to another department.

In 1948 the Minister of Labour appointed a Working Party on the employment of blind persons in industry and in public and other services. Our Secretary, W. G. Askew, was a member of the Working Party, and, of course, St Dunstan's officials were among the witnesses heard. It gladdened my heart to read the Woking Party's report. It was wholly positive, with all its emphasis on the abilities, not the disabilities, of the blind. "The fundamental fact is that blindness is a handicap which can be —and in innumerable instances is—overcome. . . . The value of employment to the blind is that it enables them to enter fully into the life of the community. The value of the employment of the blind to the community is that they represent a potential labour force capable, if properly used, of making a substantial contribution to the national economy." Only a few chapters ago these were revolutionary ideals. "We consider that when he engages a blind worker, an employer has the right to expect that it will be worth his while to do so. An employer has to make his business pay, and no plan for placing blind people in industrial employment can hope to succeed on any other basis than that the blind worker can and should do a full week's work in return for a full week's wage." How far had we come from the days, not long past, when the subsidized sheltered workshop was almost the only alternative to begging on the street. With our invasion of industry the work of our After-care Department had changed. (So had its name. We followed the general practice of calling it Welfare.) Home workers like basket-makers were a minority now, and we needed only one craftsman to go round visiting and advising and correcting any faults that had crept in. But factory-workers also needed to be visited regularly, to check against the possibility of their machines going out of use. As soon as our visitor saw this happening he would at once see the shop steward and the management and ask what work there would be for the operator if the machine was taken out of service. Usually they would all put their heads together, and we would have him back in our work-shops to retrain him for another machine. We might also have to invent a safeguard or gadget to enable him to use the new machine.

"Let us now praise famous men." So says an ancient writer in the Apocrypha, and we have not been slow to praise outstanding St Dunstaners. We owe them our appreciation, for they blaze new trails for all of us. But let us not forget to praise also the ordinary fellow who is just as blind, just as courageous, just as hard-working. We are proud of him, for it is his success that justifies the whole work of St Dunstan's.

Mike Ansell would probably call himself an ordinary fellow, although nobody else would. A professional Army officer before the War, he played polo for England, and was a prominent member of the British Show Jumping Team. At thirty-four he was promoted Lieutenant-Colonel, won the D.S.O. for extraordinary bravery, and lost his sight. He recovered it partly and precariously while he was a prisoner of war, and he could see just enough to get about when he came home after three and a half years of captivity. He could not read, but we arranged for him to take a course in horticulture at Reading University. He became a highly successful market gardener, winning prizes at the Chelsea Flower Show. He was also elected Chairman of the British Show Jumping Association. Then his remaining sight failed.

He came back to St Dunstan's and learnt typewriting and braille and the rest of it, and he wanted to go back to the organization of show-jumping. I told him it was an unlikely career for a blind man, but he soon proved me wrong. Within a few years he had become the leading figure in this sphere in Britain, reorganized the horse-jumping and other horse societies, and virtually put the horse back on its feet. Responsible more than any other person for the success of the British team in the Olympic and other international contests, he gained world-wide fame. For his work with the horse a C.B.E. was added to his D.S.O., and in 1957 he was exceptionally honoured by being appointed Colonel of the regiment he was commanding when he was blinded and was promoted full colonel. Mike Ansell is now a valued member of St Dunstan's Council.

Captain Alan Milne, a commando officer, read economics at London University and graduated in 1949 with first-class honours. He stayed at the London School of Economics as a research student until 1952, when he added a Ph.D. to his B.Sc. and went on a Commonwealth Fund Scholarship to an American university for a year. He is now Lecturer in Social Philosophy at Queen's University, Belfast.

Two Manx St Dunstaners, both from Castletown, have achieved professional success. Howard Simcocks, a qualified accountant before he was blinded in Italy, studied law and passed the finals of his examinations in 1948. He could not practise immediately, for he had finished his three years' studentship in two and a half years, and had to wait six months to be called to the Manx Bar. He soon became a well-known advocate and a public figure in the Isle of Man, and is now a Member of the Manx Parliament, the House of Keys. He is also Chairman of the local War

Pensions Committee, and has served as the British Legion's Secretary for the Isle of Man County for several years.

Norton Christal, Chairman of the Castletown branch of the Legion for some time, was elected County Chairman in 1959. Teaching is his profession, and he has been a master at King William's College for many years. He has served youth in various ways, notably in the Boy Scouts and in the encouragement of rugby. An outstanding three-quarter for Burton-on-Trent and a county player before the War, since he was blinded he has published a booklet entitled *Rugby Football for Young Schoolboys*.

George Ellis was a journalist, and a writer of great promise. Also an R.A.F. man, he was trained in telephone operating but had to give it up because of bad health. He loved writing and had a natural flair for it, and he made a success of free-lance journalism in spite of his physical handicaps. Besides writing for the national Press he brightened up the *St Dunstan's Review*. Reading any of his articles or letters you would say it was written by a happy man, and that would be true. Ellis was always cheerful and ready for a laugh. He was also always ill and in pain, but he called himself lucky for being only blind. One of his best friends, Wally Thomas, was totally deaf as well—and also cheerful and full of life, taking a keen interest in sport and current affairs. To help him keep in the picture, Ellis wrote him an eight-page braille letter every week, conveying all sort of news he had gathered from the radio and other sources. When he became too ill for any kind of work Ellis still tried to keep this up. "I must write to Wally," he said, in the increasingly brief respites from obliterating pain. For days he fumbled helplessly and tragically at his braille writing machine, refusing to admit defeat even when they took him away to hospital for the last time. He was only thirty-four when we lost this brave and splendid comrade.

Walter Thornton had been a teacher in Lancashire before the War, in which he served in the Royal Air Force. As

Education Officer he was stationed at St John's Wood Barracks, in Regent's Park, when London was bombarded by the V.1's. I was living in my chauffeur's cottage, next door to the bombed ruins of my own home, when the R.A.F. School was hit. I met Thornton for the first time, soon afterwards, in our Hospital Unit at Stoke Mandeville, where he was busy practising his handwriting.

Not many St Dunstaners, or blind persons generally, make much effort to keep up their standard of writing, because the typewriter usually meets all their needs, and takes their handicap in its stride. Unless practised very hard, a blind person's handwriting deteriorates with the years, and most of us do little more than keep our signature legible enough for our cheques to be honoured. However, there are a number of devices to make it easier to write in the dark, including a frame produced by the R.N.I.B. with elastic lines that allow the pencil to go up and down yet give guidance. Thornton tried using this, and also experimented with paper with braille lines, a plastic stencil, and other aids. When he came to Church Stretton he was still at it, but without any aids, and set aside a few minutes every day for writing by hand. He might have been thought the last person likely to need handwriting, for he was outstandingly quick to learn typewriting and braille, reading and writing shorthand. Yet the thing he was famous for at the Training Centre, and for which he is still widely remembered, was his remarkable facility in getting about alone. He used to walk from one house to another and all over the village with the greatest confidence and ease.

Thornton looked bound to succeed, and he undertook one of the most difficult jobs open to him. A few big firms had agreed to make an experiment in finding administrative or executive work for suitable St Dunstaners, and Cadbury's took him on. As in most placements of this kind, he started off a round peg in a square hole. His enlightened and intelligent employers went on patiently experimenting, and soon found a job that perfectly matched his abilities.

He became Youth Welfare Officer, and was so successful that he was soon promoted to the management staff. "I now find it much easier to write notes by hand on the small cards I had prepared for use with the braille pocket writer, and have almost completely discarded the latter in consequence," he wrote after two or three years. "The facility to make quick, short memo notes is invaluable in my work. Doubtless my writing will go worse as time passes, but I reckon it will be a number of years before it becomes illegible."

No doubt his ability to walk about unaided helped him a lot, too, especially when he was running a camp with over a hundred and fifty boys. One of his big tasks was to organize a Festival of Youth and Industry at Bourneville, with a variety of athletic activities for over 1600 competitors representing nine countries and a hundred different firms. He broadcast on his job, wrote a booklet about it, and even wrote for doctors on blindness in the *Lancet*. He revived life-saving as a Youth Club activity at Bourneville, entered his club in the National Competition of the Royal Life-saving Society, and helped it win first prize in its class year after year. When he took a party of the boys to France Thornton entered for the French National Life Saving Award—"just for fun"—passed, and inspired twelve of the lads to do the same.

Those who have gone into farming—and we have 150 men in country life to-day—have done very well too. Handicrafts have not been entirely neglected by second-war St Dunstaners, and in the craft of hand-weaving there are few people more expert than Sergeant-Major M. Lees, formerly of the 3rd (Mixed) Heavy A.A. Regiment. The M stands for Maureen, and she was in charge of a group of 1500 gun-site girls during the War—the second war, that is; for Maureen is one of the few women, and certainly the only one who has come to St Dunstan's, to have been in the Services in both world wars. Operating five looms in her coach-house workshop at Birkenhead, Maureen has not only won countless prizes for her own beautiful work but has taught weaving to many other persons who are physically disabled in some way. A Founder-Member of the Weavers' Guild, she has worked ceaselessly to encourage and raise the standard of hand-weaving in general and to bring the joys of craftsmanship to the handicapped.

Little more than a bare generation ago a blind man only had to do something a little out of the ordinary for the story to be splashed in newspapers. To-day he has to do something exceptional even in our eyes to rate more than a paragraph. This decrease in free publicity may make appeals organizers a little wistful, and it would obviously be a very bad thing if people were to start thinking that blind-welfare organizations no longer needed so much support. With this reservation, the change is wholly heartening.

When, for example, a blind hero of a fire rescue is praised just like any other man who risks his life to save others, and not as if he had performed a temporary miracle on himself, we begin to realize how far we have come. John Hughes, of Rock Ferry, was a case in point a few years ago. He found his next-door neighbour with her clothing ablaze. A woman of fifty-three, she was rushing round panic-stricken. "The only way I could stop her was to trip her up and throw her to the ground," he told a reporter apologetically afterwards. "While I stripped off her blazing clothing, I shouted to my wife to bring a carpet. I rolled her in it and my wife telephoned for an ambulance." He did not mention that his own hands were burnt through his action. The account that appeared in the *Liverpool Echo* emphasized his courage rather than his blindness.

Gilbert Stanley, one of our telephone operators, took up judo, and was accepted into the local Judo Club on equal terms as a matter of course. Bob Pringle hitch-hiked to Naples alone, without any dark glasses or white stick, and got just the same treatment as any other young man who thumbs his way along. He counted a few tumbles in ditches a small price to pay for this novel adventure in independence. It was a remarkable feat, but the trail had been blazed by men like Tommy Milligan and Walter Thornton, who took the terrors out of walking about alone.

Jock Macfarlane has made the use of public transport commonplace by commuting from his home in Essex to the City of London daily for nearly forty years. A telephone operator with the Export Credits Guarantee Department, he was awarded the B.E.M. after thirty years' service. Then in 1956 he was elected to represent Southern England for three years on the Civil Service Union's Grading Committee for telephonists. At the first meeting of the Committee he was elected Chairman—not because he was blind nor yet in spite of it, but simply as the best man for the job. And when he led a deputation to the Treasury no one raised an eyebrow.

So many things have changed, but there is one that has not, and I hope never will. This is the tendency among St Dunstaners to want to help others less fortunate than themselves. Rex Furness working unceasingly for the blind of Warrington, W. T. Scott giving his spare time talking to and helping the deaf-blind, Norman Perry helping the crippled children of Grimsby, Bob Britton giving parties for the deaf children of Blackburn—these and others, little-known and unambitious for any limelight, serve quietly but splendidly. They would not thank me for publishing the facts of their service, but—unhappily—I cannot embarrass Edward Patrick Ward by telling a little of his story. Ward is dead.

He was a corporal in the Anti-Aircraft Battalion of the Irish Army, one of three young soldiers blinded by the accidental explosion of an anti-tank mine while on manœuvres. They were taken to St Bricin's Military Hospital in Dublin, where they received the devoted care of nurses and doctors but no proper training or employment. I was asked if they could come to St Dunstan's.

The Irish Republic was neutral, so I asked myself

whether these three young men were potential friends or foes. I decided that in the dire event of the British Isles being overrun by the Germans they would be on our side, either as soldiers or as members of the Resistance Movement, and that made them potential allies. So I arranged for them to become full St Dunstaners and enjoy all the benefits of our organization. If I was politically wrong I am quite sure that I was on the side of the angels, and that it was a humane decision.

The three young men did very well at St Dunstan's, and all found useful and remunerative employment and happiness. One is now a successful physiotherapist in England, and another a very good telephone operator in Ireland. The third was Corporal Ward.

He trained as a telephonist and, being a Dubliner, went back to work on the St Bricin's hospital exchange. A laughing, cheerful easy-going fellow, earning his own living in a useful job, happily married with two fine children, his cup of happiness overspilled. Unasked and unrewarded—in material terms, at least—he made it his vocation in life to help complete the training of civilian blind people as telephonists. In this way he helped some twenty men and women to their own independence before a car accident cruelly took him away.

As Chairman of St Dunstan's and the only blind Member of Parliament I was naturally asked from time to time to try to persuade the authorities to make some special concession for the blind. Sometimes I refused to make the attempt because I thought the demand irrelevant to the handicap of blindness.

I was asked, for example, to appeal for a free television licence for the blind. I had myself advocated a free wireless licence, on the grounds that the wireless was the blind man's newspaper, his magazine, his source of entertainment in his home, and his special friend. He did not enjoy the ancient monuments, the National Trust properties, the flowers in the parks, the national galleries, and other beautiful things that, as a tax-payer, he helped to pay for: so he was entitled to this concession in compensation. I used exactly the same argument in support of a proposal to remit purchase tax from wireless sets sold to the British Wireless for the Blind Fund. In both cases we were successful because our requests were reasonable. Sound radio could have been invented for the blind, and meant more to them than to sighted persons. Nothing like that could be said of television, and I would not ask for free licences.

I took the same attitude over a request for reduced telephone charges, although there was some point in the argument that the telephone is an exceptionally useful means of communication for the blind. On the other hand, I wholeheartedly supported a plea that guide-dogs should be allowed to travel on buses, free of charge, even though other dogs were banned. Again, as a matter of duty I sat in the House of Commons until five o'clock one morning to argue the case for the removal of purchase tax from baskets because they were made largely by the disabled and blind. We were debating the Committee stage of the Finance Bill, and any foreign visitor who might have wandered into the Strangers' Gallery—perhaps curious to know what matter of great national importance was being discussed by the Mother of Parliaments while the rest of the country slept—would have doubtless been surprised to hear me protesting against the law that taxed baskets with a wooden bottom at the rate of $66\frac{2}{3}$ per cent., while the same baskets made wholly of willow or cane were taxed at only $33\frac{1}{3}$ per cent. The point was that the latter were harder for a blind man to make, and 25 per cent. of St Dunstaners could not make many baskets satisfactorily unless they had wooden bottoms. The Government conceded the point to the extent of cutting the purchase tax on wooden-bottom baskets to $33\frac{1}{3}$ per cent., so the all-night vigil had not been a waste of time.

Where should the line be drawn? It is not always easy

to decide on a particular case, but I think the essential difference lies between the handicap of blindness and the handicap of poverty. Sometimes the two go together, but they are not necessarily the same. If a claim or a request, made ostensibly on account of blindness, is really an appeal for help on account of poverty, it ought to be made as such and not confused. Others are poor besides some of the blind.

A good illustration of the distinction can be drawn from the long-established concession for railway travel, under which a sighted escort travelling with a blind person may travel free. Why, I have often been asked, is it two fares for the price of one instead of free fares for the blind? The answer is that if a blind person can travel by himself—and some do—then obviously blindness is not stopping him from travelling and he is not at any very severe disadvantage. If, on the other hand, he cannot travel by himself or he needs the company of a guide at the other end, then he is at a disadvantage on account of blindness. The issue has nothing to do with riches or poverty but solely with blindness.

Of course, on all such matters I addressed the authorities as an advocate, not a judge, and I could therefore legitimately ask for more than I expected to receive. At the same time I think it is both uncivilized and unprofitable to over-play one's hand.

The return of peace heralded the beginning of a fresh long campaign with the Minister of Pensions. At the end of the War the basic rate was still 40s., and we got our first rise in a curious way. Two or three years earlier I happened to be the first in the House of Commons to make a strong plea for the principle of Workmen's Compensation to be changed. At that time compensation was scaled down as the injured man's earnings went up, and I complained and eventually introduced a new Bill, but the General Election came before it could be passed. One of the first

X

measures of the post-war Labour Government was to bring the Bill in again. Outlining its proposals in the House of Commons, the Minister of Pensions said that compensation for injured workmen, instead of being related to the wages lost, would be fixed at 45s. a week. I immediately interrupted to say that injured soldiers must receive at least as good treatment as injured workmen.

There was no answer to this, and the only question was how much rise we would get. The British Legion and St Dunstan's thought men injured in the service of their country ought to get better treatment than civilian workmen, and a rate of 60s. seemed reasonable, with increased wife's and children's allowances. We again proposed that these should be paid irrespective of date of marriage or of children's birth. We also asked for other long-standing anomalies and injustices to be corrected, notably the need for a substantial increase in additional allowances for the most severely disabled.

In the event the Minister met most of our supplementary claims but disappointed us by raising the basic rate only to 45s. It stayed at this figure from 1945 to 1952, while prices and wages rose and rose. Successive concessions were made for those too badly injured to be able to work—about 6 per cent. of the whole—until these most deserving cases were receiving about twice as much as at the end of the War. On the basic rate, however, the Government would not budge. Whenever I drew attention to the steady decrease in the value of 45s. I was reminded that war pensioners who were employed were getting the same rises in wages as other workers. I thought this missed the point. A disability pension is a make-weight for a handicap not only in work but in the enjoyment of leisure—indeed, in the whole activity of living. If a man conquered his handicap so well that he was earning his keep it seemed unjust to allow inflation to cut his pension on the grounds that his wages were keeping pace.

I pressed continually for a Select Committee to inquire

into war pensions, and a motion I tabled in 1948 was signed by 275 Members, nearly 70 of them Labour; but the Government refused, and against all our efforts the controversy fell into party politics. Conservatives were accused of making political capital out of our grievances. Labour was accused of prejudice against the British Legion. Hot and harsh words were exchanged in Parliament and in the Press. My own position was made more difficult by my recent election as President of the Legion.

As Vice-Chairman I had served the usual term of three years, which ended in 1946. I had declined the invitation to go forward to the Chair, because with my work at St Dunstan's and in the House of Commons I had my hands full. The Presidency, on the other hand, is not a full-time administrative job like the Chairmanship, and it was a great honour to be chosen to succeed Field Marshal Earl Haig, Admiral of the Fleet Earl Jellicoe, and Major General Sir Frederick Maurice. Whether the Legion was wise in choosing an active politician instead of a professional officer is not for me to say. I only know that I was the first President to be attacked from within the ranks of the Legion itself, and there was a time when resignation was seldom far from my mind. I was not alone in these thoughts. An amendment to the Royal Charter to make any serving M.P. ineligible for the office of President was moved at two Annual Conferences, and at a third Legion history was made by a motion of censure on the President.

In some countries, notably the U.S.A. and France, there are two or more ex-Servicemen's organizations, and the differences between them are mainly political. The British Legion, as a single body, has always been carefully non-partisan. Like the Irishman, it has been 'agin all Governments' from time to time when they have seemed to be over-reluctant to meet the Legion's claims. Any organization bringing pressure to bear on any Government always gets more support from the party in Opposition than from supporters of the Government. Hence the charge, during

the two post-war Labour Governments, that we were playing party politics. After the General Election of 1951 the
parties changed sides, and as a Government supporter I
had to tackle the Minister of Pensions from the rear. I had
been doing this for many years before the War, of course,
but I had not been President of the Legion then.

The first Budget of the new Government gave the war-
disabled a rise of 10s. in the basic rate. This still did not
restore our earlier position—55s. in 1952 was worth less
than 45s. in 1945—and I said that it was less than I had
hoped, and fell very far short of what I had wished. We
were asking for 90s. Following my usual custom, I thanked
the Government for what it had done and gave notice that
we would press for more.

It was this speech of mine that brought on the censure
motion at the Legion's Annual Conference, which said I
had forfeited the confidence of the Legion and called on me
to resign. I thanked the proposer and seconder of the
motion for giving the conference an opportunity to discuss
a matter which was one of principle, but reminded them
that I had thanked the post-war Labour Governments many
times, often for relatively minor concessions. I had thanked
every Government that had ever given us anything, and I
proposed to continue to do so. When the motion of censure
was put to the Conference it was defeated by 650 votes to 5.

I had never regarded the Ministry of Pensions as anything but a friend, in spite of our numerous arguments and
disagreements. Successive Ministers and permanent officials had always been mainly helpful and sympathetic, and
over the years they had come to know our needs. I had
called the Ministry some hard names in my time, but I had
never suggested it was redundant. In 1953 the Government said it was, and decided to merge it with the Ministry
of National Insurance in spite of strong protests by the
British Legion. The Government won their motion by 226
votes to 212, and I was one of the 212.

Meanwhile we were still waiting for another increase in

the basic rate, and when the responsible Minister began lacing his answers with remarks about the majority of pensioners being employed and benefiting from wage-increases we opened a fresh intensive campaign. Our demand was still 90s., a figure that had originated in a curious way. In 1946 a judge in a civilian accident case had awarded a capital sum that would be sufficient to yield 90s. a week. After eight years of creeping inflation—which sometimes went at a pretty fast creep—this would buy a good deal less than the 40s. basic rate in 1939. A rise to 67s. 6d. in 1955 seemed at least a step in the right direction. I ventured to thank the Government, and this time my gratitude escaped criticism.

This was still the rate two years later, but a major reform now looked imminent. For this reason I offered myself for re-election as President of the British Legion for another year. I had served ten, and had thought it was time for a change, but after having been in the campaign all that time I wanted to see it through.

In the end we got 85s., which, with generous special allowances, was a good settlement. I record the grateful thanks of disabled ex-Servicemen and women to the Right Hon. John Boyd-Carpenter, M.P., Minister of Pensions and National Insurance at that time.

The following year I said farewell to the Legion and also to the House of Commons, on being honoured with a Life Peerage. My position at St Dunstan's was happily unchanged.

Since the War St Dunstan's has continued to receive a proportion of the annual Poppy Day Collection, by arrangement with the British Legion, a sum that has usually amounted to between £30,000 and £40,000. Our average total annual expenditure has been—and still is—between £500,000 and £600,000.

Shortly after the War we had a fresh actuarial calculation made to discover the value of our funds then spread over the lifetime of all our men. At that time—in 1946—we had 1673 men from the First World War, with an average age of fifty-six, and 666 young men and 20 young women from the Second. It was estimated in the next thirty years there would be 473 further additions as a result of delayed blindness attributable to or aggravated by war service. If there were no more wars the last St Dunstaner—probably a woman, for women live longer than men—would probably die in the year 2006.

This 1946 actuarial survey showed that our assets were a little under two-thirds of the sum estimated to be necessary to capitalize our future commitments. Thanks to further public generosity in the following years, we were able to raise the sum required to bridge this gap, but the severe drop in the purchasing power of money prevented us from reaching our objective. This had not been unexpected, and we had applied our judgment to the situation, using the actuary's reports as a guide. It was fortunate that we did, as otherwise we should have been unable to maintain our services to our beneficiaries.

A fresh actuarial survey in 1959 showed that our funds were still not adequate for the task we had undertaken. Nevertheless, we were doing well, and if a reasonable measure of support continued for a few years yet, and provided there was no national crisis or devaluation, we could expect to succeed. Therefore after very careful thought we decided to abate the most highly organized forms of competitive money-raising, and rely upon subscriptions, donations, deeds of covenant, and legacies. While not refusing any form of modest voluntary help that was offered to us, we announced that we should much prefer our friends all over the world to concentrate on those four forms of support during the next few years. That is still our appeals policy to-day.

Meanwhile we had seen the advent of the Welfare State.

In 1944 the Coalition Government published its proposals for the new National Insurance scheme. Ominously, from our point of view, the White Paper expressed doubt whether the social security benefits would apply to those in receipt of disability pensions and their dependants. I spoke up quickly about this. It seemed to us totally unfair that a disabled ex-Serviceman compelled to pay the full contributions should be denied the full benefits because he was receiving a disability pension that had nothing whatever to do with the scheme. I urged the principle that he who paid a full contribution should receive the full benefits. I pressed the point in and out of Parliament, and I was still having to argue it four years after the White Paper when the National Insurance scheme came into force.

In the meantime I had felt obliged to press hard for other things, including the payment of ordinary family allowances in respect of children for whom Ministry of Pensions allowances were already being paid. I had also been a member of an all-party deputation to the Minister on behalf of the civilian blind, who were in danger of receiving substantially less in allowances under the new legislation than they were already getting.

The coming of the Welfare State did not greatly affect St Dunstan's, except in an unpleasantly back-handed way. When I was in New York in 1952 I spent four hours in court giving evidence in a case in which a large legacy—worth over £60,000—was being contested on the ground that St Dunstan's had been nationalized. I explained that it had not, and that in my opinion the National Health Act did not give the Minister power to nationalize it. We won the case.

The Welfare State had caused us to make administrative changes, but it had not affected the structure of St Dunstan's. We remained a purely voluntary organization, and happily, in my opinion, State welfare did not kill philanthropy.

In 1944 W. H. Ottaway retired from St Dunstan's after twenty-six years' service. He had held many important offices since coming on the staff as Superintendent of

Workshops in Regent's Park. Almost every St Dunstaner knew him, and counted him a friend, and they all wanted to make him a farewell gift. So a fund was opened, with W. G. Askew as Hon. Treasurer, and Mr Ottaway was asked what sort of present he would like.

"I should like a fountain-pen, as a personal memento of you all," he said, "and please send the balance of the money to the National Deaf-Blind Helpers' League, for the purchase of braille watches to be issued at their discretion. May I express the hope that you will, perhaps, each year, make further gifts for the same purpose? It would be splendid if, ultimately, all deaf-blind persons could have watches by the aid of the generosity and sympathetic efforts of the men and women of St Dunstan's."

The balance was enough to buy seven braille watches for the civilian deaf-blind. The fund was kept open, and within five years over a hundred watches had been bought, at a cost of about £5 each. Almost the whole of the money had been subscribed by St Dunstaners. It had come in without any great fund-raising appeal. Our Bridge Club, for example, decided that it was just the thing to take the place of the wartime Comforts Fund. For the rest an occasional reminder by Mr Askew in the *St Dunstan's Review* was enough. Ten years after Mr Ottaway's retirement over £700 had been subscribed and the fund was still going strong. It has since gone over £1000, and over two hundred watches have been bought, and have brought happiness to doubly handicapped civilians. As I said, the Welfare State did not kill philanthropy.

Soon after the end of the War Air Commodore Dacre had invited my wife and me to dinner with Air Chief Marshal Sir John Slessor and Lady Slessor to talk over a suggestion Dacre had made that, before our vast Air Force all over the world was largely demobilized, a collection for St Dunstan's should be arranged. This proposal appealed to Sir John, and was soon authorized by the Air Council,

and in 1946 Lord Tedder handed me a cheque for
£126,000; and there was more to follow. We handed
an agreed proportion of the fund to the Scottish National
Institution for the War Blinded at Newington House.
With the agreement of the Air Council, the rest of the
fund was to be spent at the discretion of St Dunstan's
over a period of forty years on a variety of objects, in
particular for the provision and maintenance of a seaside
home for the children of St Dunstaners and for clubs for
our men in London and provincial centres. A small proportion was devoted to Technical Research. This magnificent gift—the largest of its kind we have ever had to deal
with—was a fine contribution from the men and women
of the Royal Air Force to our work for all blinded ex-
Service men and women, including, of course, a substantial
number from the R.A.F.

The children's holiday home was set up at Rottingdean,
near Brighton. Northgate House was used as a hostel for
our physiotherapy students until the end of 1947, when we
had it adapted for the use of our daughters and sons. There
was accommodation for fifteen big and little children, and
from the start it was a roaring and occasionally howling
success. In no time at all it was scarcely possible to believe
it had been used for any other purpose.

The London Club had to wait until we found a suitable
building for our headquarters. After being bombed out of
the Inner Circle of Regent's Park we had taken three
houses in near-by Park Crescent on a short lease, and we
used these for our offices until the end of 1947.

We wanted to get our works side under the same roof,
so we looked for a building big enough to hold everything.
We limited our search to the Baker Street area, because it
is so familiar to St Dunstaners and our staff and the public.
Finally we found what we wanted at 191 Marylebone Road,
which had once been used by Queen Charlotte's Hospital.
About the same time we were lucky enough to secure a
long lease at a nominal rent of a big house at No. 1 South

Audley Street, for our Appeals and Chairman's Offices and the Council's and Committees' Board Rooms.

We still kept a house in London that was used as a hostel for St Dunstaners from outside the capital. This was very necessary for men coming to Headquarters on business or passing through on their way to and from Brighton or Ovingdean. The London Club, for which rooms were put aside in the new Headquarters building, would help to make them feel at home. It would take the place of the old lounge in Regent's Park.

Run by a Committee of St Dunstaners themselves, the London Club was a success from the start. It was, as we intended, not so much a stage for entertainments as a social, friendly place where old comrades could meet. Instead of putting on elaborate shows the Committee arranged some of our traditional indoor games and outdoor sports. Walking, rowing in Regent's Park, swimming at the Marylebone Baths—all this was just like old times. Indoors there were dominoes and chess, darts, whist drives, and especially bridge. Since its foundation in 1938 our Bridge Club had grown greatly, and the London Club became its permanent home.

It also provided a headquarters for our magicians, another post-war growth. In 1947 the National Association of Magical Societies and the International Brotherhood of Magicians had decided to conduct their National Day of Magic in aid of St Dunstan's. The result was a splendid cheque—and an offer of free tuition. Members of one of the societies, the Institute of Magicians, volunteered to disclose their secrets to St Dunstaners who wanted to do some conjuring themselves.

Of course, there was a ready response. It is an agreeable paradox that one of the worst possible entertainments for the blind to attend is an admirable hobby when the blind man is the entertainer. Dannie McLoughlin, our Irish singer from the First War, had conjured professionally with great success, and Jeff Bond's success on the stage at

Church Stretton was still fresh in our memories. Led by Smudger Smith and Rees Warren—billed inevitably as "the Welsh Wizard"—enough learnt to justify forming a St Dunstan's Section of the Institute of Magicians. It was eventually merged into the London Club.

Of course, the London Club was to the especial advantage of Londoners, but that was not metropolitan favouritism. At no other centre in the country could you find two hundred St Dunstaners living permanently within a circle of ten miles. And it was a good place for men coming to London or passing through. We would have liked to provide similar premises for clubs in other large cities, but it was not practicable. Fortunately, several of them had their own clubs and ran them with great success.

There had been a St Dunstan's Club in Birmingham since 1921, and it had held regular monthly meetings—sports in the summer, socials in the winter—until 1939. It was revived soon after the War by one of our most indefatigable supporters, Avis Spurway, the wife of the Vicar of Titchfield. The problem of accommodation was solved by the generosity of the Edgbaston branch of the British Red Cross Society, who not only lent their headquarters but threw in their wonderful Hospitality Committee as well.

The Red Cross also provided a home for the revived Manchester Club, while the Liverpool Club—formed in 1949—was given similar help at the local headquarters of the British Legion. The Brighton and District Club naturally met at Ovingdean. The British Legion again helped when a St Dunstan's Club was formed at Cardiff in 1954. The youngest of our clubs is the one at Sutton, which dates only from 1957.

St Dunstan's Camps, another wartime casualty, were revived before the clubs. Again we had to thank Padre and Avis Spurway of Titchfield (now of Dorking), who had arranged annual camps for us every year from 1920 to 1939. Mrs Spurway refused to be beaten by problems of accommodation and catering in 1945. She had her eye on some huts at Lee-on-Solent, and asked the Fleet Air Arm if she might borrow them. No, they said, gently but firmly, she could not. But the Commodore of H.M.S. *Daedalus* kindly offered to put us under canvas in the grounds of Seafield Park, which was part of his land-based ship. More, he undertook to do the catering. "Done," said Mrs Spurway, and forty St Dunstaners duly turned up. If they thought the Navy had done its bit they had a shock waiting for them. Cruising on the Solent, rip-roaring parties in Petty Officers' Messes, a supper-dance at the Wrennery—there was all this, and a generous slice out of the whole ship's company's ration of cigarettes and beer. Guide wires had been put up from tent to tent and all round the camp, and the organizing officer had shown an almost uncanny insight into the men's needs although he was a stranger to St Dunstan's—a deficiency that he was to remedy quite quickly and very thoroughly, for his name was Lawrence Fawcett, and he is our present Commandant.

St Dunstan's Navy Week became an annual institution. H.M.S. *Daedalus* told Mrs Spurway that they actually enjoyed having St Dunstaners as their guests, and wanted us to come again—and again, year after year. We have done, and are still coming, thanks to Avis Spurway and the R.N.A.S.

The R.A.F. gave us similar hospitality, so long as there were enough men to take advantage of it, at Shawbury, near Church Stretton. Miss Oliphant's camp for St Dunstaners living in the south-west was revived in 1947, at Westbury, and is still going strong.

Between the wars we had set great store by our reunions in various parts of the country, and it always made me feel envious when I read of wartime reunions in the Dominions. Travelling and catering difficulties, the black-out, and risk of air raids made them impossible for us. However, from 1943 I was usually able to invite a few other St Dunstaners to have lunch with me when I visited any of the larger provincial towns. This was something—in fact, a great deal—although these reunions were only small and generally limited to men living in the centre of big cities. It made us all look back wistfully to our old reunions, when men from a whole area and from many counties used to gather together. It also made me resolved to revive reunions as soon as we could after the War.

And so we did, in spite of rationing and other difficulties. In the summer of 1946 there was at least one reunion in some part of the country every week. Attendances were very high—but a new problem underlined one of the big changes since before the War. Weekdays were better for both travel and accommodation, and they had suited home handicraft workers; but with so many more men working regularly in offices, and especially in factories, we now held some reunions on Saturday afternoons.

Reunions are very much local affairs, a fact that is specially noticeable to people who recognize one another by ear. They talk and sing quite differently in Cardiff and Birmingham, Edinburgh and Dublin. Also they have different ideas of entertainment. At one centre there is always a concert party, at another it would be unthinkable to have anything but dancing and games. But, of course, common factors outweigh the differences. Old friends meet again and swop stories about the past, and there is a happy buzz of conversation and laughter. A reunion is an unfailing tonic for anyone who is feeling a bit sorry for himself, whose stock of St Dunstan's spirit is falling low. He replenishes it from the common pool, and yet there is more in the pool after the reunion than before.

Of course, not every man's troubles can be blown away by gusts of laughter, but that is another reason for reunions. Members of the Headquarters Welfare Staff and representatives of the various departments are always present, and any man with a problem has the opportunity to talk them over at the highest level without having to

make a long journey to Headquarters. Reunions are valuable
for St Dunstan's officials, too. By mixing with a group of
St Dunstaners they learn how individuals are getting on,
and how a cross-section is affected by matters of general
concern.

A few months after the end of the War my wife and I
went to South Africa on private family business. I hoped to
confer with St Dunstan's South Africa Committee and meet
a few old St Dunstaners again as well. In the event we
were received with such hospitality that it was often difficult to get my own business done.

The preliminary training centre at Tembani had closed
down a few months before we arrived, but we went to see
the delightful house and grounds where so many men had
had their first taste of St Dunstan's. It had been the creation
of the South Africa Committee, a separate St Dunstan's
organization entirely independent of the Mother Country,
but working in the closest sympathy and harmony with the
parent body. Ovingdean was now the training-centre for
South African St Dunstaners, and we were glad to go on
trying to repay a little of the unbounded hospitality that
had been lavished on St Dunstaners, and on all British
troops who were fortunate enough to call at South Africa
during the War. The South Africa Committee, under the
chairmanship of H. M. Alers-Hankey—and still with the
expert advice of secretary Mrs Chadwick Bates, carried
on the after-care of St Dunstaners from both wars.

Our visit would have been exhausting if it had not been
so invigorating. We travelled thousands of miles in the
Union, and at every town the local committee and St
Dunstaners gave us a wonderful reception. They asked me
to give many talks, interviews, and lectures, and every-
where I was delighted to find what a splendid name for
themselves the South African St Dunstaners had won.
Besides meeting many of them I saw most of the parents,
wives, and sweethearts of the South Africans still in train-

ing at Ovingdean, and collected a lot of messages for personal delivery when I got back. We managed to take time off for a brief riding trip in the Basuto Mountains, and I was glad to find I could still stay on a horse. We only did a hundred miles in five days, but it was a great adventure to us after no more than a couple of dozen short rides in the previous five years.

We flew back home, stopping at Nairobi, where I made contact with a Salvation Army institution that was looking after a number of blinded African soldiers. It was a thrill and pleasure to touch down in England on a beautiful spring day and smell the sweet fresh air, so different from the desert.

We have made many more visits to South Africa since then, almost every year, and always there have been happy reunions with St Dunstaners from both wars. As telephone operators and physiotherapists, farmers and shopkeepers, and in many other walks of life—stonemason and wood-turner, wholesale merchant sock-maker, cartage contractor —our South African comrades have achieved splendid successes.

I have mentioned Michael Norman, who entered the Church. With him at Cambridge University was a fellow-countryman, Ken McIntyre. Already a B.A. of Rhodes University, Grahamstown, McIntyre took a B.A. Honours degree at Cambridge. Back in South Africa he was appointed Lecturer in History at the University of Natal. Now he is Senior Lecturer in History at Durban University—one of our outstanding academic successes.

Then there was Jimmy Ellis, the almost handless trumpeter of Tembani and Church Stretton, and founder-editor of the *Tembani Times*. While in South Africa he had met and married V.A.D. Laura Mullins, of Rondebosch. He had also started going out to schools and meetings to talk about St Dunstan's work. So when he had finished his training in England we took him on our Appeals staff, and he travelled all over Britain lecturing. That lasted five years. Then in 1950 he brought his wife back to South Africa, to take up the appointment of Appeals Representative for the Union. He soon started a new magazine, the *St Dunstan's (S.A.) Review*, and we had some fun spotting which of the unsigned articles he had written himself.

It was almost like going back home for Ellis as well as his wife. He had spent the first year and more of his new life with Batey as his philosopher and guide, and had the benefit of this until 1952, when Batey retired. She had worked for St Dunstan's from the start, given it thirty-seven years. It was hard to imagine it without her. But she had been ill for nearly a year, and within a few months she died. We had lost one of the builders of St Dunstan's and one of our best friends.

Jimmy Ellis carried on as Appeals Organizer for nearly ten years. Then, in 1959, he was appointed National Public Relations Officer for the South African National Council for the Blind. "Life for me is people," he said once. There are 30,000 blind people in South Africa, where this doubly handicapped St Dunstaner is following the old tradition of helping less fortunate civilian blind.

In 1947 I wrote to the Governments of Australia and New Zealand renewing our invitation to provide training for any blinded Servicemen they might care to send. The first reaction to this was a welcome visit by our old friend Joe Lynch, the St Dunstaner President of the Federal Australian Blinded Soldiers' Association. He came to see how things had changed since his own days at Regent's Park, and to talk the whole matter over.

There were, I knew, some sixty-five to seventy Australian Servicemen who had been blinded in the Second World War. I knew also that although geographical difficulties had prevented centralized training and research in Australia itself, the Repatriation Committee under Gilbert Nobbs had done brilliantly in getting men back into normal life. They had placed several men in industry, mainly as process workers or telephone operators. But there were still many who wanted and needed training, and in 1948 a party of nineteen of them arrived.

They all made good in their different ways. Eric Hailes took up an occupation rare for a St Dunstaner, that had yet been popular among the blind for over a hundred years. Ever since two blind music students in Paris succeeded in restoring a "wreck of instrument" to a playable condition, in 1830, piano-tuning had been learnt and practised by blind persons with a musical ear. After his preliminary training at Ovingdean we entered Hailes as a student at the Northern Polytechnic. Two years later he passed his finals, receiving a Silver Medal for taking first place in the examinations out of a class of fifty.

New Zealand did not need us to the same extent, the 'little St Dunstan's' set up at Auckland—the Blinded Servicemen's Trust Board—had been able to look after its own. One or two New Zealanders came to us after the War, but most were trained in their own country. Donald McPhee was still in charge. Sir Clutha Mackenzie was still at Dehra Dun.

After the end of the War a new St Dunstaner had gone out to help him in his work. He was Major Ronald Bridges, a professional soldier, an officer of the 7th Gurkha Rifles, who had been blinded in action in Burma in 1945. Meanwhile Clutha Mackenzie visited Nepal, at the invitation of the Maharaja, to discuss the resettlement of blinded Gurkha soldiers on completion of their training at Dehra Dun.

This was the beginning of a succession of missions by Mackenzie to many parts of Asia and Africa. Next he went to China, not yet under Communist rule. Mackenzie reported on blindness in the country in general, and advised on the training of war-blinded soldiers. Then he went to Malaya and Singapore, at the invitation of the respective Governments, to advise on the setting up of a blind welfare service. At Mackenzie's suggestion the post of Adviser on Blind Welfare was given to Major David

Y

Ronald Bridges, who had spent part of his boyhood in Malaya, where his father was in the medical service.

Bridges followed in his father-in-law's footsteps—he married Elizabeth Mackenzie, Sir Clutha's daughter— and created Malayan history when a blind girl was placed as a telephone operator for the first time. Bridges was awarded the O.B.E. for his work in Malaya, where he stayed for ten years before going to Manila in 1958 as Director of the newly formed Far East Regional Office of the American Foundation for Overseas Blind.

Meanwhile Mackenzie had continued the work he had begun in India on the development of a system of braille reading and writing suitable for the main Eastern languages. This led to his appointment as braille consultant to U.N.E.S.C.O., and to the spreading of the use of braille throughout Asia and Africa. In the course of this work Mackenzie was invited by the Turkish Government for consultations on the modification of Turkish braille and to survey and report on general blind welfare problems in the country. It was his first visit to Turkey since he was blinded there in 1915.

Africa came next, beginning with a thorough survey of the blind in the four territories of British East Africa. Reporting that about one out of every two hundred was blind in the area, he set to work to plan and develop welfare services for thousands to whom blindness was indeed a calamity until he brought them the message he had himself received at St Dunstan's.

He found a remarkable exception to this in the blind women of Uganda. Most of them were married, and many had married after loss of sight. Evidently blindness was no bar to marriage, the dowry price for a young blind woman being the same as that for a sighted girl. It was taken for granted that she would be able to do all the normal duties of a housewife and mother, and invariably she did.

"In no other country within my experience, where no extensive blind welfare service exists, do blind women occupy such a relatively equal status with the sighted and have such normal marital life," reported Mackenzie. "In fact, unmarried blind girls in advanced countries stand much less chance of marriage than those of Uganda."

He asked their husbands why they had married blind girls.

"Because a blind girl is less apt to run away," he was told.

In all other respects, he saw, there was no appreciable difference between blind and sighted wives. The blind wives cooked, cleaned, washed clothes, bore and brought up children, cultivated crops, and made the usual types of household matting and domestic basketware. Mackenzie found two blind women, middle-aged, who had married a second time after the deaths of their husbands, in each case to a brother of the dead husband. Mackenzie estimated that 80 per cent. of all the blind women of Uganda enjoyed this gallant independence.

Sir Clutha Mackenzie was awarded the Kaisar-i-Hind Gold Medal for public services in India. For his unique missionary work in two continents he received the 1957 award for Outstanding Services to the World Disabled presented by the World Veterans' Federation.

When India and Pakistan became independent Dominions we followed the general trend by transferring the responsibility for the care of their war-blinded to their own national committees. The last Indian who came to us for training was Petty Officer Copal Krishna Unny, of the Indian Navy, who had forty-nine operations while in our care. He stayed to take London Matriculation after twelve months' study. Nine months later he gained the Diploma for Public Administration of the same university, completing his training brilliantly before returning home.

Ahmed Abdullah el Eissa came from Sudan. Handless as well as blind, he came into training with his brother as his attendant. Captain Bekhradnia came from Iran. Samat bin Samat was Malayan, but from North Shields. Zofia

Ksiazek-Bregulowa, a Polish dramatic student, had lived through the Warsaw rising. Major Alexopoulos was Greek, and had been blinded by an Italian mortar bomb while fighting in Albania in 1941. He did not come to St Dunstan's until 1950, and then it was in a curious way.

Princess Eugenie of Greece paid a visit to St Dunstan's. She was not an ordinary visitor, for she had worked as a V.A.D. at Tembani during the War. Now she wanted advice on the care of the blinded Greek soldiers, of whom there were about a hundred and fifty. So far, she told me frankly, very little had been done for them. Nobody in Greece had much idea of what to do. Except herself, although she did not say that.

I gave her a sample of our new braille writing-machine, and one of our striking watches for handless men. It would serve as a model that Greek craftsmen would doubtless be able to copy. The Princess was interested in the talking book, but I explained that the machine was useless without a most complex and costly organization for making and handling the records. I took her round the Training Centre, where she spent several hours inspecting the various departments and meeting the men under training. Finally I said this: "If there is a young Greek who was blinded in the War, and who is capable of becoming a leader or the head of an organization for welfare of Greek blinded ex-Servicemen, I shall be very pleased to have him over here for a time and train him for the job."

She thanked me, and shortly afterwards Major Alexopoulos arrived. He stayed six months, and then returned to Athens to teach braille and typing and the other things he had learnt to 150 other blinded Servicemen.

One of the first of our post-war visitors from overseas was Helen Keller, an old friend of mine, who came and met our members of the deaf-blind world, which she has served in her unique way all her life. "We have nothing like this in America," she said when she left. "I'm going back to tell them about this."

That could not have been said about Canada, where the Sir Arthur Pearson Association of War Blinded, as it was now called, flourished as strongly as ever. Eddie Baker and I exchanged visits and ideas. Still head of the highly advanced Canadian National Institute for the Blind, Baker took time off to go to Trinidad, at the request of the authorities, to review the position of the blind in the colony and advise on their future welfare.

We ourselves broke new ground in West Africa. In 1945 the Colonial Office invited us to send a representative out to consider how blinded West African Servicemen could best be helped. Our Commandant at the time, Air Commodore Dacre, took on the job, and toured Gambia, Nigeria, Sierra Leone, and the Gold Coast—as Ghana was then—studying conditions and interviewing blinded men from the Royal West African Field Forces. The upshot was the establishment of a training centre for them at Lagos, to which we gave a quantity of equipment. Its deeper significance was the heralding of a new era for the much more numerous civilian blind in West Africa, whose status and outlook were still far behind that in Britain in the bad old days before Pearson.

Workers for the blind from far and wide came to see what we were doing at Ovingdean. Some visits were sponsored by the British Council, others by U.N.E.S.C.O.; some were sent by Governments, others by voluntary welfare organizations of our own kind. They came from Uruguay and Finland, Yugoslavia and Korea, Turkey and Zanzibar—all over the world. They had nothing in common except a desire and resolve to help the world's blind.

Eventually they came from Germany.

Hans Voigt, of Hamburg, came in 1948. He was especially interested in our gadgets for handless St Dunstaners, for he had many such doubly handicapped men in his care too. Voigt was an old friend of mine. Like myself, he was blinded in action in the First World War, and he was head of the German War-Blinded Organization in the years between. We exchanged news and views several times, in England and in Germany. Round about 1938 he was a guest at one of our regatta dinners in London.

I have told how Lord Normanby established a branch of St Dunstan's in German P.O.W. Camps. German blinded prisoners of war in Britain had no such organization of their own, and at my suggestion we rendered them what small services were possible. Towards the end of the War a few of them were transferred to a camp near Church Stretton, and I asked Tommy Milligan to see if he could help them. Milligan, then an instructor at our training centre, was not only a very good braillist but spoke German fluently. Soon he was going over regularly to give these men lessons in braille and typewriting.

Very soon after the end of the War in Europe I wrote to Field-Marshal Lord Montgomery, who was commanding British troops in Germany, asking him to do what he could to help German blinded soldiers, and suggesting that he should get in touch with me, asking for my help to overcome the great political difficulties that stood in the way of reconstituting a German war-blind society. I did all I could, and our Military Government approved the creation of a new war-blind society that soon had 4000 members in the British occupation zone and in Hesse.

Towards the end of 1946—well over a year after the end of the fighting in Europe—I received a letter from a German blinded soldier who wanted to correspond with a British blinded soldier. He also asked for help and advice. I published his letter in the *St Dunstan's Review* and invited comments. Nearly all the St Dunstaners who wrote were in favour of helping him, and several said they would be pleased to enter into correspondence. John Proctor's letter was typical: "I think St Dunstan's should, as far as possible, be international, and we ourselves are apt to forget how very fortunate we are."

*   *   *

At the end of 1951 Matron Dorothy Pain retired, and the good wishes and affection of countless St Dunstaners went with her. No stranger could have taken her place adequately; happily, we did not have to ask one to try. Miss Frances Ramshaw had been on our staff for eight years, first as a braille teacher and then as Education Assistant and Training Officer. She had worked for the National Library for the Blind before coming to us, and had all the necessary qualifications and experience. Still more important, she knew most St Dunstaners, had helped many, and was much respected and loved; as she still is to-day.

When Matron Pain left, Ovingdean was in a period of slow transition back to its pre-war state. It was still a busy training centre, but admissions were dropping steadily, and there was enough room at last for the convalescents and holiday-makers. Port Hall, the girls' hostel, even had a few vacant beds out of season for St Dunstaners' wives who needed convalescence or a rest. By the end of 1953 our home at Blackpool was no longer necessary, and we had to shut it down. It was a regretful decision, because it had given great happiness to many St Dunstaners in its twelve years of life.

As the number under training dwindled further, Ovingdean became again primarily a place for St Dunstaners wanting a holiday or convalescence. Soon we had room for them all, but not if they wanted to come at the same time, as most of them naturally did. Many of those working in industry had no choice, so we reserved beds from mid-July to mid-August for them. Later we introduced also a scheme of special fortnights for St Dunstaners who wanted to spend their holiday at Ovingdean with men who had been in training in the same year as themselves.

In 1953 we saw the Coronation. St Dunstan's was allotted 70 seats on the route of the Procession and 4 in Westminster Abbey itself. A ballot was held for the places on the route. In the Abbey, Captain F. J. L. Woodcock represented Canadian St Dunstaners and Joe Lynch the Australians, while the United Kingdom was represented by Mike Ansell and Tommy Milligan. (I attended as a Member of Parliament, and so did not come out of our quota.)

Tommy Milligan was, and of course still is, our earliest surviving St Dunstaner. Wounded at La Bassée in December 1914 while serving with the Irish Guards, he entered St Dunstan's on February 11, 1915, the second man in. The first, the late Jimmy Batchelor, entered on February 10. Tommy first qualified as a masseur and then studied languages, and became foreign correspondent for a London firm. He has long been a legend for the ease with which he walks all over London by himself.

Tommy Milligan was, of course, one of the select band who became a St Dunstaner before St Dunstan's got its name. It was the Blinded Soldiers' and Sailors' Hostel when he entered, not in Regent's Park but in Mrs Lewis Hall's house in Bayswater Road. In those days the name of St Dunstan was associated only with the church in Fleet Street—and with the goldsmiths, who consider him their patron saint. This was something I did not know until after Alfred Noyes had given him to us and I had accepted him.

This happened in 1951, the millenary of the saint's appointment as Archbishop of Canterbury. Alfred Noyes wrote a moving and beautiful occasional poem called St Dunstan's Prayer, which was published in the Sunday Times on May 27 with the comment "Yesterday was the feast day of Saint Dunstan, the 'Minister of Eternal Light' to those in darkness." In my regular monthly column in the St Dunstan's Review I expressed our gratitude for the lovely lines, while recalling that St Dunstan had not taken any special interest in the blind and suggesting that if any group could claim his patronage it would be craftsmen. "However," I wrote, "the behaviour of saints is not only a matter of history but also of the imagination, and I like to think that St Dunstan's and St Dunstaners have succeeded in establishing that Saint Dunstan could be our patron saint. Let us then agree with Mr Noyes that he is."

The Goldsmiths' Company not only improved my knowledge but kindly invited me to their banquet in honour of their patron saint. Dr Geoffrey Fisher, who had eventually succeeded St Dunstan as Archbishop of Canterbury, proposed his immortal memory. I still hoped we could share him with the Goldsmiths' Company, but there were objections from one or two St Dunstaners. What about St Cecilia, I was asked, the acknowledged patron saint of the blind as well as of musicians?

As a matter of fact, I was strongly attached to St Dunstan for practical reasons. During my early chairmanship I had often thought about the name and wished that it belonged exclusively to our organization. I did not, of course, expect to rob the Archbishop of Canterbury of a thousand years ago, or to deprive the church in the City of London of its name either; but in Regent's Park there had been two buildings called St Dunstan's—the old original Georgian villa on the Outer Circle, which had been our main building during the First World War, and had since reverted to private ownership, and our organization with its headquarters in the Inner Circle. This was slightly confusing to postmen, taxi-drivers, visitors, and others, and I set about trying to remedy it.

I made a personal approach to all the successive owners of the villa and asked them to give up the name. The first three refused on the grounds that the name had historic associations, which, of course, I respected. The fourth owner was Miss Barbara Hutton, the American millionairess. She had pulled down the old villa and built on the site a magnificent house in which she lived for a time, but which she subsequently gave to the American nation to become the Ambassador's home. Miss Hutton received me most kindly, said she was willing to give up

z

the name, and asked if the house might be called Winfield instead. This was agreed to by the Office of Works.

By 1959 over 5000 blinded Servicemen had come to St Dunstan's. A total of 2500 still survived—1300 from the First World War, and 1200 from the Second or after—of whom 550 were living overseas under the care of our affiliated organizations. We now had men who had lost their sight in the post-war fighting in Malaya, Korea and Kenya. In 1958 we admitted 36 men, of whom 24 had lost their sight as a result of service in the First World War. Mustard gas was a short-lived military weapon, but after over forty years its toll is still not complete.

The oldest man we have admitted was William Smith, of Eastbourne, who came in 1953, when he was eighty-five. He had lost his sight in the Second, not the First World War. He had enlisted in Civil Defence at seventy-three, and been injured by incendiary bombs. Too old to undertake any training, he died peacefully at Pearson House at the age of ninety.

To be too old for training at St Dunstan's generally means long past middle age. Captain John Oriel was fifty-two when he came, and he had been told that he was too old to learn braille. He learnt it quickly enough. Never a grumbler, he used to say that after his shock in 1917, when he thought he was blind, he had enjoyed twenty years of good sight and ten years of indifferent sight, and now there was an end of operations and pain. He thought that everything connected with his old life was finished, and his inclination was to go away from all he had known. We persuaded him to go back to it.

John Oriel, C.B.E., M.C., M.I.Chem.E., was an eminent Chemical Engineer. He went back to his profession and became still more eminent. In 1955 he was elected President of the Institution of Chemical Engineers. He is now a Fellow of Churchill College, Cambridge.

Arthur Bell was also gassed in the First World War,

when serving in the Army, only two months before the 1918 Armistice. His sight was affected, but not enough to stop him from training hunters on a horse farm, serving in the Police, practising as a solicitor in London, and finally —in 1939—joining the R.A.F. He came out a Squadron Leader, and could still see in 1947 when he read an article on mink-breeding and decided this was what he had wanted to do all the time. He started in his back garden, but there was not enough space and the neighbours objected, and after two years he practically lost his remaining sight. He came to St Dunstan's while his wife tried to carry on.

We found another more suitable farm for them, and arranged for Bell to go to Scandinavia to learn more about mink-breeding. He came back and became one of the leading mink-breeders in the country. By 1955 he had over eight hundred head of stock, and was elected Chairman of the Fur Breeders' Association. Shortly afterwards at the Hudson Bay Fur Company's Show he swept the board, collecting five out of ten cups and eight Class Champions.

Oriel and Bell are exceptional men. But so is A. V. Law, who passed his Morse test as a radio amateur at the age of fifty-eight. So is Tim Healy, for long a tireless worker for the civilian blind of Blackpool, who wrote his first novel, *While Apples Grew*, at the age of eighty. No sooner was it published than he began work on a second. St Dunstaners do not grow old before their time.

I have been blind for forty-five years, and have been Chairman of St Dunstan's for thirty-nine years. These are long periods of time, during which I have met with and, to a large extent, I think, overcome the handicap of blindness and watched others doing so and helped them.

There have been 5000 or more St Dunstan's families, and I have known very large numbers of them personally, having studied with them, walked, rowed, played bridge, danced with them and their friends, and argued incessantly. I know them as friends, and I have been concerned with their professions, handicrafts, entertainments, family and economic affairs. I have met most of the leaders of the blind world in many countries, and have read most of the books and articles written on the subject of blindness. Looking back, what do I think of it all? And, looking forward, what do I foresee?

My most certain impression is that, great as the handicap of blindness is, it is not the principal reason for unhappiness or failure where either has occurred among the blind. It has been said that money, or a large amount of money, does not make for happiness, but a cynic has added that it is a great help. I would say that blindness of itself does not make life unhappy or a failure, but it certainly provides or accentuates opportunities for both.

Nothing is more certain from my experience than that men are not equal. Even brothers and sisters with the same inheritance and the same environment are not equal in temperament or ability. Some are extroverts and find it easy to make friends. Others are introverts, and are lonely. Some are hard-working, some idle; some soft, some tough. Such characteristics are found in all human beings, whether they are blind or otherwise disabled or physically normal. The question is not so much how do the blind behave or get on, as how are men affected by blindness? And the answer is that to some it is a spur to greater effort than they might otherwise have made, often leading to success and satisfaction, whereas to others it is so heavy a burden that they only just manage to achieve a tolerable contentment. Some cases—fortunately few—give up the fight.

I would say that the overwhelming majority of St Dunstaners have made a very good show and, according to their lights, have led a good life, keeping pace with their neighbours or professional fellows or workmates.

Those who can see are often moved to pity or fear by the sight of a blind man fumbling his way along the office corridor or standing on the threshold of a busy road listening to know when to cross: pity for his plight and fear that so dreadful a calamity as blindness might one day overtake them. These emotions are worthy and understandable, but I think they are misplaced, and the blind man will probably get on all right if left alone. On the other hand, it is possible to accost him even if he is a stranger and say, "Let's cross the road together." If the sighted person is wise this is the form he will use rather than "Can I lead you across?" If the blind man is wise he will take the proffered arm and save himself a few seconds or minutes of anxiety, and he may make a new friend.

Men are gregarious by nature. Even those who like to be alone, or say they like to be alone, are sometimes lonely. The most common method of making contact with another person, be he friend or stranger, is a look and a smile, and this means of communication is not available to us. So a blind person has only half a chance of meeting a friend already known to him, or of making a new friend, or of just passing the time of day with a casual passer-by. Thus a great deal of the small pleasure of life and warmth of companionship is lacking, and I would think that most blind people are lonely from time to time.

I doubt if anyone could claim more friends and acquaintances in the House of Commons than I had for nearly forty years, whether among Members, lobby journalists, messengers, policemen, and others who frequent that busy place, but there were times when I was lonely. Most Members of Parliament are busy; all have important work to do, though some exaggerate this and pass you by because they are busy with their affairs or are hurrying to catch somebody. Those who have passed me by may well have included persons I knew well, whom I liked and who liked me, but I missed the message of the eyes as we passed each other in the corridor. A few, with greater sensibility, say, "Hello, Ian" as they pass, believing or hoping that I would recognize the voice or perhaps merely wanting to exchange a word instead of a glance. I have known many great men in the Palace of Westminster who hardly ever smiled at anybody or passed the time of day, but I have known others—and Sir Winston Churchill was notable among them—who never passed a friend, senior or junior, without a smile of recognition. In my case he always said, "Hello, Ian," and then added, as if it were necessary, "This is Winston." If ever there was a voice that did not need to tell its name his was one.

But I learnt that it is no good being sorry about this relative loneliness, and especially fruitless to be sorry for oneself. It is just one of the things that every blind man has to meet in his daily life.

Sometimes I would enter the Smoke Room of the House of Commons. I would not know where there was an empty seat, or who was sitting here or there, some alone, some in groups. I would pause for a few seconds and listen in the hope of distinguishing a familiar voice, or I would go to a familiar chair hoping it was empty. I would sit down and perhaps find myself alone or perhaps among a group of Tories making a plot which they did not want me to hear, or of Labour men talking about some vital business of their own, not for the ears of others. An awkward silence would tell me that I was an intruder, and I would move on; or, alternatively, I would be made welcome and have a drink.

These things could be so irritating and so embarrassing that a man could be forgiven if he stayed in his own arm-chair and did not try to go into the House of Commons or the local Council or his club. I preferred to take these minor misfortunes for what they were worth as small coin better disregarded, and I was very happy during my long years at Westminster. As the years passed, I fancy scores of friends came to know exactly how I was feeling, and unostentatiously and with real grace helped me on my way. I am deeply grateful to them.

I think the truth is that behind their business with their own affairs and the self-importance which afflicts all of us, most people are very kind and want to be as helpful as possible if only they know how. A blind man should tell his friends how they can help him. This is better for both, and often relieves an embarrassing situation.

What do I think of St Dunstan's? I suppose I am hardly an impartial or objective witness. I think it is a wonderful organization that has done more materially and spiritually for its members than any other body of its kind in any part of the world—and not only for its members, for it has by its example and by its members' activities inspired and encouraged work for the blind generally and a more hopeful attitude among the blind themselves. It has been for nearly fifty years, and still is, a proud part of Britain's story, which has exemplified some of our people's finest characteristics: courage, doggedness, and adaptability among the St Dunstaners, and kindness among those who have worked for the organization on our staff and among thousands of others who have helped St Dunstan's or individual St Dunstaners in some way or another.

Some good comes out of evil, and even war itself has produced its highlights of human conduct. Britain, and indeed the world, is the better for the existence of St Dunstan's, and its message will go on.

APPENDIX

ST DUNSTAN'S

(Registered in accordance with the National Assistance Act, 1948)

FOR MEN AND WOMEN BLINDED ON WAR SERVICE

IN ASSOCIATION WITH THE BRITISH LEGION

Founded by the late SIR ARTHUR PEARSON, Bt., G.B.E.

Patron: HER MAJESTY THE QUEEN

President: *SIR NEVILLE PEARSON, Bt.

Vice-Presidents:

THE MOST REV. AND RIGHT HON. ARCHBISHOP LORD FISHER OF LAMBETH, G.C.V.O., D.D.

HIS EMINENCE THE CARDINAL ARCHBISHOP OF WESTMINSTER

HIS GRACE THE DUKE OF SUTHERLAND, K.T.

THE RIGHT HON. THE VISCOUNT AMORY OF TIVERTON

Chairman of the Council	*THE LORD FRASER OF LONSDALE, C.H.
Honorary Treasurer	*SIR CECIL ELLERTON
Secretary	A. D. LLOYDS, Esq., F.C.A.

In addition to the above names marked with a star, the following are members of the Council:

Colonel M. P. ANSELL, C.B.E., D.S.O.

Colonel THE LORD ASTOR OF HEVER

The Rev. F. DARRELL BUNT, C.B., O.B.E., M.A.

Vice-Admiral SIR CHARLES CARPENDALE, C.B.

SIR BRUNEL COHEN, K.B.E.

Air Commodore G. BENTLEY DACRE, C.B.E., D.S.O., D.L.

JOHN FRY, Esq.

ION GARNETT-ORME, Esq.

LONALD G. HOPEWELL, Esq., M.A., LL.B.

Lieut.-Gen. SIR BRIAN HORROCKS, K.C.B., K.B.E., D.S.O., M.C., LL.D. (HON.)

WALTER G. HOWARTH, Esq., M.B., F.R.C.S.

SIR FREDERICK LISTER, C.B.E.

THE MARQUESS OF NORMANBY, M.B.E.

JOHN G. OSBORNE, Esq.

ALAN PITT ROBBINS, Esq., C.B.E.

GODFREY ROBINSON, Esq., C.B.E., M.C.

THE RIGHT HON. LORD TEVIOT, D.S.O., M.C.

INDEX